THE FALLEN VEIL

MATERIAL TEXTS

THE FALLEN VEIL

A Literary and Cultural History of the Photographic Nude in Nineteenth-Century France

RAISA ADAH REXER

PENN

University of Pennsylvania Press
Philadelphia

Published by
University of Pennsylvania Press
Philadelphia, Pennsylvania 19104-4112
www.upenn.edu/pennpress

Printed in the United States of America on acid-free paper
2 4 6 8 10 9 7 5 3 1

Library of Congress Cataloging-in-Publication Data
Names: Rexer, Raisa, author.
Title: The fallen veil : a literary and cultural history of the
    photographic nude in nineteenth-century France / Raisa Adah
    Rexer.
Other titles: Material texts.
Description: 1st edition. | Philadelphia : University of Pennsylvania
    Press, [2021] | Series: Material texts | Includes bibliographical
    references and index.
Identifiers: LCCN 2020022862 | ISBN 978-0-8122-5286-6 (hardcover)
Subjects: LCSH: Literature and photography—France—History—
    19th century. | French literature—19th century—History and
    criticism. | Photography of the nude—History—19th century. |
    Photography—Social aspects—France—History—19th century. |
    Nude in art—History—19th century.
Classification: LCC PQ283 .R48 2021 | DDC 840.9/357—dc23
LC record available at https://lccn.loc.gov/2020022862

✥ CONTENTS ✥

CONTENTS

⟁ PREFACE ⟁

In the mid-1850s in France, magistrates began to see an influx of new offenders appearing before the bench. These defendants, "young women of every profession, milliners, seamstresses, or laborers," were alarmingly frequent recidivists but were not typical career criminals.[1] They had "found easy profit in the atelier [. . .] in letting fall for a few moments the veil that hid their beauty."[2] Unlike the models who worked with painters or sculptors, however, these young women were sacrificing their modesty in a new kind of studio, subjecting them to the punitive gaze of the law. They were nude photographic models, working in a medium only just in its infancy and still shockingly unprecedented to its contemporaries. By the end of the century, however, the nascent commerce in nude photography to which they contributed their likenesses would grow into an international industry producing millions of photographs of the naked body — usually female — unshielded by any veil of modesty.

Photography as a medium has long been understood as, in Jonathan Crary's terms, a "systemic rupture" in perception and representation with vast cultural implications.[3] Nowhere is this disruptive and revolutionary "photography effect" more apparent than in the case of the nude image, whose controversial content threw all of the social and artistic fault lines radiating out from photography into sharp relief. Yet despite their rapid proliferation, we have placed our own veil over these nudes, concealing their immense historical importance along with the many truths they still have to tell about representations of the body. The American art historians Abigail Solomon-Godeau and Elizabeth Anne McCauley did groundbreaking work on these images in the 1990s, and the photographic nude was the subject of a major exhibition at the Bibliothèque nationale de France in 1997.[4] However, since then, these photographs have been largely overlooked in literary and historical studies of France, even those that examine the relationship between photography and literature explicitly.[5] In this book, I undertake to build on the work of art historians to offer the first comprehensive overview of the historical development of these images and their central role in nineteenth-century French culture. The nude photograph generated its own discourse, its own anxieties about society, obscenity, and art. No account of attitudes toward sexuality, the rights of women, the history of censorship, or the history of art in the nineteenth century can be complete without accounting for these photographs.

This book necessarily involves the visual analysis of the photographs themselves and their unique patterns of representation. Its focus, however, will not be on the images as much as the narrative about nude photography that emerges out of their inscription—whether through allusion or ekphrasis—into a wide range of nineteenth-century texts, including newspapers, magazines, government records, and fiction and nonfiction books. As it turns out, nude photographs exerted a particularly marked influence on contemporary literary production. In the works of the authors in this study, the photographic nude stands at the nexus of concerns about changing modes of artistic representation, about the limits of art and obscenity and the government's role in setting those limits, and about modern industrial capitalism's effect on both art production on the one hand and sexual mores on the other. Although they worked in text rather than image, these authors felt the shock of this novel way of representing the body. The nude photograph provides a new set of terms by which to reconsider some of the century's most well-known literary figures, including Charles Baudelaire, Émile Zola, and the Goncourt brothers.

At the same time, these literary voices also expand on discussions of the images going on elsewhere in nonfiction print media, exploring many of the same issues as these other historical sources but in greater depth. The other goal of this book, in addition to illuminating the influence of nude photography on literary production, is to trace the arc of these changing perceptions of nude photography in the broader cultural sphere over the second half of the nineteenth century. In the period immediately after photography's invention, nude photographs were vitally connected to the question of the medium's artistic aspirations and to questions of artistic representation more generally. By the end of the century, however, their status had radically shifted. As the industry expanded internationally and nudes became ubiquitous on the streets and in shops, such photographs were increasingly viewed as one of many problems plaguing the fledgling Third Republic. By 1900, the genre was overwhelmingly discussed in social and moral rather than artistic terms, and the germ of some twentieth- and twenty-first-century debates about photographic nudity had begun to emerge out of the nineteenth-century ones. In a very fundamental way, then, we live with the legacy of nineteenth-century attitudes as we continue, even with new and revolutionary photographic technologies and modes of dissemination and often in language that feels very different, to confront many of the same questions that initially arose with the first nude photographs.

The representation of the body, particularly the sexually explicit representation of the body, is always a difficult and complicated topic. The very language used to designate these representations was contested in the nineteenth century and still is today. In the 1880s, a great controversy erupted over the meaning of the word "pornography" (discussed in Chapter 5). Both for the sake of clarity and because it was the more commonly used term at the time, I have generally tried to use "obscenity" in its place. I also in many cases refer to images by their legal status (licit or illicit) rather than their content. Nevertheless, there are times when derivatives of pornography as we now employ the word (e.g., pornographic, pornographer) are unavoidable or better suited to the context. I use both "obscenity" and "pornography" in their most familiar definitions, even as I recognize how fraught these definitions are. Complexities of language aside, I also recognize that any given image—or the text alluding to it—has the potential to elicit very different reactions from different people. In my analyses, I have tried to be clear about my own position while respecting the positions of other viewers, readers, and scholars, because the issues raised by pornography and nude imagery can be viscerally personal. I will not make any claim of objectivity; I know that my own perspective runs through the book. I have, however, tried to let the voices of the nineteenth century speak for themselves, even when I disagree. This means that the book's narrative tends to be heterocentric and overwhelmingly focused on the representation of women's bodies, reflecting the gendered, normative sexuality of the period. Yet even if it reflects historical blind spots, it can also offer historical insights. In so allowing the nineteenth century its voice, I hope the book offers a new perspective from which to understand our continuing debates about art and the pornographic image, the signifying potential of the photographed body, and, by extension, the symbolic value of the body itself.

The book proceeds chronologically, divided into two parts (1839–1870 and 1870–1900) by the regime change from the Second Empire to the Third Republic. Each of the two sections opens with its own historical introduction. The first chapter, "Art, Obscenity, and Censorship: 1839–1870," presents the history of the photographic nude in the era of Second Empire censorship. Scholarship of nineteenth-century photography has minimized distinctions between different categories of the nude, ascribing meaning instead to an eroticizing photographic gaze that transcends particularities of content. During the Second Empire, however, nude photography was defined by a conflicted double identity. Under the censorship laws of Napoléon III, the government approved hundreds of photographs for legal sale as artistic nude studies, even as a burgeoning illegal obscenity industry was blackening the young medium's artistic reputation. The two categories were enshrined absolutely in the law, but their boundaries were alarmingly muddled in reality, provoking great anxiety over both the pernicious social effects of illicit nudes and their troubling artistic consequences. This preoccupation with the intertwined artistic and social consequences of photographic nudity reappears throughout discussions of photographic nudity during the period, in both literary and nonliterary texts.

In Chapter 2, "The Judgment of Phryne, or, The Model's Meaning," I examine periodical and other nonfiction sources in greater depth to show how the model's body defines the nude photograph in the cultural imagination of the Second Empire. Whereas existing studies focus almost exclusively on the relationship between models and prostitution, I argue that the double preoccupations of the Second Empire — the artistic status of the photographic nude and its dangerous socio-sexual significance — are both projected onto the body of the model. The exposure of the model's body posed difficult questions about female sexual agency, subjecting models to comparisons with prostitutes. It also, however, came to (quite literally) embody photography's artistic potential, as the model took center stage in the debates over whether nude photography — and the medium more generally — could be art.

Chapters 3 and 4 then turn to the literary record, examining the works of two authors who grappled with the artistic problems posed by nude photography. Chapter 3, "Baudelaire's Bodies," argues that, despite being accused of obscenity in 1857, Baudelaire was reacting against, rather than participating in, the rapid evolution of representational techniques, particularly those of the body, that came about with the invention of photography. Baudelaire uses metaphor to recover the naked poetic body from the obscene photograph's threat of nonsignification. Chapter 4, "*Manette Salomon* and Anti-Modernity," argues that the Goncourt brothers' novel about a painter's model turned nude photographic subject approaches the nude photograph as a sign of the failure of the Baudelairian concept of the modern artist to theorize adequately contemporary artistic production. The brothers instead propose a kind of anti-modernity in response to the representational problems posed by the photographed body. Baudelaire and the Goncourt brothers have opposing but interconnected reactions to nude photography that situate the photographic nude at the heart of aesthetic debates prefiguring the emergence of modernism at the turn of the twentieth century.

In the fifth chapter, "The Rise of an International Industry: 1870–1900," I introduce the historical developments of the first decades of the Third Republic. The period from 1870 to 1900 saw a rapid international expansion in the traffic of illicit photographic nudity as well as an increased presence of nudity in public spaces and its spread to new formats. At the same time, the repeal of the censorship laws eliminated the category of the legal photographic nude as it had existed under the Empire. As the art nude consequently became increasingly indistinguishable from other forms of nudity proliferating in France, its artistic credibility was called into question. Although the Pictorialist movement revived the art nude at the end of the century, questions of artistry had already receded from the public consciousness. The nude photograph finished the century consigned firmly to the realm of obscenity and vice, targeted by the morality leagues and campaigns of the fin de siècle.

In the sixth chapter, "The Dangerous Streets," I return to nonfiction and periodical sources to explore in greater detail the rhetoric of the photographic nude's declining reputation. Between 1870 and 1900, social reformers and members of the government increasingly focused their attention on the presence of photographic nudity in the public spaces of the city streets. As a result, the nude was associated with a variety of other deleterious objects and behaviors plaguing public thoroughfares. Nude photography's particularly intimate relationship with two of those street vices, prostitution and pornography, illuminates the terms and the stakes of its fall. As nude photography became more closely integrated into the structures of prostitution, contemporaries treated the two industries as theoretically similar and practically interconnected sexual economies. Meanwhile, a "pornography crisis" erupted in France in the 1880s, as a surge in cheap, lubricious periodicals inundated the streets of Paris. During the crisis, the newspapers harnessed fears about photographic obscenity to fan the flames of anti-pornography hysteria as the very meaning of the word "pornography" was being reshaped. Nude photography was positioned as even worse than pornography, indicating just how far its reputation had fallen. The photographic nude's descent into the gutters at the fin de siècle transformed it from an artistic genre hovering at the edge of obscenity to a social problem to be cleaned up by the government, like any other.

The turn toward nude photography as it was embedded in the contemporary sexual economy is then explored in two chapters on the literary record. Chapter 7, "*Nana* in the Nude," shows how Zola's novel takes up this social problem. Using ekphrasis and allusion, Zola represents Nana's body through the lens of nude photography, aligning prostitution and photographic nudity as two sides of a coin in the sexual economy of the Second Empire. The novel's photographic aesthetic, however, also exposes the continuity of this economy from Empire to Republic, implicating Zola's Republican contemporaries (and incurring their fury). Chapter 8, "Maizeroy and the Feminist Photo-Novel," examines the photo-illustrated novels of René Maizeroy, disciple of Alphonse Daudet and close friend to Guy de Maupassant. In the heyday of his wild popularity from 1880 to 1910, he was known as a "master feminist," an author of books written for and about women. I argue that even as Maizeroy's fiction testifies to the consequential social force of the nude photograph at the end of the century, his distinctive "feminist" style—which focused on writing female experiences—complicates his own use of the genre in his photo-novels. Maizeroy genders text and image as opposed representational modes of desire, ultimately rejecting "male" photographic representation in favor of voicing the nuances of female desire through the written word.

By way of conclusion, I turn to a recent personal encounter with censorship. In the summer of 2017, I wrote a review of an Irving Penn retrospective that was censored by Facebook because the header image was one of Penn's nudes. I argue that this episode not only reveals the enduring effects of the attitudes toward nude photography that emerge out of the nineteenth century, but it also clarifies the consequences of those attitudes for our continued attempts to come to terms with photographic representations of the body. At the end of the nineteenth century, as reformers condemned photographic nudity for the way that it trafficked in the body, they did so in terms that forbade the very possibility that photographic nudity could be art. In the context of photography's truthful relationship with the real body it represents, this position implicates not only the image but the body itself, and carries with it the foreclosure of the body's signifying possibility. In a world where all photographic nudity is obscenity, the body, too, only signifies as obscene, trafficked, exploited—an object of fear that should *not* be exposed. Ultimately, we must ask ourselves whether an awareness of the negative social and economic structures of photographic pornography can coexist with artistic photographic representations of the body. If there is no way around this impasse, what are the consequences of living in a society that cannot find a way of protecting the body's potential to signify as art?

PART I

The Second Empire

[FIGURE 1]
Alexandre Quinet
(possibly Félix Jacques Antoine Moulin
or Auguste Belloc), 1861.
Salt print from glass collodion negative.
Bibliothèque nationale de France.

✑ CHAPTER 1 ✑

Art, Obscenity, and Censorship: 1839–1870

The photograph is arresting. A reclining young woman turns toward the camera, her head propped in her hand, her gaze subdued but unflinching. She is naked. Despite the garish draperies and drab wall behind her, there is something striking and graceful in her posture. She defies her cheap surroundings. A piece of gauze adorns her lower body, its purpose unclear, as it covers only her lower leg and leaves her more suggestive curves and shadows uncovered (Figure 1). Like any photograph, particularly an old photograph, this image teases us with questions. When was it made? for whom? by whom? Why? Who is this woman? Why did she pose? And finally, in the face of her nudity, we must ask, What is this photograph? Is it art? Is it pornography? What does it mean and for whom?

Some of these questions are relatively easy to answer. We know, for instance, that this photograph was made sometime around 1861 because it was registered with the government for legal sale as an *académie*, a figure study for use by artists. But others of these questions are quite difficult, even impossible, to answer. The photographer who registered the photograph, Alexandre Quinet, may not actually have taken it.[1] More substantively, what we make of this woman's pose, and her nudity, is both a personal and a historical affair; not surprisingly, many conflicting "meanings" of images like this one have already been proposed by photographic and art historians. For some, the sexual, social, and representational realities embodied in this and similar images mean that they necessarily objectify and eroticize the women they depict, despite the images' approval by the government and their official designation as artistic studies. For others, photographs like this are very much art, despite the social realities of their production.[2] And whatever stance one might be inclined to take, many images are impossible to read and classify in the face of ambiguities about content, context, and audience. Perhaps more importantly, whatever scholars from the late twentieth and early twenty-first centuries may make of nineteenth-century nudes, their opinions do not necessarily align with—and may even obscure—the ways that such photographs signified for their nineteenth-century viewers. The goal of this book is precisely to try to uncover the complexities of signification in the nineteenth century by examining the written traces of these images. Before turning to those textual inquiries, this chapter will offer a general overview of the history and aesthetics of nude photography through 1870 (Chapter 5 will do the same for 1870–1900), so as to contextualize the detailed discussions that follow.

In the earliest days of nude photography, among the most important forces shaping both the meaning and the history of nude photographs were the peculiarly overlapping censorship and indecency laws. In December 1851, the soon-to-be emperor Louis-Napoléon Bonaparte took power in a coup d'état. In February 1852, he decreed that the publication, display, or sale of any visual materials would require prior authorization by the government.[3] Among the images approved for sale under the auspices of the law were many hundreds of nude photographs, purportedly for the use of artists. The copies submitted for approval made their way into the archives of the Dépôt légal (now, essentially copyright registration) and are still preserved in the Bibliothèque nationale today. Yet even as censorship allowed for the production and distribution of government-sanctioned photographic nudes, other photographs that had not been authorized, but were not necessarily more sexually explicit than authorized photographs, were targeted by the police for prosecution and eradication. The conflicting jurisdiction of the censorship and the indecency laws allowed for the simultaneous authorization and proscription of photographic nudity, creating a double system of illegal and legal nudity in France that influenced how images were produced, distributed, consumed, and perceived by contemporaries.

Not only did this dual system of legal and illegal nudity play an essential role in the early history of these images, it gave them their first written history. Just as the censors left a record of legal nudity via the Dépôt légal, the Paris police created their own records in pursuit of those circulating illegal nudity, a large register known today by its call number in the Paris police archives, the BB3. Between 1855 and 1868, the police tracked investigations, arrests, and convictions connected to photographic nudity in its pages. This first chapter will look closely at the written and photographic records of the Dépôt légal, the police register, and contemporary nonfiction sources to lay out the early history of nude photography (focusing on Paris, the center of production) while at the same time mapping out the terms in which they were understood by contemporaries. These documents outline a shifting and substantial industry in nude photographs from the mid-nineteenth century onward. From its earliest days, the nude photography industry implicated a wide swath of French society, its influence and public reach only expanding as time went on. The documents also testify to the ways in which contemporaries had begun to grapple with this new kind of image making, as they asked questions about how these images signified and what they meant for society. Napoléon's censorship decree authorized the genre of artistic photographic nudity just at a moment when the art value of the medium was itself hotly debated. In the decades after photography's invention, photographers and critics defended the artistry of photographic nudity. However, at the same time, the nascent commerce in illegal images as well as the unclear and variable aesthetic standards of the censorship law called into question the artistic aspirations of the photographic nude, and even those of photography as a medium. During the Second Empire, the problem of how nude photography should signify artistically was as much disputed as the question of whether it was a detriment to society.

Because of the central importance of the censorship law to this early history, this chapter will be organized around the categories of legality established under that law, rather than categories of artistry or obscenity. It begins with a brief legal overview and discussion of the first decade of nude photography, roughly from 1839 to 1851. It then addresses legally authorized nudity before proceeding to illegal images, in each case touching on the facts of production and distribution as well as public perceptions. Finally, it turns to the more complicated realities of this system, including the frequent overlap between legal and illegal imagery, and the influence of this overlap on the emerging discourse about photographic nudity. By grounding evolving attitudes toward the photographic nude in the historical realities of the nineteenth century and in the legal structures that produced them, the goal is both to offer new insight into how such photographs were understood at the time and to provide a guide for the three chapters that follow, which will elaborate on the contested meaning of the photographic nude introduced here.

⚐ Legal History ⚑

Before Napoléon III's rise to power in 1851, the most important law governing nude photography was an 1819 statute that targeted the public sale, exhibition, and distribution of any written or visual materials offensive to public and religious morality or to public decency and that sent offenders to a jury trial.[4] The first known conviction of a photographer under this statute for affront to public decency, or *outrage à la morale publique et aux bonne mœurs*, occurred in July 1851.[5] Notably, this and the other laws of the Second Empire did not criminalize the *private* production and exchange of nudes. Moreover, the law's focus on public sale and distribution was such that, as Dominique de Font-Réaulx notes, the optician who sold the images received a harsher sentence than the photographer.[6] The 1819 law was the basis for prosecution of images and texts suspected of indecency until 1881, with one significant change. In December 1851, Louis-Napoléon Bonaparte eliminated jury trials for crimes of the press, including for affront to public decency; photographs would not be tried for that crime in front of a jury again during the nineteenth century.[7]

Although the 1819 statute remained in effect, the censorship law of 1852 completely transformed how nude photographic images were treated under the law, bringing with it restrictions, complications, and opportunities for their commercial production. The law had a broad scope that was primarily intended to limit political debate, *not* to control distribution of nudity, but it ultimately ended up doing just that.[8] Under the 1852 law, nude photographs could be submitted either to the Minister of Police in Paris or to local prefects in the provinces to be authorized for sale.[9] Because the government did authorize certain nudes, it effectively created an officially sanctioned genre of legal "artistic" photographic nudity. The law of 1852 continued to hold joint jurisdiction with the 1819 law even after the fall of the Empire, for it was fully abrogated for images only in 1881. And despite its political origins, in the case of photography, the censorship law was overwhelmingly used to prosecute unauthorized photographic nudes.[10] When legal action was brought against those involved with the production and sale of nude photography, it almost always involved simultaneous charges under both the 1819 and 1852 laws, although not everyone could be charged under both statutes: those responsible for authorization or who were directly engaged at the point of sale, such as photographers and vendors, were prosecuted under both statutes, while other accomplices, such as models, were charged as accomplices only under the 1819 law.[11]

The two laws often shared jurisdiction imperfectly and unclearly, as the same image might conceivably be unauthorized without offending standards of public decency. Over time, legal precedent prioritized the 1852 censorship law over the 1819 indecency law. In an 1863 case, a photographer charged under both laws was acquitted of affront to public decency. Then, in the 1864 appeal of a photographer convicted under both statutes, the judge ordered sentencing under only the harsher penalties of the censorship law and ruled that sentencing under both statutes violated the prohibition on cumulative punishment.[12] Ultimately, while unauthorized images might or might not be considered indecent, authorized nudes were not prosecuted for affront to public decency. As one legal commentator remarked in his summary of the 1864 case, if photographers wanted to make nudes, "The only way for the photographer to lawfully exercise this right [. . .] is to submit the académies created as art studies to the examination of the prefect."[13] During the Second Empire, in other words, the legality of a photographic image was primarily determined by authorization rather than a judicially negotiated standard of obscenity.

≫ First Nudes ≪

The first decade of nude photography (approximately 1839 to 1851) predates the complex legal regime of the Empire's censorship law and many records, so it is also the most shrouded in mystery. The earliest nude images would have been either daguerreotypes, one-of-a-kind positive images printed on photo-sensitized silver-coated copper plates, or salt prints from paper negatives (often called calotypes).[14] Both the first surviving nude photographs and the first references to the genre in print date to the 1840s. In 1848 and 1849, the photographers Gustave Le Gray and Charles Nègre produced calotype nudes (Figure 2).[15] Around the same time, in 1847, a reporter for the newspaper *Le Corsaire* reported that a boutique in Paris was already selling in daguerreotype form "a number of Parisian odalisques in the simple costume of Titian's *Venus*."[16] Sylvie Aubenas has argued that early daguerreotypes could not have operated as artists' figure studies because of

[FIGURE 2]

Gustave Le Gray, 1849.
Salt print from paper negative.
Société française de la photographie.

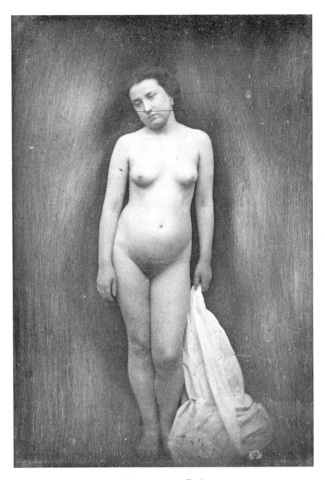

[FIGURE 3]
Anonymous, 1842–1855.
Daguerreotype.
Bibliothèque nationale de France.

their small size and reflective surface.[17] However, the exact function of these early nudes remains unknown. And whatever the drawbacks of the daguerreotype format, an 1843 instructional treatise by Noël-Marie Lerebours on the daguerreotype includes a section on nude figure studies, indicating that artists may well have worked from daguerreotypes.[18] Extant images do little to further clarify the genre's aspirations, for very few photographic nudes that can be definitively dated to the 1840s still exist. We can only deduce from the extant corpus of daguerreotype images from the 1850s—including some that have been tentatively dated back to the late 1840s—that the earliest nudes probably ran the gamut from tasteful, well-composed figure studies to scenes of explicit sexual activity (Figures 3–6).[19] Beyond this, we know, and can say, little about them with any certainty.

[FIGURE 4]

Auguste Belloc, ca. 1851.
Stereoscopic daguerreotype.
Musée d'Orsay, Paris.

[FIGURE 5]

Bruno Braquehais, 1850s.
Daguerreotype. Metropolitan
Museum of Art, New York.

[FIGURE 6]

Anonymous French, after 1850.
Stereoscopic daguerreotype.
Rheinisches Bildarchiv, Cologne.

⚜ The Legal Académie ⚜

Photographic Forms

In the 1850s, the history of the nude comes suddenly into clearer focus. The decade brought new photographic technologies, such as wet-collodion glass plate negatives and albumen paper prints, and new formats, such as the stereograph and the *carte-de-visite*.[20] It also brought vastly increased photographic production, as paper prints from glass plate negatives, which could yield images by the hundreds or even thousands, gradually replaced the daguerreotype, which was expensive and produced single positive images. And with that increased photographic production came an increase in nudes. In the 1850s and 1860s, drawing on the long tradition in the visual arts of the academic figure study, photographers began to produce nude photographs as private commissions for artists. As long as they were not publicly displayed or commercially distributed, such commissions could have skirted the bounds of the 1819 and 1852 laws, but some of them were nonetheless registered for sale or otherwise made their way to the Bibliothèque nationale collections. A number of painters of the period worked from académies: Gustave Courbet probably worked from a photograph by Julien Vallou de Villeneuve for

The Bathers and certainly did so for *The Painter's Studio*, Eugène Delacroix commissioned a series of nudes from the photographer Eugène Durieu, and Jean-Léon Gérôme commissioned a nude from Nadar in order to finish *Phryne Before the Areopagus* (Figures 7–9).[21] These well-known examples are all paper prints, but as previously mentioned, most extant daguerreotype nudes date from the early 1850s, and some of them may have been commissioned as artist's studies as well.

[FIGURE 7]

Julien Vallou de Villeneuve, 1854.
Salt print from paper negative.
Bibliothèque nationale de France.

[FIGURE 8]
Eugène Durieu, 1855.
Albumen print from glass collodion negative.
Bibliothèque nationale de France.

Nadar, 1860–1861.
Salt print from glass collodion negative.
Metropolitan Museum of Art, New York.

ÉTUDE D'APRÈS NATURE.

Autorisée sans exposition à l'Étalage

[FIGURE 10]

Henri Voland, *Étude d'après nature*, 1861.
Albumen print from glass collodion negative.
Bibliothèque nationale de France.

Along with these private commissions, a new genre of commercially produced artist's nudes sprang up after the passage of the 1852 censorship law. Photographers quickly began to take advantage of its protections to submit "photographic studies" or "studies from nature" for authorization, leaving behind via the Dépôt légal an encyclopedic catalog of government-sanctioned, commercially distributed, and ostensibly artistic photographic nudity, most of it depicting women (Figures 10–16). Académies submitted for government approval were usually larger-scale paper prints, although they do include some small formats, such as half or full stereographs. In general, they follow two different visual approaches. One type hews closely to advice dispensed by Lerebours in his 1843 treatise. Lerebours urges photographers to be "sober in the use of accessories, as a great simplicity often adds to the merit of such a tableau."[22] Only occasionally employing props, this set of photographs largely exploits the stark contrast that black-and-white photography created between the body's luminescent white curves and the murky dark background of the studio, or between that body and the texture of simple draped fabrics, to create a subgenre of simple and austere figure

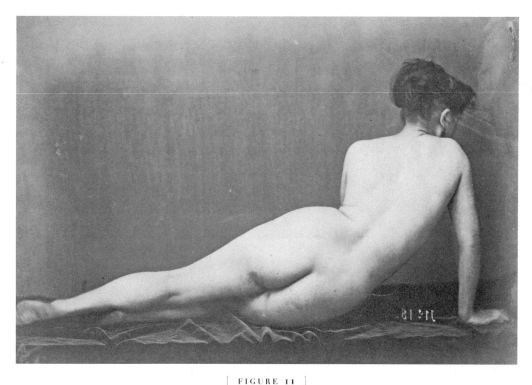

[FIGURE 11]

Guglielmo Marconi, 1869.
Albumen print from glass collodion negative.
Bibliothèque nationale de France.

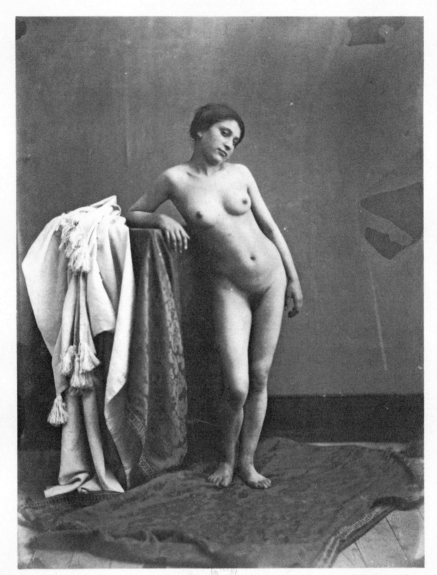

[FIGURE 12]

Louis Camille d'Olivier,
Étude d'après nature, 1854.
Salt print from glass collodion negative.
Bibliothèque nationale de France.

studies (Figures 10–13). Another category of académie, however, took the opposite approach, using more or less elaborate props and sets to justify the model's nudity (Figures 14–16). Some of the most common scenes are of boudoir or various "oriental" and exotic settings (Figure 15). At their most complex, these photographs veer into *scènes de genre*, elaborate tableaux that included costumes and painted sets. Surpassing their supposed role as a helpmate to other visual arts, these set pieces betray photography's aspirations to rival the status of painting, even when those aspirations required a certain generous suspension of disbelief.

The many académies submitted for authorization deploy an emerging visual language that includes the use of specific tropes, such as masks, mirrors, or the unpinning of the models' hair, and an obsession with the visual effects of gauze.[23] But they also demonstrate a more fundamental shared visual lexicon that has nothing to do with props or accessories. In 1843, Lerebours' final counsel was "not

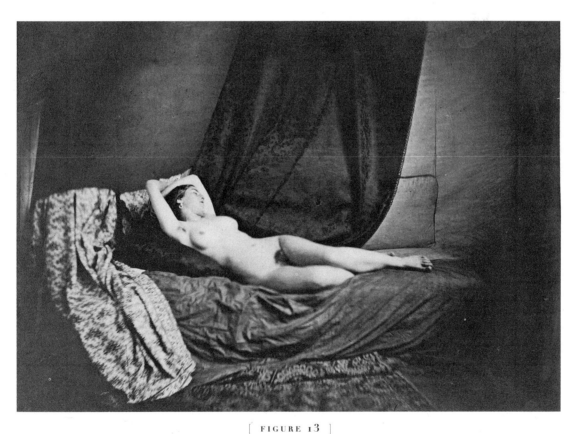

[FIGURE 13]

Alexandre Quinet,
Étude d'après nature, 1861.
Albumen print from glass collodion negative.
Bibliothèque nationale de France.

[FIGURE 14]
Bruno Braquehais,
Étude académique, 1854.
Albumen print from glass collodion negative.
Bibliothèque nationale de France

[FIGURE 15]

Julien Vallou de Villeneuve,
Étude d'après nature, 1853.
Salt print from paper negative.
Bibliothèque nationale de France.

[FIGURE 16]

Félix Jacques Antoine Moulin,
Paysanne à la fontaine, 1853.
Salt print from glass collodion negative.
Bibliothèque nationale de France.

to place oneself too close to the model, and as much as possible to avoid that different parts of the body be at too widely variable distances from the lens."[24] Lerebours' advice is at least partially technical; achieving a clear image without distortions of perspective required a flat visual plane. But the admonition also points to the académie's unifying principle. It relied on both this uniform flatness and on the distance between the viewer and the naked model to mitigate the eroticism of its subject. In painted nudes, pubic hair was expected to disappear so as to conform to standards of decorum.[25] A photographer, however, could not paint away such unsightly incursions of corporeality. Instead, pose, composition, and perspective had to mitigate the dangers of the body, countering any suggestion that the model might open her legs and offer herself up for delectation. Consequently, though photographic conventions were most certainly inherited from painted salon nudes and do much the same work of transforming nakedness into nudity (in T. J. Clark's formulation), they tend to be even more rigid.[26] To the extent that any photographic art nudes succeeded at rising above prurience in the eyes of nineteenth-century viewers, they did so only through an uneasy compromise between the model as a real body and the model's body as the substance of art achieved via these rigid compositional proscriptions.

Production and Distribution of Académies

While the photographic record of the legal académie is exceedingly rich, the written record is relatively laconic (especially in comparison with the police records). The entries that accompanied prints deposited for authorization by the government include only the name and the address of the person (the photographer, editor, or head of the commercial studio) seeking authorization for sale, the title of the work, and whether any conditions were placed on the sale of the photographs. No other information was gathered because no more was needed for what was, once approved by the government, a legitimate commercial product. Still, these records offer some sense of the production and consumption of legal nudes. The production and distribution of académies was fairly straightforward. Like nude studies in any other established artistic medium, they were produced by artists— in this case, photographers—working out of a studio. Photographers of varying talent registered nude images, but this group did include some well-respected photographers of the day. In at least one case, a female photographer produced académies.[27] Modeling for authorized nude photographs was not illegal, and the best photographers often used the same pool of models used by painters.[28]

Commercial académies were also fairly easily obtained. Some nudes received authorization that limited the conditions under which they could be sold: they might be sold only in the École des beaux-arts, or were not to be publicly displayed, or were only to be exported; violation of these terms could still lead to prosecution.[29] Yet despite these limitations, many were available in photography shops or from photographers around Paris. Photographers even advertised nudes in photographic publications.[30] And académies were shown in early photographic exhibitions. The Société française de photographie banned nudes from its first two exhibitions, in 1855 and 1857, but no such explicit injunction was levied in 1859.[31] Other photographic societies organized informal exhibitions including nudes, and nudes were discussed in photography journals of the period.[32]

The Académie and the Question of Art

It is impossible to know why the French government authorized nudes for legal sale under the censorship law. Some measure of pecuniary motivation may well have been involved, as the government collected registration fees for authorization. At the same time, the high quality of many images and the visual conventions governing the académie suggest some investment in defining the representational terms of the "artistic" photographic body. Whatever the government's intention, these artistic images did come to play an important role in contemporary debates about photography's art value. At the time of its invention, photography had many vociferous detractors, including some of the authors considered in this study (Baudelaire and the Goncourt brothers). In the 1850s, article after article in the major photographic publications — *La Revue photographique*, *La Lumière*, and the *Bulletin de la Société française de photographie* — took up the argument of photography's art value against those who believed that the medium could aspire to no more than scientific accuracy.[33] For these defenders of photography, the corpus of sanctioned art nudes was a new genre that had the potential to elevate the art status of the entire medium. Whether the creation of the académie spurred discourse about art and the photographic nude or the other way around, the académie was integral to arguments in favor of photographic artistry. Académies were discussed in the photographic press in terms of their artistic qualities and their contributions to the progress of the visual arts. Articles in photography journals applauded nude photography as an essential tool for painters, allowing painters easy access to "all the attitudes, all the types, all the variety of nature" of the human body for use in their work.[34] The critic Francis Wey declared that the photograph's unprecedented ability to capture the body in motion would transform painting, starting "a revolution against the system of *clichés*, in favor of reality. Thanks to an invention of science, modelling will cease to be technical [*savant*] work, and will return to the domain of the arts."[35] Paradoxically, for Wey the precision of the medium had the potential to liberate art from realism by relieving the pressure for perfect execution, thereby freeing the exercise of "modeling" the body for artistic interpretation.

Many defenses of the photographic nude laud it as a tool for painters, but some notably describe académies as works of art in their own right. Reviewing the daguerreotypist Gouin, Charles Gaudin wrote that "He tends to an image [*épreuve*] like a painter tends to a favorite work. He has talent's patience. Nothing is more beautiful than his académies. They are so skillfully posed, so artistically lit, the tones are so true and so natural, that they could serve as prized studies for painters."[36] Although he praises Gouin's images as studies for painters, Gaudin also attributes to them the same measure of talent and care required by painting. Less than a year later, Gaudin would revise his praise upward, writing of other Gouin académies that "These figures live, this flesh palpitates under your gaze. It is nature caught in the act by photography and poeticized by the painter's talent."[37] In his discussion of the nudes of Bruno Braquehais (Gouin's son-in-law), the critic Ernest Lacan deploys similarly artistic praise.[38] Although he commences with a discussion of the utility of the photographic nude for the use of *other* artists, by the time Lacan describes Braquehais' académies, he has abandoned the language of utility: "These images [*épreuves*] are of an extreme limpidity. The lines are delicately shown, without being too harsh; the tones have a great transparency united with a remarkable vigor; the rendering of the model's form is at once firm and soft; the lighting, skillfully economized, gives striking relief to the forms, making their smallest detail comprehensible."[39] In all of these reviews, the académie's utility is subordinated to its beauty, making clear that the medium's unparalleled realism also had the potential to be the standard for artistry.

⚞ The Unauthorized Nude ⚟

Photographic Forms

All the while, other kinds of nudity had also begun to proliferate in Paris outside the watchful gaze of the law. Beginning in 1855, these illegal images made their way into the government records by way of the BB3 (Figure 17). Supplemented by contemporary visual and print sources, the BB3 provides a remarkably detailed snapshot of the illegal photographic industry at its inception. First and foremost, the BB3 demonstrates the quantity and variety of these images. It does include some other illicit sexual objects, such as lithographs, drawings, *cartes transparentes* (a transparent card depicting obscene images), statuettes, paper dolls, pipes, snuffboxes, the odd *consolateur* (dildo), and condoms, but the vast majority of its entries concern photographs.[40] According to the BB3, in the 1850s, illicit

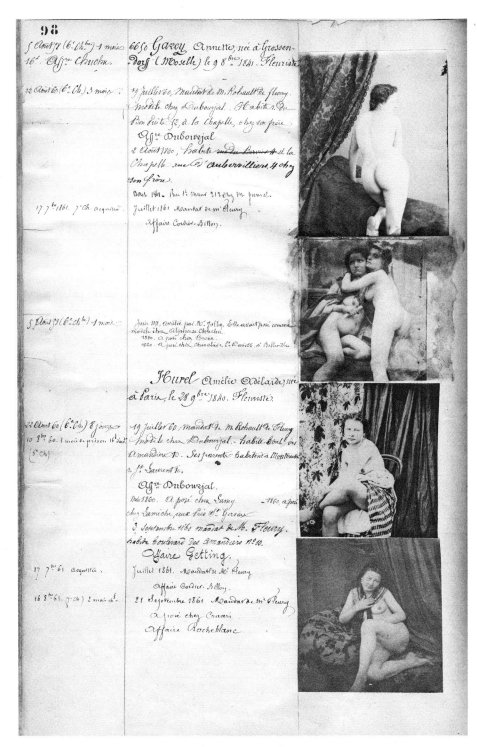

[FIGURE 17]

Pages from the police register BB3, Second Empire.
Archives de la Préfecture de police, Paris.

99

Courtault — Louise Victorine Françoise; née à Paris, le 25 Avril 1843; brocheuse. Célibataire.

Securieux Joséphine Eutrope née à Fère en Tardenois (Aisne) le 6 Janvier 1841.

photographs still included daguerreotypes, although no confiscated daguerreotypes have been preserved. However, as the technology changed, daguerreotypes were soon largely replaced by cheaper and more reproducible paper prints in a number of small formats like the carte-de-visite and the stereograph; the photographs preserved in the BB3 and in the Enfer of the Bibliothèque nationale fall into this group. Tiny microphotographs called "stanhopes," which required a special lens to be viewed, were also popular. Stanhopes could be embedded into a variety of everyday objects, such as lorgnettes, canes, boxes, and even jewelry, transforming these into erotic novelty items.[41] Illicit photographic nudity circulated in large numbers. Police raids yielded hundreds or thousands at a time.[42] In October 1860, nearly 5,000 images and plates were discovered in the studio of the photographer Auguste Belloc.[43] And Senate proceedings allege that 15,000 stanhopes and 300 plates were confiscated in one single raid in June 1865.[44]

Many, if not most, of these unauthorized images have disappeared. Those that remain are often held in private collections and can be difficult to date and attribute. However, the police did preserve some nude and seminude photographs in the pages of the BB3 in order to identify participants in the illegal nudity industry, and they gave some confiscated images to the Bibliothèque nationale in the 1860s. These photographs represent only a fraction of total output, and may not be entirely representative of all illicit production; the images in the BB3, for instance, were primarily chosen to aid in identification of models, not as examples of illegal images in circulation. But we can assume with some certainty that they are examples of illegal (unauthorized, obscene, or both) photographs seized by the police.[45] Despite their limitations, the BB3 and the Bibliothèque nationale collections constitute the largest corpus of attributed and dated illegal nudity and are the best basis for an assessment of what such images looked like. As noted above, these photographs are small-format paper prints (stereographs or cartes-de-visite). Their heterogeneous content ranges from gauze-draped women that might have been mistaken for legal académies to graphic depictions of sex and masturbation (Figures 17–21). These images, too, participate in the emerging visual language of gauze, cascading hair, and mirrors, adding to that repertoire what art historian Abigail Solomon-Godeau has described as a fetishistic erotics of the stocking-clad leg (most forcefully expressed in images of women putting on or taking off stockings).[46] Where the académie, however, flattens and distances the body so as to minimize its sexual charge, these photographs collapse that distance and engage the viewer in the model's physicality. The models often open their legs for the camera, or they are framed in a foreshortened perspective thrusting their pelvises toward the viewer, as if to emphasize (were there any doubt) exactly what the purpose of the image is.

Like académies, unauthorized nudes predominantly depicted women. As a group, the extant examples of illegal images are governed by a characteristic way of looking that for Solomon-Godeau defines erotic photographic representation against older forms of nudity or obscenity: the emphasis on the female body as an object of visual desire.[47] The epitome of photography's new "scopic consumption" of the female body is a pose that Solomon-Godeau calls the "beaver shot," a perspective that she argues is coeval with the medium (Figures 18 and 19).[48] While Solomon-Godeau maintains that masturbation and lesbian scenes are likewise staged for consumption by male spectators, she excludes images of heterosexual coitus from her analysis.[49] Yet they, too, conform to this visual agenda, for when women have male partners, their bodies are turned unnaturally toward the cam-

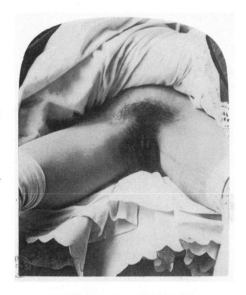

[FIGURE 18]

Auguste Belloc, *Les Œuvres de Buffon*, 1860.
Right half of a photographic
print on stereo card.
Bibliothèque nationale de France.

[FIGURE 19]

Anonymous, Second Empire.
Photographic print on stereo card.
Bibliothèque nationale de France.

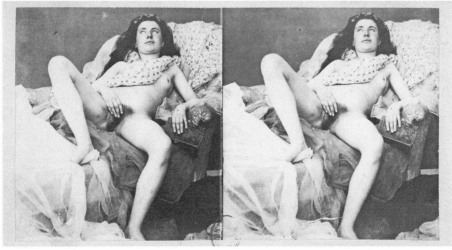

era, legs up, torsos twisted, genitals awkwardly exposed precisely so that the viewer can take pleasure in sight *alone* — and above all, in the sight of a woman (Figure 20). One of the best examples is a photograph from the Enfer of the Bibliothèque nationale, part of a series that invokes older tropes of erotic lithography.[50] Two women are laid out for the viewer, one on her front and one on her back, offering the spectacle of sex in two positions and from both sides all at once (Figure 21). If the men in this image, dressed as soldiers, are types from lithography, the women are the products of photography. In the thousands of photographs circulating in Paris in the 1850s and 1860s, *women's* bodies were on display for visual pleasure and consumption; in contemporary reactions to these images, anxieties about the dangers of the obscene photograph centered around the female body.

[FIGURE 20]

[Vincent?], early 1860s. Photographic print from the police register BB3, Archives de la Préfecture de police, Paris.

[FIGURE 21]

Anonymous, Second Empire. Colored photographic print on stereo card. Bibliothèque nationale de France.

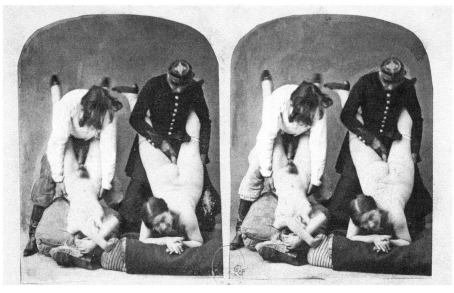

Production of Unauthorized Nudes

Despite the many photographs that grace its pages, the primary purpose of the BB3 was to catalog not these images but rather the people involved in making and selling them. In its entries, the police traced out networks of conspirators that began with the photographer. Approximately half of the seventy-odd photographers whose names can be found in its pages were professional photographers who also registered many other kinds of photographs for legal sale.[51] On the whole, however, the illicit nude was an amateur affair. The professional photographers recorded in the BB3 often had legitimate businesses that their nudes supplemented. Some of those arrested for producing nudes were not even photographers by trade. One ran a wine shop, another was a marble worker, another a peddler.[52] Dealers might take up photography themselves, such as a traveling salesman who eventually decided to take his own photographs with the help of a sea-captain friend.[53] Three known photographers were women.[54]

Photographers were aided by a host of other collaborators, including glaziers, colorists (often women), polishers of photographic plates, and jewelers who fabricated objects containing stanhopes.[55] The accomplice who loomed largest in the collective imaginary during the Second Empire was the model. After 1857, models were tracked, prosecuted, and charged under the 1819 statute.[56] They were no more professional than anyone else in the industry. Male models were usually already involved in the photographic scheme in another capacity and selected by proximity. Their ranks included domestic servants, commercial courtiers, soldiers, a lemonade seller, an accordion maker, a florist, a tailor, a rug maker, a pharmacy student, an actor, a wine merchant, a mirror maker, and a male colorist; photographers themselves also posed.[57] Because of the genre's focus on the female body, however, most models were women. Female models, who were only marginally more carefully chosen, made on average 4F50 or 5F for a multihour session (approximately $12 today).[58] A number of female models appear in both illegal and authorized nudes, but only one said modeling was her profession.[59] Many models were under the age of legal majority (twenty-one), but none in the BB3 were under the age of sexual consent (which was set at eleven in 1832 and raised to thirteen in 1863).[60] In one 1860 case, an eleven-year-old was used as a model, but the models were generally in their late teens and early twenties and employed in the various trades available to young working-class women of the time.[61] They included hat makers, servants, seamstresses, boot pickers, female colorists, and shopgirls; the most common professions were florists and laundresses (*blanchisseuses* and *lingères*).[62] Some were *filles publiques* or *filles soumises*, different terms for prostitutes.[63] Even those who didn't list prostitution as their profession may well have derived some income from it. As Elizabeth McCauley notes, the professions of the models in the BB3 rarely provided enough income to survive, and the women practicing them often turned to prostitution to make ends meet.[64] The model, and her real and perceived connections to the prostitute, would be one of the great preoccupations of Second Empire discourse (see Chapter 2).

Distribution of Unauthorized Nudes

By 1851, the *Gazette des tribunaux* was protesting that "images [*épreuves*] presenting the most licentious subjects, reproduced with all the precision, with all the truth that the daguerreotype alone can achieve" were openly displayed in shop windows, a complaint repeated throughout the 1850s and 1860s.[65] Shops might not always be so brazen; sometimes they instead hid "in a gloomy corner of the shop, some carefully concealed boxes not meant to be opened until after the door was closed, to serve a special clientele, admirers of obscene subjects."[66] Displayed or concealed, however, illicit nudes could indeed be obtained in photography or print shops, where authorized images provided cover for illegal distribution.[67] Some photographers worked on commission or sold out of their studios.[68] Photographs might also be found in other commercial establishments, (for example, jewelers' shops, a store for chemical products, and one selling optical instruments).[69] The *bouquinistes* that continue to line the Seine today sold obscene engravings at the time and likely sold photographs as well.[70]

In many cases no storefront was used at all, as photographers, colorists, glaziers, and models were arrested peddling their wares on the street.[71] More frequently, photographs were sold by various street merchants and itinerant peddlers also selling other wares, such as books, prints, (legal) photographs, canes, umbrellas (sometimes with microphotographs in the handle), jewelry, perfume, and toiletries.[72] One young man was arrested for selling obscene photographs outside of the Exposition universelle of 1867.[73] From the streets, photographs also spread into public gathering places, like cafés, cabarets, and wine shops.[74] They became so common in public spaces that the 1869 definition of a creamery in the *Dictionnaire universel* included a toiletry merchant who concealed obscene photographs among lace, toothpaste, glue, and other bric-a-brac.[75] For many, selling illegal nudity supplemented the low wages of legitimate employment. A list of the different people arrested for peddling provides a remarkable glimpse into contemporary French society. An army of commercial deliverymen (*courtiers* and *commissionnaires*) were joined by a musician at the Théâtre de Belleville, artists and painters, a hat maker, an *expert comptable*, a former *chef de gare*, a bronze worker, *tabletiers*, a *passementier*, a mirror maker, a florist, a grocer's errand boy, a framer (who hid photographs behind lithographs in their frames), a bookbinder, a former *sergeant de ville*, a tailor, and even an omnibus driver caught ferrying obscene *cartes transparentes* across town in the omnibus.[76] Most but not all of those involved in the sale of images were men. Some of the shopkeepers and street merchants were women, and one laundress was arrested for selling images.[77] In addition, the structures of prostitution were important distributional channels for nude images. Arrests in the BB3 show that nude photographs were bought, sold, given, and stolen by prostitutes and their clients (again, see Chapter 2).[78]

Consumption of Unauthorized Nudes

Far less information is available about consumers, who were not targeted by the law as producers and vendors were. The limited entries of the BB3 suggest a varied male clientele, including a twenty-six-year-old without a listed profession, a painter, a cook, a pharmacy student, and even a former French consul with a large collection of photographs (which he was contemplating selling after falling on hard times).[79] In only one court case was an enthusiast of nude photography implicated as a criminal (a counterfeiter).[80] Rather, these photographs were widely consumed by the French male population. By 1869, they were so popular with schoolboys that a reference to obscene photographs also appeared in the definition of "Collégien" in the *Dictionnaire universel*.[81] And if one is to believe the journals of the Goncourt brothers, many members of the French elite, too, had a fondness for nudes, including the sculptor Jean-Pierre Dantan (who possessed a collection of some 1,200 photographs), Aurélien Scholl (the future editor of *Le Voltaire*, who had a taste for "nudities"), and the duc de Morny (illegitimate half-brother to the emperor, who commissioned nude photographs of his lovers).[82] Such was the genre's popularity that in 1864, *Le Figaro* humorously reported that during one trial, the defense attorney asked to reexamine some of the "evidence" against his client, only to be stopped by the judge as he reached for the photographs: "'As honest as you all are, gentlemen,' scolds the magistrate, leaning over with a smile, 'experience has taught us that in this kind of expert assessment some copies always disappear.'"[83] Even those tasked with upholding the law, it seems, were not above a peek.

"Networks of Complicity"

By the 1860s, illegal nudity was omnipresent, if underground. Although most records from the era focus on Paris, French photographs had already begun spreading into the provinces and around the globe.[84] Newspapers and periodicals reported regularly on trials of photographers and models for violations of the 1819 and censorship laws. By 1865, the government had already received multiple petitions asking them to take action against the spread of photographic nudity.[85] And the language used to discuss illegal nudity reflects a growing sense of menace. Gabriel Pélin, who described the contemporary industry in detail, condemns the shopkeepers who displayed obscenity in their windows as "agents of depravation," who "push cynicism and shamelessness to their very limit."[86] In 1860, the satirical newspaper *Le Tintamarre* published an article entitled "Photographies érotiques" ("Erotic Photographs") that featured a fictitious "Monsieur Prud'homme" (Mr. Prude). Prud'homme describes with horror the old men and adolescents, mouth agape at the photographs on display in shop windows, asking rhetorically, "Where do they go after feasting their eyes on these cynical tableaux? God only knows!"[87] In Pélin's real and Prud'homme's fictional outrage alike, there is a fear that consumption of nude photographs was a gateway to social and sexual depravity of all kinds. The implied answer to Prud'homme's question — that these men go to satisfy themselves with prostitutes — would take a central role in the anxieties and fantasies about these images, anxieties that coalesced around the model, her motives, and her sexual status (again, see Chapter 2).

The greatest perceived danger of these images was precisely their broad reach. In 1863, a judge lamented while handing down a sentence that "This commerce corrupts everyone, from the unhappy women who sell the image of their body for almost nothing, to the young people whom these images will, in the schoolhouse, initiate and solicit into debauchery."[88] No one, from the models to the schoolboys who bought such images, could escape their nefarious influence. The sense of sexual danger and social disintegration is even more pronounced in a discussion of obscene photography that appears in Charles-Jérôme Lecour's 1870 study *La Prostitution à Paris et à Londres, 1789-1870*. Lecour asserts that the obscene photograph is the cause of a dangerous decay of social mores (and an encouragement to prostitution) because of its insidious pervasiveness:

> The photographic reproduction of obscene groups, the extreme ease offered by microscopic prints called Stanhoples [*sic*] for clandestine commerce, the necessary complicity of the girls who serve as models in these groups, whose indecency defies the imagination, complicity that extends to the workers, colorists, pasters, cardboard vendors, etc., employed at this fabrication, constitute elements of demoralization that penetrate everywhere, even in educational establishments, and about which we cannot be silent in examining the excitations that provoke and develop public debauchery.[89]

Echoing the judge from 1863, Lecour outlines a "necessary complicity" that spreads throughout society. He focuses on those involved in production, from the models who pose in photographs to the craftspeople who finish them, but this complicity could also be said to spread from the photographers who take the photographs to the merchants who sell them and to the men who buy them. Try though the police might to curb the spread of such images, ultimately, they could not regulate everyone tainted by complicity.

◢ Between Art and Obscenity ◣

During the Second Empire, the law thus enshrined two categories of nudity. The one, legal and ostensibly artistic, undergirded the art aspirations of the medium; the other, illegal and often obscene, inspired anxiety about the social dangers of photographic nudity. Because of the absolute jurisdiction and enforcement of censorship law, the two should have remained fairly separate. Yet there was in reality a third group of photographs, consisting of the many images that hovered between obscenity and artistry, thereby revealing just how porous the legal (and aesthetic) boundaries between them could be. This final group was as influential as it was nebulous, for the most consequential debates about the meaning of nude photography arose out of its challenge to the law's categories.

Absolute though it was, the censorship law had not been intended to legislate obscenity and included no explicit aesthetic standards. Consequently, alongside académies, the government also authorized hundreds (perhaps even thousands) of other photographs of women that had no clear artistic purpose at all. These included stereographs and cartes-de-visite of suggestive scenes or of actresses, demimondaines, and dancers in revealing or formfitting costumes (Figure 22).[90] They inundated shops and regaled passersby from displays in shop windows, and were wildly popular. In 1860, the photography magazine *La Lumière* joked that the quantities of actresses' photographs hidden in the desks of schoolboys were making it impossible to teach.[91] Without descending into complete nudity, these early talismans of celebrity often played on the erotics of the exposed stockinged leg just as illegal images did (indeed, for Solomon-Godeau, photographs of dancers and entertainers define this erotic paradigm).[92] The government also authorized other seminude photographs without even the justification of celebrity portraiture, such as photographs by Lamiche and Augé depicting women lolling about in various states of undress, revealing their nipples and lifting their petticoats (Figure 23). These kinds of photographs often inspired the same disdain as illegal images. Gabriel Pélin indignantly decried window displays where "the noble figures of virgins, of empresses" were "exposed pell-mell next to nude courtesans."[93] They did nothing to reinforce the artistic aspirations of the photographic nude, and yet the government had sanctioned their sale.

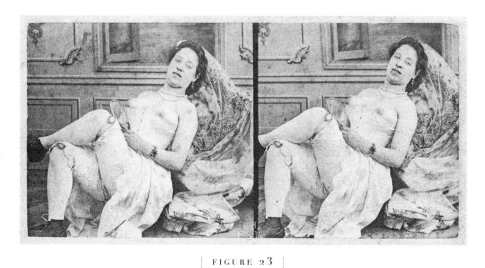

Indeed, even académies inspired confusion about the bounds of artistry and decency. They shared a number of motifs (gauze, mirrors, and cascading hair stand out as examples) with contemporaneous illegal images.[94] Some were also produced as stereographs, a format better suited to titillation than artistic inspiration (Figure 24).[95] Sometimes they also betrayed some of the marks of the model's real body, in dirty feet or unwashed hair, dirt that, according to some scholars, might remind viewers of the prostitutes who modeled in illegal images.[96] In other cases, Elizabeth McCauley has argued that the poses and the gaze of the model, so essential to cordoning off the space of the legitimate artistic nude, violated the boundaries of that artistic space.[97] An instructive set of images are those of Louis-Camille d'Olivier. D'Olivier was known for striking académies that were "*honestly* done," yet even his large-format académies occasionally use poses that mimic the foreshortened perspective of explicit illegal imagery.[98] Moreover, he also produced a questionable series of authorized stereographs and hundreds of authorized half-stereographs in the mid 1850s, some of which quite salaciously depict groups of nude women sprawled about a boudoir caressing each other and gazing into mirrors. These racier scenes share certain compositional traits with illegal images, including their format, a fixation on the erotic potential of the mirror, implied lesbianism, and, again, a foreshortened perspective on the body (Figure 25; see also Figures 75 to 78 for more from the series). If we add to this the fact that some photographers did produce illegal images that looked very much like académies (thus hoping to avoid prosecution), the status of the académie becomes far more muddled.

A dozen or so photographers who appear in the BB3 also registered nudes for the Dépôt légal, and a pair of photographers who straddled the legal line are particularly instructive of the cross contamination the censorship law could not eradicate.[99] The first is the photographer Pierre Eléonor Lamy. In January 1861, he submitted a series of forty stereographs depicting women engaged in domestic activities for government approval. With the exception of one nude, they all play on the erotic charge of semiundress without actually exposing much skin, but they were authorized with different restrictions depending on variations in how much they did show. The least daring could be sold but not displayed (Figure 26). Those showing nipples or lifted skirts were authorized for export only, and some of this group required special dispensation by direct order of the *conseiller* (the case for Figures 27 and 28). Often only a few inches of fabric distinguished these shades of legality (as in Figures 26 and 27).[100] Furthermore, Lamy also produced photographs that either were not approved or were never submitted for authorization. In these illegal images, examples of which can be found in the BB3, in the Bibliothèque nationale, and in private collections, hemlines and

[FIGURE 24]

Alfred Billon (possibly Auguste Belloc), 1860s.
Photographic print on stereo card.
Bibliothèque nationale de France.

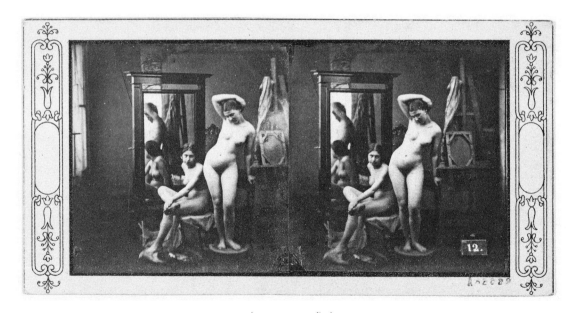

[FIGURE 25]

Louis Camille d'Olivier, 1856.
Photographic print on stereo card.
Bibliothèque nationale de France.

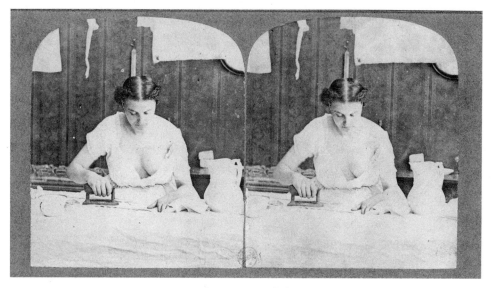

[FIGURE 26]

Pierre Eléonor Lamy, 1861.
Photographic print on stereo card.
Bibliothèque nationale de France.

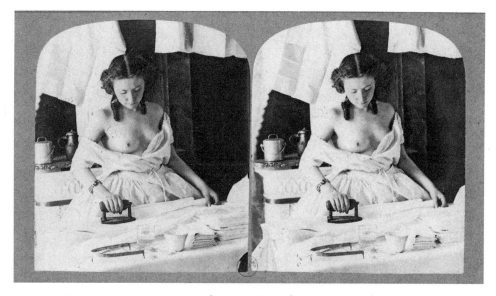

[FIGURE 27]

Pierre Eléonor Lamy, 1861.
Photographic print on stereo card.
Bibliothèque nationale de France.

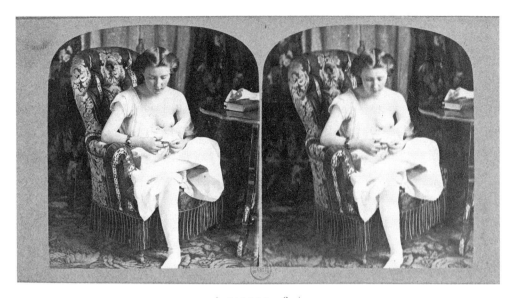

[FIGURE 28]

Pierre Eléonor Lamy, 1861.
Photographic print on stereo card.
Bibliothèque nationale de France.

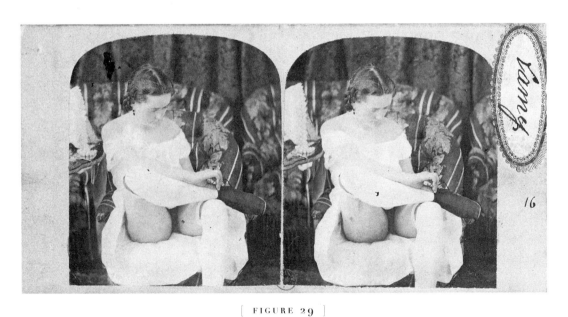

[FIGURE 29]

Pierre Eléonor Lamy, 1860–1861.
Colored photographic print on stereo card.
Bibliothèque nationale de France.

necklines have shifted enough to make the implicit unacceptably explicit (Figure 29). They reveal that legality and illegality could be nearly as close as the different levels of legal authorization.[101] Many of the legal and illegal images from Lamy's series (like Figures 28 and 29) are unnervingly similar to each other, and none look like the kind of "art" that would propel photography to the lofty realms of artistic glory.

Perhaps the most extreme example is that of Auguste Belloc, another photographer who appears in both sets of records. Belloc was the photographer responsible for the largest single police seizure recorded in the BB3, including a series of examples of the "beaver shot" packaged in cardboard boxes designed to look like books entitled *Œuvres de Buffon* (see Figure 18).[102] But he also appears in another entry in the BB3, as a signatory of an 1857 petition to the emperor defending unauthorized nude images as art.[103] He was a widely respected photographer who (among other things) produced art nudes, some of which he submitted for authorization under his own name and others of which were submitted by other photographers before and after his death (Figure 30).[104] He also developed scientific advances in the photographic process and wrote treatises on photography.[105] Belloc was considered one of the best photographers of his generation, and his photographs were held up as the gold standard of art photography. One 1857 article declared that Belloc's very name would one day be synonymous with photographic greatness: "One will say a Hanfstaengl, a Périer, a Nadar, a Belloc, a Ferrier, a Bisson, a Jeanrenaud, a Legray, a Billordeau, a Reylander, a Whyte, as one says a Raphaël, a Carache, a Guide, a Corrège, a Titien, etc., and that in all genres, in all branches, in all applications of photography."[106] During the Second Empire, it was possible for one man to be both an innovator of art photography and a threat to its very existence.[107]

Nor were the difficulties posed by the spread of these new forms of nudity limited to the sphere of photography. Courbet, for example, did not work only from the images by Villeneuve. Others were found in his studio on his death, and many photographic historians have remarked on the closeness of his painting *The Origin of the World* and "beaver shot" photographs.[108] Indeed, in May 1867, the BB3 reported that Courbet had been "reported as possessing and placing in a personal show that was open to the public . . . an obscene painting. Upon verification, nothing more than an académie was observed."[109] Based on the dates, Dominique de Font-Réaulx has argued that this painting was likely the *Origin*.[110] Courbet may well have worked so closely from illegal photographs that he ended up in the BB3 alongside them. A number of art historians have also linked the critical scandal that erupted around Manet's *Olympia* to its allusions to the visual

[FIGURE 30]

Auguste Belloc, 1852. Salt print
from glass collodion negative.
Bibliothèque nationale de France.

language of illicit nude photography.[111] And Solomon-Godeau has argued that
the broader "crisis of the nude," described by T. J. Clark in relation to *Olympia*,
was probably "integrally related to the proliferation and dissemination of pornographic and erotic photography."[112] Nude photographs did not merely violate
the boundaries of the legal classifications into which they were placed, their influence seeped into other media, exerting new pressure on the conventions governing the representation of the body.

A Menace to Art and Society

Unsurprisingly, this confusion of the categories of legality and decency also left
its mark in discussions of photographic nudity. The very terms used to designate
the nude are a testament to how uncomfortably indistinguishable legal and ille-

gal photographs could be. Illegal images might be called "obscenities" or "nudities," but they might also be described as perversions of the académie: "académies of the street" or an "académie whose models are not always academic."[113] At times, it is very difficult to deduce what kinds of images are actually being discussed by commentators; when newspapers complained about photographs that "under the pompously artistic title of académies, present the eyes with images that are too often licentious," they could mean illegal images masquerading as académies or académies that pushed the boundaries of obscenity.[114] The two categories were so entangled that many twentieth-century art historians ultimately consider them fundamentally the same, the académie little more than legally sanctioned smut.[115] During the Empire, however, the censorship law nonetheless maintained the status of the académie as a genre, no matter how difficult it was to define. And likely as a consequence of this fact, the entanglement of art and obscenity was not figured at the time as a collapse of the two categories into one but rather as an attack by obscenity on the artistic potential of photography. In the 1850s and 1860s, anxieties about the artistic dangers of obscene photography go hand in hand with fears about its nefarious social influence.

One striking example comes from an 1858 *La Lumière* article by a photographer, Georges d'Apremont (one of few negative articles about art nudes in that publication). D'Apremont heaps scathing criticism on photographers of human subjects. He asks sarcastically, "Where are the artistic studies, the scènes de genre [photography] has given us? [. . .] I see here and there a few well-composed groups; I see a few nudities or anacreontic ideas having brushes with the law; but I do not see therein the elements of serious studies that might please the eye and render actual service. [. . .] There is a whole revolution to undertake in this area."[116] His directive to other photographers is clear: the photographic figure study was in disrepute, but it could be art, and photographers had a responsibility to make it so. He finishes the article by exhorting his compatriots to "understand properly their civilizing mission; set aside for a bit their Opera dancers, orgies under the table, académies equally without shame and without art, to fight hand-to-hand for national imagery, and, instead of fearing the penal code, they will soon open immense and fruitful prospects."[117] D'Apremont is throughout explicitly concerned with photography's social role, with its potential importance for the national character, but photographers' obligation to "moralization" and "good taste" is bound up with their obligation to photography as an "entirely new art."[118]

More remarkably, this same concern with the art status of photography appears in nonphotographic publications, similarly mixed in with condemnations of the detrimental moral effects of obscenity. The newspapers frequently invoke the dangers that obscenity poses to photographic art. "Monsieur Prud'homme," for instance, is equally indignant over their affront to art as he is over their affront to decency: "The effrontery of these exhibitions, which are in my opinion the shame of a profession whose Nadars, Disdéris, and Vaillatonts have made into art, equals, if not exceeds, the impudence of Aretino."[119] Elsewhere, a piece in *Le Figaro* goes on at length against photographers who produced obscenity, opening with a scene at criminal court and an expostulation to an imagined photographer:

> What, you wretch! You have in your hands the marvelous tools of photography, and this is all you know to make of it! You see no other fruit to pick, in this art born only yesterday, then the forbidden fruit? You find nothing else to reproduce, in the infinite spectacle of creation, then naughtiness [*grivoiseries*] and indecency! To live, you must make yourself into the cowardly courtesan of the blasé libertines to whom you sell your filthy prints; you must become the shameful corrupter of unemployed female workers; you must work in the shadows, conceal yourselves, run the risk of prison and pillory! You are truly forced, you say, there is so much competition in photography! There remains absolutely nothing else to do . . . except harm![120]

Again, the author's reaction is a mix of artistic and moralistic indignation. His diatribe against the "false artists" who make obscene photographs invokes "indecency" and "shameful corruption," but the crimes of decency that they commit are also against the fledgling "art born only yesterday." In this declamation against obscenity, its moral dangers become artistic, and the damage they incur is done to photography's art potential and to society alike. After lauding Disdéri's accomplishments as embodying the medium's best social and artistic applications, the incensed author concludes with an imperative to would-be pornographers: "Let them become brains; let them cease to be purely machines and from this day we will cease to see—to the shame of the arts—photographers appear in criminal court."[121] Above all else, photographic obscenity was a shame to the "arts," and to photography's place among them.

Such explicit denunciations of obscenity as an attack both on art and on moral decency would nearly vanish with the Empire, giving way to a discourse about the photographic nude that, until pictorialist photographers revived the nude at the very end of the century, almost entirely ignored art. But during photography's early years, art was at the heart of the debate about the nude. Even the greatest detractors of the medium, including Baudelaire and the Goncourt brothers, situated it in the context of wide-ranging artistic debates rather than merely addressing the nude as a problem of social good. And as we will see in the next three chapters, these artistic concerns even invaded the discourse about the sexual availability of the model's body. Whatever we may think of it now, at its inception the photographic nude simultaneously evoked for contemporaries the most exalted realms of art and the lowest depths of prurience all at once.

⚜ CHAPTER 2 ⚜

The Judgment of Phryne, or, The Model's Meaning

In 1859, the French satirical newspaper *Le Charivari* published a remarkable drawing (Figure 31). The tableau is set at the water's edge. In the foreground, two young women bathe, submerged nearly to their necks in the water. On shore, a camera has been set up, its lens trained on the pair of bathers, the photographer already in place under his hood. Underneath the title, "Captured . . . by the daguerreotype," a caption reads, "Ah! . . . Clarisse. Look at that great machine . . . one might say there's an eye watching us!" Who are these women frolicking in the nude, seemingly still so naive in 1859 that they do not realize that the "machine" observing them is a camera and that they have become models? Are they complicit? Are they the victims of photographic voyeurism? Even as the cartoon pokes fun at the popularity of the female body as a photographic subject, it also reveals a fundamental discomfort about the relationship of the camera to the women it so often "captured" for prying eyes.

In an industry defined by the ways that it defied conventional artistic and social classifications, the female model was in many ways the most troublesome figure of all. She *was* the nude. Whether academic or obscene, Second Empire photographic nudity was dominated by images of women. Even as she exposed her body completely for the camera, however, her identity and motivations remained shrouded in mystery. In fact and in public perception, she was often a prostitute, and most scholarship has emphasized the model's ties with prostitution.[1] Yet reality was more complicated. In many cases, even when the image of her body was for sale, her real body was not. The model might be a prostitute, a shopgirl down on her luck, an artist's model, someone's lover, or a victim forced into participating in the burgeoning obscenity industry; it was impossible to know from her picture. Indeed, precisely because the nude photographic model defied the contemporary boundaries and categories of female sexual behavior,

CROQUIS D'ÉTÉ.   1

PRISES...... AU DAGUERRÉOTYPE
_ Ah !..... Clarisse ......vois donc cette grande machine ......on dirait qu'il
y a un œil qui nous regarde !......

[FIGURE 31]

"Croquis d'Été," *Le Charivari*, 27 July 1859.

she inspired anxieties about the nature and limits of female sexuality. As she did, her body became the object of scrutiny and regulation by which contemporaries sought to understand and contain the dangers of these images.

The female photographic model was not alone in thus standing in as a symbol for other concerns; her sister, the artist's model, also became, according to Marie Lathers, "a figure on whose body the anxieties, fears, hopes, and fantasies of a culture and a century were painted and sculpted."[2] These models, too, were often associated with prostitution.[3] The photographic model, however, offered a body to the camera that could not be "transformed" by her medium into a projection of cultural preoccupation the way other models' bodies were painted or sculpted. Instead, the battle lines were drawn directly onto that real body both within and outside the camera's frame. The photographic model thus came to (quite literally) embody myriad anxieties and fantasies, not merely fears about prostitution. She represented an entire range of dangerous and disruptive sexual possibilities, in-cluding, on the one hand, the coercion and exploitation of young women and, on the other — remarkably, and contradictorily — the expression of sexual agency and desire. Meanwhile, the model's body also took on an entirely different, although not unrelated, set of meanings within the context of contemporary debates about photography's art value. The significance of a given photographic image came to reside in the model herself, burdening her body not only with fears about female sexuality but also with the aspirations of an entire medium. She alone could make the difference between a photograph that was prurient filth and one that was a work of innovative beauty. The Second Empire model was seductress and victim, accomplice and muse, abject and exalted all at once. Her body could be the *corps du délit* (literally, the body — "corps" — of the crime, and legally, the physical evidence of it), even as it could also be a work of art.

The Model as Prostitute: The Corps du Délit

In 1865, the socialist Pierre-Joseph Proudhon wrote that the trade in obscene photography was turning Paris into "the *great prostitute* of nations."[4] By that time, the prostitute had already become, in T. J. Clark's words, a "cultural signifier of modernity" and a metaphor for a variety of contemporary preoccupations in visual and literary works of art.[5] In the case of nude photography, however, the pairing of prostitution and the incipient trade in photographic obscenity was far more than metaphoric. As described in Chapter 1, many models for illicit images were prostitutes, and the system of prostitution was part of the distribution chain of images. Prostitutes possessed these images, passed them along to clients, received them from clients, allegedly stole them from clients, and even participated in their commercial distribution.[6] One of the more active photographers in the police records, François Lamiche, recruited women to distribute his images by hiding "the obscenities that they go to sell in brothels" under their skirts, a perfect image of the fledgling relationship between the two industries (and one that would become even more apt later in the century).[7]

Perhaps not surprisingly, then, the nude photographic model as prostitute was a leitmotif of early reactions to nude photography. She appears cloaked in varyingly euphemistic language almost from the very invention of photography. An 1847 article in the newspaper *Le Corsaire*, for instance, describes an imagined customer, enticed into a photography shop by a nude photograph, who inquires about "the name of the seductive model" only to be met with blushes and lowered eyes that confirm that the shopgirl herself is that model. Upon this discovery, the author marvels that "this innocent boutique no sooner became something like the grotto where Dido lured Aeneas."[8] Later, the same Gabriel Pélin who described those selling photographs as "agents of depravation" (see Chapter 1) claimed that shopkeepers went so far as to facilitate prostitution: "Certain merchants would give, if needed, the address of the model! . . . Ruffiano!"[9] The pimp photography merchant resurfaces again in the scandalous (though likely fictionalized) memoirs of Monsieur Claude, chief of the *Sûreté*, wherein he recounts the case of an erstwhile cook turned obscene photographer who was a "pimp by way of his lens," and used photographs to arrange sexual liaisons for women of the upper classes.[10] There was a pervasive perception that Second Empire photographic models were prostitutes and that the sale of a photograph was directly related to the availability of the model's body itself.

Nude photographs need not even facilitate prostitution so directly for the model to be condemned as a prostitute. The model was often simply assumed to *be* a prostitute because the nature of her work—exposing her body for the sexual pleasure of a consumer—made her so much *like* one. This, for instance, is the logic of another former police chief, Charles-Jérôme Lecour, in addressing nude photography in *La Prostitution à Paris et à Londres, 1789–1870*. When (as discussed in Chapter 1) Lecour describes "the necessary complicity of the girls who serve as models for groups, whose indecency exceeds anything one could imagine," he assumes that this complicity means that models were prostitutes; no one but a prostitute would doff her clothes for the camera. This same assumption lurks in endless offhand references to prostitution peppering discussions of nude photographs, such as an 1861 article in *Le Figaro* about nude photography wherein the author snidely remarks that a photographer "collected his *posers* at random in the gutter, on the sidewalk [*trottoir*]."[11] Wherever these models actually came from, as a category, the photographic model was to be found on the *trottoir*, the emblematic space of nineteenth-century prostitution. And finally, this assumption would take striking form in the 1863 legal ruling wherein the judge referred to photographic models as "unhappy women who sell the image of their body for almost nothing"; only the words "the image" (and the implied presence of the camera) differentiated them from the long tradition of women who sold their actual bodies for the same pittance.[12]

Indeed, the body took on enormous significance in the assumed equivalence, becoming the fundamental link between the two groups of women. This was not merely because both women betrayed the same willingness to expose themselves for profit, but because, for many, their nudity revealed vaguely defined physical traits that substantiated their sameness. Take, for instance, an 1857 article in *Le Triboulet* denouncing public displays of nudity: "For some months, one sees displayed, in the front windows of certain bookstores and print shops, hideous *photographic académies*, each in more abracadabrical poses than the last. The commerce of these stupid nudities—whose models seem to have been chosen in the best-stocked [*les mieux achalandés*] *establishments* of Paris,—is not authorized, but merely tolerated."[13] The author associates models and prostitution with his italicized reference to certain establishments of Paris and pointedly uses an adjective ("achalandé") that means simultaneously "well-stocked" and "highly frequented" in French. To make sure no one misses the point, he finishes with the word "tolerated." Tolerance defined the legal status of prostitutes at the time, and the use of the word to describe photographs therefore relegates them to the same legal and social position as prostitution.[14] At the same time, he prioritizes the body in thus binding the two together. Rather than focusing on the models' "abracadabrical poses," he emphasizes the way that the model's bodies, which "look like" they have come out of a brothel, undermine any pretense of artistry. This simultaneously vague and essential characteristic of the model's body both marks her as a prostitute and marks the images as obscene.[15]

Other reactions, such as *Le Tintamarre*'s outraged "Monsieur Prud'homme," emphasize the body even more. Describing the eager public clamoring around window displays of nude photographs, the author writes, "In these museums of feminine charms, there are nothing but femurs and bouncing bosoms, and a son dares not take his father there without danger. But they each go on their own. The public who presses up to the display windows of which I speak, is almost exclusively composed of old men and adolescents. One goes to reignite the dust of extinguished passions; the other to fan the flames of juvenile desire. Where do they go after feasting their eyes on these cynical tableaux? God only knows!"[16] While it is meant to be sarcastic, the reaction of "Prud'homme" is nonetheless revelatory. Again, it presumes models to be prostitutes because of the public display of their naked bodies; the implication is that these photographs are driving men off to find prostitutes to satisfy the desire that they inspire. In this scene, however, the dangers posed by these kinds of photographs have been localized onto the bodies of the models. The museums of "feminine charms" are described in terms of the forbidden body parts they display, the "femurs" and "bosoms," not in terms of their lascivious poses. The language about the body is stronger still in Pélin's discussion of photographic nudity. Pélin argues that those who produced photographic obscenity chose only the most lascivious bodies because "They already know, these intrepid speculators, that the virgin form, the pure, severe, form is not Aphrodite . . . As a consequence, they recommend to photographers the reproduction of figures worn out by orgies and indecency.—This tempts customers and sells well! . . . Oh! If they could gain their living from it, they would transform their window displays into advertisements for brothels without hesitation."[17] For Pélin, the bodies of the models are chosen precisely because they have been visibly tainted by sexual activity; this same body that betrays them as prostitutes constitutes precisely their appeal to consumers. The implication is that however demurely they might be posed, their bodies condemn the photography shop as little better than a front for prostitution.

Even the legal approach to photographic models was predicated on their bodily connection with prostitutes. In 1857, six years after the first trial of a photographer for affront to public decency, the government changed its approach to the execution of the 1819 law. In that case, Ernest Pinard (the very man who prosecuted Baudelaire and Flaubert for the same crime) argued that

> These women having gone to offer themselves to photographers, thus bringing them the means to commit the crime, they should be made to bear their share of the guilt; they were arraigned and fined, a penalty subsequently recognized to be completely illusory, given that behind these girls are people who pay their fines for them; these same people are the ones who exploit them: the photographers, who pay, on average, the feeble sum of 5 francs for five hours of posing. The deputy prosecutor therefore calls for prison time for these models commensurate with the greater or lesser gravity of the actions imputed to each of them, gravity appreciable at the sight of the poses reproduced in the photographic prints before the Court.[18]

Even as the government acknowledged that models were "exploited" by photographers, it also justified charging them as accomplices by claiming that they willingly offered their bodies up for exploitation. Having been offered in this way, the body seems to take on a life of its own, independent from the model as such. It becomes both the means and then, once in photographic form, the proof of the crime, the literal corps du délit. If the pose indicates the degree of the offense, the body is its substance. Imprisonment may well have been more practical than fines, but it also fits within these new parameters for understanding the model's crime: a bodily punishment for a bodily transgression. This classification of the model's body under the law linked her even more closely to the prostitute, for the prostitute was the only other kind of woman whose body was the essential means to a crime. Moreover, the two shared a precarious legal status as a consequence of their criminalized bodies. Neither prostitution nor modeling in photographs was explicitly illegal (models were actually accomplices to the *distribution* of the photographs), but women who engaged in both activities were nevertheless actively pursued by agents of the law.[19]

This insistence on the shared body of the model and the prostitute under the law took striking visual form in the police records. Beginning in the 1850s, and

[FIGURE 32]

Photographic print and entry
from the police register BB1.
Archives de la Préfecture de police, Paris.

continuing through the end of the century, the police kept a register known as the BB1 as part of their efforts to control prostitution. The BB1 contains hundreds of entries of prostitutes, nearly all of which are illustrated with photographic portraits of the women in question (Figure 32). In the pages of the BB1, the body is controlled and kept under surveillance through a combination of image and text that includes information about the background, whereabouts, and activities (clandestine or otherwise) of these women. The same urge to classify the threatening female body structures the entries of the BB3. While more men than women appear in the BB3, there are far more photographs of women

[FIGURE 33]

Anonymous, 1860s.
Photographic print from the
police register BB3.
Archives de la Préfecture
de police, Paris.

[FIGURE 34]

[Vincent?], early 1860s.
Photographic print from the
police register BB3.
Archives de la Préfecture
de police, Paris.

than men in its pages, an imbalance likely explained by the fact that the majority of models were women; their role as models meant that their photographs were readily available to the police.[20] In both the BB1 and the BB3, the police used photography to place the bodies of these women under the complete control of the law. The main difference between the two is that the BB3 perhaps exposes more violently the law's intentions in relation to the body because it used confiscated nudes. In the BB3, the government obtained a full accounting of the body and of its deleterious sexual power, right down to images of that body engaged in its troubling work. In some group photographs, the police even scrawled the names of the women directly onto their naked bodies or drew lines through women irrelevant to a particular entry (Figures 33 and 34). In these photographs, the hand of the law marked the model's bodies quite literally with an indelible guilty stain. No matter what might subsequently happen to these young women, their bodies would remain forever branded in the annals of the police records as the record and proof of their crime.

⚐ The Obscure Object of the Camera ⚐

Yet even as the government codified the guilty body of the photographic model-prostitute, reality defied this syllogism. In June 1857, the police arrested a seventeen-year-old photographic model named Julie Elisabeth Parant. At the time of her arrest, Parant was living in Montmartre under an assumed name. According to the BB3, Parant stated that she was married but was hiding from her husband, who wanted her to take a *carte de fille publique* (a card registering her as a prostitute). The implication of this brief biographical note is that Parant had decided to pose for nude photographs to avoid prostitution.[21] Parant's case, and the questions it raises about coercion, choice, and the distinction between posing naked and prostituting oneself, embodies the conflicting and often troubling realities of who was modeling and why. Despite all the rhetoric about the models whose bodies betrayed them as prostitutes, there is much evidence to suggest that models came from a variety of backgrounds and that they came to modeling for many different reasons. The model might well be a prostitute, but she also might be an exploited young person, or she might even (in a possibility far removed from Parant's sad situation) be a woman freely posing for her lover. As the model embodied these conflicting possibilities, she inspired fears about the boundaries between pure and fallen women and the nature of female sexual agency. Her exposed body represented the potential not only for honor lost but also for sexual agency gained, both by way of photography.

As Parant's case suggests, the same records that testify to the links between illicit nude photography and prostitution also testify to these complexities. While many models admitted to being prostitutes, scores of models *did* tell police that they were engaged in a variety of different professions, and they probably were. Moreover, although the press frequently descended into incendiary remarks about prostitution, it also corroborates these claims, describing the women appearing regularly in court as a "troupe of young women, laundresses, florists, seamstresses, boot makers," who, according to *La Presse* in 1860, "had the deplorable idea to augment, in posing for these shameful tableaux, the modest salary that their work procures."[22] *Le Figaro*, for all its use of the euphemistic trottoir, also describes the young women brought up on charges as a "waistcoat maker, flower girl, boot maker, feather worker," to emphasize that they weren't models "by profession"; whether intentionally or not, the same list simultaneously reinforces the idea that they weren't prostitutes by profession, either.[23] Of course, these were exactly the young women who probably did turn to occasional prostitution to support themselves, but not necessarily so, as the case of Parant attests.[24]

Indeed, what made these photographs so troubling was precisely the fact that modeling for photographs and engaging in prostitution *weren't* always the same. One place this tension appears is in Lecour's treatise on prostitution, which seems to argue that models were prostitutes because of their "necessary complicity." If that complicity made the models like prostitutes, that should make the photographs just like prostitution. The deleterious effects of nude photographs, therefore, could be potentially quarantined from the realm of "good society" in the same way that prostitution could be. Lecour, however, insists that the complicity of the models extends "to workers, colorists, gluers, paper sellers, etc., employed in [the photographs'] fabrication" and that this complicity is one of the "elements of demoralization that penetrate everywhere."[25] What at first looks like an attempt to contain the dangers of these images by summarily classifying them together with prostitution ultimately gives way to an acknowledgment that their dangers actually lie in the way that they infiltrate portions of society where women (and men) are not engaging in prostitution directly. In other words, that photographic obscenity *could not* be equated with prostitution is precisely what made the model the subject of so much anxiety. She was her own category, as problematic as the prostitute and associated with her, but one that stubbornly resisted assimilation into this existing paradigm.[26]

One fear at the time was that the model might be a victim. The reality was that many (if not most) of the working women who posed for commercial nudity were "victims" in a broader sense of their poverty; they modeled only because of extreme financial need (no matter how "willingly" the government prosecutor might claim they did so). Some, however, were probably more directly coerced at the hands of photographers, whom (as we have seen) *Le Figaro* called "the shameful corrupter[s] of unemployed female workers."[27] As noted in Chapter 1, an eleven-year-old model appeared in court in 1860.[28] Although she was just at the age of sexual majority, she was a child, and many models were under the age of legal majority (twenty-one). There are also a few entries in the BB3 that suggest that young women were tricked or otherwise forced into modeling.[29] One such case was described in detail in *La Presse* in 1857. According to the newspaper, a pair of respectable married dairy workers were walking in the passage Valentino one day when they stopped to look at some photographs, including a reclining nude. "One can understand," the newspaper opined, "the surprise of the husband and wife upon recognizing the features of their daughter, Virginie Brault, aged seventeen."[30] Worse still, Virginie's younger sister, Joséphine, had also been involved. At the ensuing trial of the photographers—a married couple who were longtime neighbors—more questions were raised than answered: "Did the two young women, Virginie and her sister Joséphine, aged fifteen years, solicit the photographer to have them pose thusly, as the two accused and a witness declare, or was it M. Rideau who requested that the young women pose, as they report? What is certain is that they posed unbeknownst to their parents and in a poorly enclosed atelier, as several neighbors reported having frequently seen the interior of the atelier from their windows when the models were there."[31] At the recommendation of the prosecutor, the two photographers were sentenced to jail time, and there is no mention that the sisters were charged as accomplices. However, the article never resolves whether they chose to pose for the photographers or were forced to do so, whether they were paid, or why they would have agreed to the arrangement in the first place. The whole affair offers only a series of questions to the reader, questions behind which lurk fears about sexual agency and exploitation that run deeper than tarnished reputations.

The judge presiding over the 1858 trial of a photographer named Eugene Darnay expressed these fears even more explicitly. As he passed down his sentence, the judge opined that Darnay's greatest crime was not the pictures he created but the process of sexual corruption that creation entailed: "You have committed an even greater fault in bringing young women into your atelier, in perverting them, in exciting them to debauchery, in making them pose as models for your shameful productions. Among these young women, for the most part between the ages of sixteen and seventeen, there are some who belong to honest families, and who arrive by your actions at police court, under a stain that will never fade away."[32] The logic for charging models as accomplices rested on the supposed equivalence of the model's and the prostitute's body, and yet the judge of Darnay's case casts doubt on both this legal standard and the logic that underpinned it. It was all very well to try "fallen" women or prostitutes as accomplices, he seems to be saying, but these models don't fall into that category. Indeed, even as the young women were sentenced as accomplices, Darnay was convicted of "debauching of a minor." Of course, the "honest family" whence they came is a vague category, but, in this case, these models are very clearly presented as young women who, before being enticed to take their clothes off, were the polar opposite of someone who might be found on the trottoir.

They probably weren't alone. The *Gazette des tribunaux* reported in another case, for instance, that some models were accompanied by their mothers to the sentencing.[33] And Darnay's case was not the only one in which photographers were charged with debauching minors, nor was it the only one where legal minors were charged as accomplices for modeling.[34] As Darnay and his ilk used these young women as models, they chipped away at the boundaries distinguishing the model who was a prostitute and she who was not, at the boundaries of consent and coercion. In an 1860 report of yet another trial, the writer bemoaned those who "speculate on immorality and drag down with them into the perils of their clandestine commerce young women already lost, no doubt, but who achieve, in these impure ateliers, the complete abdication of all modesty."[35] Try as he might to convince his readers (and himself) that the women in these photographs were already long "lost," this is the very case where the eleven-year-old was among the models; despite his feeble "no doubt," there was a great deal of doubt, indeed.

As with the perceived connection between the model and the prostitute, these doubts were also projected onto the body. Another government-sanctioned attempt to classify the legal and sexual status of the model's body instead betrays the profundity of worries about their difference. In his *Étude Médico-Légale sur les attentats aux mœurs*, the doctor Ambroise Tardieu recounts that in August 1861, he was called to help the police deal with some particularly disturbing images (likely examples of the "beaver shot") that were part of "a truly innumerable mass of obscene photographs."[36] These images stood out because "the exhibition the models made of their most secret parts appeared exacerbated by a unique refinement of obscenity; the eye penetrated so far that it seemed that the opening was maintained with the aid of some artificial process."[37] Tardieu was asked by the police to verify whether it was physically possible for the women in the photographs to have spread their legs without the use of a "foreign object" to force the pose.[38] If Tardieu determined that their position had, in fact, required physical restraint, the implication was that the photographer might be charged with a more severe crime, likely indecent assault (*attentat à la pudeur*) rather than affront to public decency. Tardieu went to St. Lazare prison, where convicted prostitutes were imprisoned, and, with the aid of another doctor, systematically placed "a great number of women" in the necessary position, determining that the women had not been forced and "the opening of the sexual parts results either from the natural anatomy of women or from the manner in which they were posed."[39]

That Tardieu was asked to make this study on real women to confirm what he already suspected — that the pose was not forced — indicates the degree to which the body had become the corps du délit. Only after Tardieu had forced the truth from the body could the matter be laid to rest. Tardieu's experiment, however, also indicates just how shaky the assumption of consent and complicity that justified the prosecution of models (and their association with prostitutes) might be. It may have been the case that the police would have been concerned for the models even had they been supposed to be prostitutes, but the fact that Tardieu recreated the photographs on incarcerated prostitutes without qualms about *their* violation suggests otherwise. The fallen bodies of the prostitutes, the logic seems to have been, were already corrupted, so there was nothing wrong with using those bodies to make sure that the women in the pictures (perhaps not so fallen after all) had not been unlawfully coerced. In this strange and futile attempt to locate victimization or guilt on the body itself, Tardieu was working to quiet lurking fears that models and prostitutes were not the same, and that not all of the bodies the law had cataloged as guilty in the pages of the BB3 actually *were* guilty. Or, we might say in more pointed terms, the bodies of the prostitutes were already accepted as objects of the law's most dehumanizing penetration; the question was, had the photographic model already become this kind of object, or might she still be a "real person," worthy instead of the law's concern?

◁ Women as Desiring Subjects ▷

Fears about prostitution and coercion largely focused on the women who modeled in commercial images. Yet these were not the only kinds of images in production at the time. Photographers also produced private commissions, which, as previously noted, were not illegal. Because these images were not for sale, they defied the claim that the real bodies in nude photographs were for sale, adding yet another layer to the model's complexities. These photographs represented the possibility of yet another erotic body, equally difficult to classify and even more difficult to contain: that of the sexually desiring woman who offered herself to the camera not for money but for pleasure. During the Empire, the figure of such a woman begins to circulate in anecdotes in the press, accompanied by very specific worries about sexual exposure and agency—worries that would be, once again, mapped onto the bodies of the models in the photographs.

Because private images circulated extralegally, there is very little archival evidence of what they looked like or who was making them during the Second Empire (later in the century, on the other hand, they would abound). The only photographs that we know to be examples of a woman participating in her own seminude photographic representation in the period are those of the Countess de Castiglione. Mistress to Napoléon III in the 1850s, she notoriously commissioned a series of images of her naked legs in the 1860s from the firm of Mayer and Pierson (Figure 35). Her motivations for doing so remain unclear to this day. Solomon-Godeau argues that the countess's photographs are defined by the convergence of fetishizing forces—commodity, photography, and patriarchy—onto her body, not by any demands of her own self-expression.[40] Be this as it may, the countess's decision to photograph herself seems to have been a personal one. And although she is one of very few recorded examples of how these images might have been appropriated by women on their own terms, she does not ap-

[FIGURE 35]

Pierre-Louis Pierson, *Les jambes*
(portrait of Countess de Castiglione), 1861–1867.
Albumen print from glass collodion negative.
Metropolitan Museum of Art, New York.

pear to have been alone. The press coverage of one trial in 1861 also indicated that certain obscene photographs in that case were commissioned by the female model herself; although those photographs did end up in public circulation, it remains unclear to this day whether this was her intention.[41]

Moreover, contemporary sources suggest that at the very least there was a public *perception* that women like the countess existed and that their motives were their own pleasure. One place where this kind of woman appears is a September 1859 "Chronique" from *La Lumière*. The author coins the phrase, "discreet as a photographer," because, he says, of the popularity of a new kind of love token: photographic portraits, wherein "ladies, not at all *aux camélias*, go so far as to represent themselves, as true daughters of Eve, in the primitive costume of our first mother."[42] To take these photographs was not without a certain risk (whence the reference to the photographer's discretion), for, should they fall into the wrong hands, the consequences could be catastrophic. In one case, we are told, only chance "prevented a certain husband from attending one evening an exhibition of académies of this kind, where he might have been able to convince himself, in studying an admirably executed print, that his wife had taken for the camera, if not the most natural pose, at least the most natural costume possible! Happily, only two or three of the husband's friends came to this gathering, and they had the generosity not to speak of it except to everyone they knew."[43] Such images, taken behind the backs of unsuspecting husbands, and possibly even displayed publicly as artistic académies, may not have been widely distributed for sale, but they risked sullying the reputation of a very different kind of woman from those being hauled in before magistrates on a daily basis.

As the same article continues, its increasingly overwrought author elaborates on the protocol for photographic cuckoldry with another cringe-inducing story of failed recognition. He claims that the more seasoned practitioners of the photographic arts of love made sure that "it's only from behind that Romeo can contemplate his Juliette" so as to avoid recognition.[44] In this second case, the wife is both wise enough to follow this prescription and brazen enough to bring her husband along with her to retrieve her commission (so as to assuage any potential suspicion). The poor photographer, however, flustered by the delicate situation, mixes up the woman's nude with the photographs intended to distract the husband from his wife's transaction.

> Terror for the wife upon recognizing the incriminating reproduction, embarrassment for the disciple of Niepce. M. de X. examines the image at length and cries: "It's not possible that such a Venus exists in flesh and bone; this one is more beautiful than nature; undoubtedly artful retouching was used to achieve this masterpiece! I defy you to find a woman so genuinely perfect from a statuary perspective. In any case, I am seizing this superb photograph for myself at any price, and I want it to adorn my study."
>
> The story is authentic; it proves that husbands will constantly make us laugh and wives not always.
>
> It would have been easy for us to embellish his personality and to lend to M. de X a clairvoyance that he did not have. Everyone would have applauded the conduct of a husband who thus contented himself with preventing the imprudence of his wife. That was not at all the case: M. de X. did not recognize the original of that photograph today so luxuriously framed, placed in his study, and shown with pride to all his visitors. [45]

The poor husband in this story is the object of more open ridicule than the first, but both stories once again turn on the body and its revelations of guilt or innocence, this time by way of bodily recognition. So incapable is the second husband of recognizing the body he "possesses" as a husband that he proudly displays the evidence of his cuckolding to all of his friends. His story does not, moreover, reflect well on the poor unsuspecting husband of the first anecdote either, for it suggests that the various male friends who *did* recognize the wife in that first photograph probably had more intimate knowledge of the model's body than did her husband. Aided by the camera, the women in both stories outsmart their hapless husbands via photographs that paradoxically put their bodies (and their desires) on display for all to see while at the same time anonymizing them just enough to save them from the worst consequences of this subversive exhibitionism. The objectifying and dehumanizing characteristics of which the camera is often accused, particularly in relation to representations of the nude female body, are, instead, appropriated by these women to serve their own ends and to protect them from detection. Little wonder that the author admits to finding these two stories "full of terrifying reflections for a columnist who does not want to remain forever a bachelor."[46] The column palpitates with this terror as it recounts its "lesson for the husbands who are always the last to recognize the perfections of their wives, [and] lesson for those who hide these perfections with such care from their husbands."[47] By deriding the subjects of the story, the author tries to defuse the repercussions of such images, but his sarcasm is inadequate to the task of containing the dangerous bodies in these photographs.

The woman who has her nude picture taken for her lover may well have been a phantasm of sexual anxiety and alarm about technological advancement and social change. But even, or, perhaps, all the more so, if she is, she still reveals much about photography's power to generate discourse about desiring women and the free circulation of their bodies. The women of these stories are frightening precisely because they are not prostitutes, because they are using these photographs of their bodies outside the usual transactional economies of sex (that is, marriage and prostitution). These photographs truly operate at the blurry edge of art and eroticism, outside of even the two nebulously demarcated commercial categories of legality and illegality. And their bodies—those bodies in which the meaning of the image continues to inhere—are also more difficult to read. They refuse to give up their meaning. There is no BB3 to catalog offending wives, no Tardieu to examine them for signs of coercion or guilt, and the men who have legal ownership over the bodies in question prove ridiculously ill-equipped to the task of monitoring them. These men are incapable of recognizing their wives' identities in their naked bodies, let alone their motivations and desires.

Jann Matlock has argued that in the nineteenth century, "Fears about women's looking [. . .] have a strange way of slipping onto accounts of women's exposure."[48] In these stories of photographs of desiring women, the reverse is true; accounts of women's exposure give way to fears about women themselves looking with desire. This fear often surfaced as jokes about women looking at photographs of naked men.[49] In 1860, seminude photographs of the acrobat Léotard *en caleçon*—which would lead to the prosecution of the photographer Pesme for failing to authorize the photographs—were all the rage.[50] They inspired a tableau in Cogniard and Clairville's *Revue de l'année 1860* called "Ne Bougeons plus" about a husband and wife who each have photographic portraits taken in semi-undress to rekindle the affections of the other; in this story the female appetite for these pictures of Léotard aligns with the male taste for revealing photographs of actresses.[51] Léotard aside, however, this fear about women looking and desiring did not require that they actually have photographs of naked men to see. Rather, their own nudity contains the disruptive possibility of a desiring gaze that threatens to upend marital structures, social order, and hierarchies of desire. Precisely this dangerous potential erupts to the surface in one final example of a woman's nude photograph from a chapter of the memoirs of Monsieur Claude, appropriately entitled "Les Dangers de la photographie." One day, Monsieur Claude is called to the office of his protector, a certain senator. Claude's men had recently raided the premises of this senator's former cook-turned-photographer, whose wares included nudes peopled by "wives of *orléanistes* and of opposition journalists who pass today as highly respectable."[52] This raid not only threatened the reputation of Claude's mentor, it portended a political fiasco, for various husbands would not hesitate to make trouble for the government in avenging their wives' reputations. The senator begs Claude to blackmail one of the most vociferous opposition-journalist husbands into silence. Claude little cares for the politics but agrees to aide his former mentor, who then hands him a nude photograph and proceeds to recount the sordid tale behind the image.

According to the senator, the woman in the photograph is the daughter of a wealthy merchant who was married off to her widowed mother's lover. Prevented by her jealous mother from consummating her relationship to her husband (whom she nonetheless loves), the young woman exacts her revenge by taking lovers and engaging in upper-class prostitution, whence her nude photograph. Nude photograph in hand, Claude visits La Farcey (the proprietress of the young woman's brothel), who finishes the story. Like the other cuckolded husbands, this one discovers his wife's photograph in less-than-ideal circumstances: in the brothel's photographic catalog. Unlike the other husbands, however, he recognizes his wife, and, what's more, he takes the opportunity to sample the conjugal goods of which he had hitherto been deprived. The outcome is that "his wife was so amiable that once returned home, the husband wanted nothing more of his mother-in-law!"[53] The two then conspire to rid themselves of her mother, and after this murder, the daughter is transformed into the most loving and chaste of wives. Only the photograph remains to betray her past as a prostitute and as a murderer. When Claude visits La Farcey, she presents him with the identical image to his own, on the back of which another of the young woman's erstwhile lovers has written, in a fit of jealousy, "'This is the woman who, in cahoots with her husband, killed her mother to grant herself a new stamp of virtue.'"[54] Armed with this last piece of evidence, Claude successfully blackmails the husband, preserving the reputations of his friend and of the "unveiled women," bringing the anecdote to a close.[55]

Yet if everyone's reputation emerges intact, that does not lessen photography's transgressive force in this story. Once again, the nude model's body is understood to reveal the photograph's meaning. Her pose and nakedness should signify that she is a prostitute. The damning inscription written on the photograph emphasizes the idea that guilt could be read *directly* on the photographed body, for this note unlocks the story and exposes the woman's murderous plan. In this case, however, the meaning of her body is not at all what the photograph suggests. While she has engaged in prostitution, she is not a prostitute, but a wronged wife hoping to gain back her husband; once he is regained, her fall is erased by her marital virtue. The image ultimately obscures as much about the wife's desires and motivations as it appears to divulge. The paradox of photographic exposure is almost too perfectly represented by the fact that the inscription exposing her guilt is written not on the front of the photograph but the back, and is, therefore, simultaneously revealed and concealed by the image. The photograph disrupts the institution of marriage as it objectifies and commercializes this woman's body, turning her into sexual merchandise at the brothel. At the same time, it also empowers her, and, ironically, precisely in empowering her to wield her sexuality outside the bounds of the marriage contract, it restores the social equilibrium it seems to overturn. It returns the woman to her husband, her home, and her respectability (and neutralizes the equally troubling quasi-incestuous coupling of mother-in-law and son-in-law). What are we to make of a genre, and a medium, that simultaneously perpetuates and undermines social structures, sexual relationships, and models of sexual agency?

Real though the connections were between nude photography and prostitution, these stories about images that function as personal expressions of sexual desire point to other explanations for the narrative of their supposed sameness. The assumption that the real body of the photographic model was also on sale rests on—and reinforces—the equation of the photograph and the reality it depicts, an equivalence underpinned by the unique verisimilitude of the medium.

This equivalence, in turn, offered a framework for understanding the bodies on display because it allowed nineteenth-century viewers to integrate nude photography into preexisting discourse about social ills such as prostitution. What people found, however, was that the actual relationship between reality and its photographic copy was far less clear. The woman behind the photograph could be very different from the woman she *seemed* to be with her clothes off. One might never know whether that living woman was also for sale, where the sidewalk ended and the trottoir began. The pages of the police records with their columns of identifying photographs offered a comforting fantasy of comprehension and control, but in reality, their bodies could not be regulated as their photographs were. The more these bodies were exposed, the less they revealed, except inasmuch as they demonstrated the futility of parsing the photographic image by means of the model's body.

⚔ The Model as Art ⚔

During the Second Empire, the problem of the photographic nude came to be figured through the body of the photographic model. As the photographic body was condemned as the means of the crime, it became essential to the terms and definition of obscenity and was treated as a problem to be contained and eradicated. It was also scrutinized for insight into the motivations and sexual status of the real women who had posed, reflecting fears about female desire and agency. At the same time, the model's body was also asked to answer a final and very different set of questions about agency and representation. For the photographic nude did not merely exist as an illicit or personal erotic object; it could also be an art object. The final set of concerns projected onto the model's body are precisely the artistic issues born of the difficulty of reaching a consensus about what constituted photographic art. The model whose exposed body invoked the illicit pleasures of prostitution or the frisson of female desire did not merely threaten public mores, she also undermined pretensions of artistry. That body had to be deciphered in terms of not only its social and sexual status, therefore, but also its artistic status. In the model's body came to inhere the very boundary between obscenity and art, the essence of the image's signification, and the artistic aspirations of an entire genre.

Photographers were well aware of the stakes of the nude and of the crucial role that the model played in the success of a nude photograph. They were so aware, indeed, that one of the great photographers of the day urged against even trying to make nudes. In his 1862 opus, *L'Art de la photographie*, André-Adolphe-

Eugène Disdéri devotes a lengthy section entitled "Des scènes animées—Sujets de genre—Sujets historiques" to addressing the burning question of the "sad nudities" that "display, with dreadful truth, all of the physical and moral ugliness of models paid by the session."[56] Disdéri, like others who sought to use the nude to elevate photography's status, argued that "the representation of the human body is the most interesting and the most elevated of the imitative arts."[57] In the artistic representation of the human body, "reality is sanctified and as if consecrated by beauty."[58] Moreover, Disdéri asserts that the best works of art always embody "moral beauty" along with "plastic beauty"; this is precisely what makes a work like the Venus de Milo so moving.[59] For him, the nude photographic model poses an insurmountable problem rooted in the overlapping and conflicting imperatives of morality and reality in photographic representation. Photography's realism allowed for no mistakes, no alterations where the body was concerned; moral beauty therefore had to be found in the physical substance of the model herself, which was for Disdéri an impossibility. As he puts it, "How can a photographer obtain truly beautiful images with the Venuses and saints of the street-corner [*Vénus des carrefours*]?"[60] In a now-familiar rhetorical turn, Disdéri, too, reverts to imposing prostitution on the model's body ("Vénus des carrefours" is a euphemism for "prostitute") as a way of marking out nude photography's failure to transcend reality.

This time, however, the danger is not sexual but artistic. In Disdéri's eyes, because models are prostitutes, no model exists who might embody both the physical and moral beauty demanded by art, who could stand up to the "marvelous perfection [with which] photographic instruments express the most delicate nuances of reality":

> One therein sees immodesty playing at chastity, incredulity parodying faith, a visage imprinted with all the traces of our prosaic life forcing itself in vain to attain an ideal expression. Should one add to all of this moral turpitude a few signs of physical imperfection in even the most beautiful model, the inadequacy of her legs, the triviality of the joints in her foot, in the knee, poorly disguised callouses, and one will understand that the photographer must renounce representing the nude from the point of view of art, unless he has at his disposition a model wherein is allied to the most perfect physical beauty a grand and appropriate moral character. But this would be an exceedingly rare exception.[61]

Like so many others, Disdéri grounds his objections to the nude in the model's body. As though through a magnifying glass, he identifies parts of that body as potential sites of artistic failure: legs, feet, knees. There is no freedom for the

[FIGURE 36]

Stamped "Disdéri" on reverse.
Second Empire. Carte-de-visite.
Bibliothèque nationale de France.

imagination, no delicacy, no modesty in front of a camera's lens, which means that, for a photographic nude to signify as art, a model's body had to be of unprecedented perfection, unrivaled by the models in other media. The photographic model had to embody moral and physical beauty in her unaltered material substance. Bound to these standards, any photographic art nude was more or less doomed to failure from the start, whether the model was a prostitute or not.

Disdéri's rejection of the nude is somewhat puzzling given that at least two seminude photographs exist with his studio's stamp (although it is possible they are fakes) (Figures 36 and 37). It is equally strange that, as one of the great photographers of the period, he invokes the language of "truth" and "reality" so often wielded against the medium's artistry. Yet even as it condemns the genre as a failure, Disdéri's rejection of the photographic nude also contains crucial insights. First, it reveals once again just how simultaneously important and treacherous the nude was. It venerates the nude, even as it argues that very few pairings of artist and model could produce a successful work of art, no matter the medium. Moreover, it suggests that if a photographic nude *did* manage to cast off the

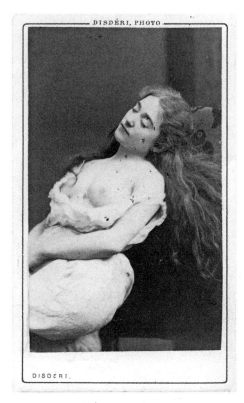

DISDÉRI, PHOTO

DISDERI.

[FIGURE 37]

Stamped "Disdéri." Second Empire.
Carte-de-visite.
Les Archives d'Eros, Paris.

shackles of realism (and prostitution), it would be all the more remarkable a testament to the medium's artistry. Second, it is by far the most explicit acknowledgment of the exceptional burden of meaning borne by the female body in arguments about photography and art. In photography (the logic goes), there is no way for the artist's imagination to gloss imperfections, so every tiny detail of the model's body has heightened signifying value. Even the smallest flaw could ruin an image. Where elsewhere the choice of model is a difficult one, in photography it is the defining one, perhaps the only one. In photographic nudes, the model *is* the signifier. Her body alone was enough to condemn an image as an "académie whose models are not always academic."[62]

The critical reaction to Félix Moulin is an excellent example of the photographic body's artistic stakes. Moulin was one of the most lauded photographers of the Second Empire, his atelier described in 1855 as "the most productive and the most popular, perhaps, in the capital of France, and in the world."[63] He exhibited at both the Exposition universelle of 1855 and the 1859 exhibition that, for the first time, saw photography and painting displayed together in the Salon.[64]

At the latter, he displayed primarily photographs he had taken on a two-year sojourn in Algeria at the emperor's behest, which led to his enduring fame after their publication in the three-volume *L'Algérie photographiée*. He was also known as one of the most prolific producers of legal académies (see, e.g., Figures 16, 38, and 74).[65] Moulin's work garnered high praise. In an 1853 review of his scènes de genre, Ernest Lacan declared that if Moulin continued his great work, "not only will he make a name for himself among artists, he will powerfully contribute to undercutting the objection still raised about photography in saying that it is only a mechanical operation, and that imagination and sentiment have no role in its results."[66] Moulin, surely, could elevate the nude.

At the start of his career, however, Moulin turned to unauthorized nudity to make money. He was the first photographer convicted of affront to public decency in 1851 and subsequently publicly admitted to his illicit activities.[67] In an 1855 biography published in the *Revue photographique* on the occasion of the Exposition universelle, Moulin expressed regret over his earlier "académies of the street" and declared that, henceforth, he would "sing a more elevated song."[68] For some, however, his work was still besmirched. Paul Périer, reviewing Moulin's contributions to the Exposition for the *Bulletin de la Société française de photographie*, was unconvinced. He described Moulin's photographs as monotonous, cold, mannered, ugly, vulgar, and even obscene, using Moulin's model as proof: "If, at a minimum, the scant propriety of the subject were redeemed by beauty, by grace; but how, to the wrong of indecency, he adds so gratuitously those of ugliness and of vulgarity! Look at that Hottentot: she does not have, like those of M. Rousseau, the excuse of being rare. What need is there to show us that a woman can have that right arm, that shoulder blade, that knee-hollow and those feet?. . . M. Moulin has granted us the right to tell him in the name of taste, if not in the name of modesty: 'Cover up this object that one *cannot bear to see.*'"[69] Which Moulin one saw in his work—a pornographer barely disguising his obscenity as "unseeable" académies or a genius whose talent incarnated photography's highest artistic aspirations—was a question of personal perspective. Périer, however, could not be clearer about which Moulin *he* saw in the photograph of the "hottentot" model. Like Disdéri, Périer claims that the real female body without the aestheticizing pretense of paint, pencil, or stone does not stand up to artistic scrutiny. On that premise, he deploys the flaws of the model's body against Moulin, using a succession of her body parts to discredit the work. Because his attack is so fixed in the bodily reality captured by photography, it easily extends from the particularities of one image to photography more generally, with the "hottentot" standing in for the systemic problems of photography's realism, and the way that the medium is incapable of covering the body with the veil necessary for artistic signification. Perhaps this accounts for the strange hysteria of his response, which is incommensurate with the kind of image that would have appeared at the Exposition universelle.

In these examples, the same flawed body that was deployed to accuse models of sexual promiscuity or prostitution acquires another layer of meaning. It simultaneously signifies sexual impropriety and artistic impropriety. In thus doubling the body's meaning, these cases point to perhaps the most remarkable quality of the model. She does not merely come to embody all of the strands of discourse about the photographic nude under the Empire (social, sexual, artistic). She reveals the way that they are fundamentally linked. The body of the "hottentot" not only proves that Moulin cannot produce art, it condemns her as an "unseeable" object of sexual desire. Conversely, the women whose bodies are "unseeable" because they look like they have been selected from the most debauched places of prostitution do not merely prove that all models are prostitutes; they also prove that the "hideous *photographic académies*" hanging in shop windows could not have possibly been real works of art. As *Le Figaro* opined of the photographer who found his models on the trottoir, "he thus condemned himself all alone, for does not this indifference in the choice of models prove, right up to the very evidence, that these nudities are pure indecencies and have absolutely no relationship with art?"[70] The common bodies of working-class women turned models precluded any possibility for artistry, regardless of their poses. The implications for the artistic status of photography are seemingly devastating. The exposed body of the model having thus been transformed into the battleground over photography and art, each body that "looked like" a prostitute implicated photography's artistic failure, even in images that had no pretense to artistry to begin with. Indeed, for photography's detractors, even the most exquisite nude model might *always* prove that photography wasn't art. The photographic model was a woman, and not an idealized abstraction; there was always a sign to be found somewhere on her body that she was not pure, that she might be a prostitute. Clinging to this body as the only site of signification, critics of photography could turn it into a battering ram against the medium.

In the face of this overwhelmingly negative language about the photographic model's body, it is tempting to see the model only as a figure of all of the sexual and artistic fears inspired by nude photography and of the insidious ways in which these fears fed each other. Yet ultimately, the nude's potential was not confined to the body's danger. In positive reviews of photographic nudes, that body set the standard for artistry with as much power as it could set the terms of obscenity. In a lengthy justification of the photographic nude written in 1854, Ernest Lacan addressed the difficulties posed by a realistic medium that allowed no physical flaw to go unnoticed. Noting that "the model, man or woman, as beautiful as they might be, is always far from being perfect," Lacan acknowledged that "it is necessary, for comprehensive studies, that the photographer, make the most of the beauties of the model and that he dissimulate their imperfections."[71] Yet even as he urged photographers to do their best to disguise the body's blemishes, Lacan also venerated that body as fundamental to the art of photography. For Lacan, the photographer's most essential and basic task was "to cast light on the model" and reveal, "the grandeur and the grace of the model, as well as the play of muscles and the outline of contours."[72] In the best photographs, the same models who were assumed to be prostitutes could instead become the substance of (as another review described photographic nudes) "masterpieces" with their own "incredible charm," embodiments of "life and movement" rather than signifiers of sexual depravity.[73]

In this view, the artistic potential of the nude (and of photography more generally) is not limited by the real body's obscenity but instead is as unlimited as that body's beauty. And indeed, despite Périer's indignant denunciation of the "hottentot," for one ecstatic reviewer it was precisely one of Moulin's nudes that ultimately best embodied his remarkable talent (Figure 38): "In depriving himself of the aid of any accessories, M. Moulin creates the most remarkable work. Naked as Eve in Eden, modest as innocence itself, a young half-kneeling woman raises at once her head and arm towards the sky, one might say an angel of Milton or Klopstock, or even more so Elsa of Alfred de Vigny; there is something simultaneously sweet and proud in this woman, something melancholy, mystical, dreamy."[74] However much Moulin's skill was responsible for transforming a naked body into an austere scene of melancholy and mystery, it was still the case that, "nude as Eve," these real bodies might also be mistaken for angels. Perhaps this is what was most terrifying of all about the photographic model: the possibility that, even with all of its imperfections, her body might still be art; that its flawed and tainted physicality might signify something grand and transcendent; in short, that the real, sexual female body had its own sublime and human beauty.

Perhaps the best way to understand the significance of the model's body during the Second Empire is to look forward for a moment to the decades after 1870. Many of the same paradigms for understanding the model persisted. She was ever more frequently connected to prostitution (see Chapters 5 and 6) and the two other explanations for her appearance in front of the camera—coercion or her own desire—harden into caricature. By the end of the century, the voyeuristic photographer had become a stereotype of both fiction and newspaper reportage (one infamous real case involved a man who photographed women on

[FIGURE 38]
Félix Jacques Antoine Moulin,
Étude photographique, 1853.
Salt print from glass collodion negative.
Bibliothèque nationale de France.

— Oh ! alors, si monsieur est photographe...
Donnez-vous donc la peine d'entrer, cher monsieur !

[FIGURE 39]

Mars, detail from "À la mer:
indiscrétions de cabines,"
Le Charivari, 14 July 1881.

the beach at Dieppe without permission).[75] Meanwhile, satirical amateur photographers were paired off with willing model-mistresses.[76] Indeed, by the end of
the century, another caricature from the *Charivari* suggested a broad complicity
between the model and the photographer, in a scene of a woman inviting a photographer into her bathing cabin (Figure 39). As these different figures of the
model solidified into types, the model herself lost her power of fascination, and
her body lost its heterogeneous signifying value. Whereas during the Empire
Claude's memoir suggests the currency of fears that a photograph of one's wife
might appear at a brothel, during the Third Republic, a "true" tale recounted in
Pierre Delcourt's *Le vice à Paris* indicates, instead, the currency of fears that a
fake photocollage of one's wife's face pasted onto another's body might circulate

at a brothel.[77] Once the model became an illusion, her body could no longer speak to her motivations, her sexual status, or even the image's artistic meaning. At the end of the century, Paul Bergon and René Le Bègue, the pictorialists who took up the defense of the art nude, wrote tellingly about warding off the dangers of photographic materiality in the nude: "It is necessary to add that the photographic artist can, through the sentiment in which he composes his tableau, through the choice of the model, through a certain blurriness of focus, attenuate the impression of materiality and even make it disappear. Svelte, elegant and young models are to be recommended in this sense; voluptuous types will only very rarely lead to good results."[78] By the end of the century, the model's physical body had to all but vanish in order to signify photographically, as she herself faded from the cultural consciousness.

Her later disappearance is part of what makes the model's early presence all so remarkable. In 1857, as it reported on the very case wherein Pinard first prosecuted models as the means of photography's crime, the *Gazette des tribunaux* reached back into the annals of classical history to describe the young women disrobing for photographers. If only, the author opined, all of the defendants appearing before the magistrate were instead appearing, as the ancient Greek courtesan Phryne had, in front of the Areopagus in Athens, there would have been little doubt of their acquittal. But, he continues, "times and mores have changed; nary a one of the accused's beauties is hidden, photographic prints having reproduced them with scrupulous exactitude and in a considerable quantity, and that is what, contrary to Phryne, exacerbates their position."[79] Accused of impiety, Phryne was acquitted because of the beauty of her naked breasts, which her lawyer bared to her judges in a bid for clemency. Once photography had entirely revealed its secret beauties, however, the body that had formerly been the subject of art could no longer be anything but the proof of guilt. The author would have his readers believe that under photography's piercing eye, the Phrynes of yesterday had given way to the seamstresses and prostitutes of his day, casting off their veils for all to see. And yet, if these young women's bodies could consign photography to the gutter, they could raise it up as well. Photography could and *did* produce art through the accurate and faithful portrayal of the female body. Despite their total exposure, these models were not so very unlike Phryne after all. The object equally of intense scrutiny and of fierce desire, they, too, might ultimately be redeemed by a body that could be at once the means of a crime and the pure stuff of art.

CHAPTER 3

Baudelaire's Bodies

Charles Baudelaire does not belong to a school. He falls into his own
category. His principle, his theory is to paint everything, to lay everything
bare [*tout mettre à nu*]. He will rummage through the most intimate recesses
of human nature; he will use, in order to render it, vigorous and striking
tones, he will above all exaggerate its hideous aspects; he will inflate it
beyond measure in order to create impressions, sensations. One might say
that he thus creates the opposite of the classic and the conventional.

—Ernest Pinard, Imperial Prosecutor

In 1857, while the *police des mœurs* were pursuing photographers and models
around Paris for the production of photographic nudity that had slipped
between the cracks of France's censorship system, another more famous
trial was taking place. That year, the poet Charles Baudelaire was accused of affront to public decency for six poems in his collection *Les Fleurs du mal* and
brought to trial by the very same prosecutor who was prosecuting many photographers and models: Ernest Pinard.[1] In his public statement, Pinard denounced
Baudelaire's artistic "principles" as little more than the urge to "lay everything
bare" and "rummage through the most intimate recesses of human nature." Although Pinard's language is euphemistic and indirect, it sounds very much as if
it alludes to photography. Pinard, moreover, was not alone in suggesting that
Baudelaire's poems were visually obscene. Many contemporary critics agreed
and were even more forthcoming in their condemnation of the poet. A reviewer
for the *Revue contemporaine*, for instance, likened Baudelaire's poems to an "obscene engraving" and deplored the "sordid postures" represented therein.[2] Another went even further. He opened his review of the poetry collection with an

allegory about cynical contemporary "Diogènes" who rush toward the worst of human experience "expressly to hold up their cynical lanterns, in order to be able to exhibit, with a hope of profit, ignoble photographs."[3] For this reviewer, Baudelaire's poems were little better than the worst kind of photographs, produced only with an eye toward financial profit milked from humanity's basest instincts. He clarifies precisely the implications of Pinard's charges. In the eyes of many readers, it seems, Baudelaire's poems were intimately entangled with the new kind of obscenity taking over the streets of Paris. Baudelaire was "laying everything bare" in a new and unprecedented way, much like these photographs of the body.

Despite his subsequent reintegration into the French literary canon, Baudelaire has still not entirely exonerated himself of these first accusations of obscenity. Because of its semantic similarity to the title of Baudelaire's own collection of squibs, *Mon Cœur mis à nu*, modern critics have appropriated the language of Pinard's accusation, "laying everything bare," to characterize his poetic project.[4] Indeed, *Mon Cœur mis à nu* is particularly fertile ground for self-incriminating declarations; it is there that Baudelaire famously wrote, "woman is natural, that is to say, abominable," leading many scholars to focus on Baudelaire's woman as a figure of inferior nature as opposed to that of masculine art.[5] In these readings, women are fundamentally sexual, corporeal beings who only come to symbolize "art's power to redeem matter" through the complete suppression of their bodies, whether through desexualization into the unnatural dandy (the lesbian) or sublimation into a metaphoric signifier for some superior abstract concept (such as art itself).[6] In other words, before being desexualized, sublimated, abstracted, or otherwise released from the bondage of their bodies, the women of Baudelaire's poetry are still considered obscene. The legacy of Baudelaire's trial is the assumption that what he does lay bare is not his heart (*cœur*) but the body (*corps*) of a woman.[7]

There is no question that an eroticized female body is essential to Baudelaire's artistic project, but the exact status of that body is difficult to characterize. Baudelaire's poetics, like his theories about the visual arts, are grounded in his unique understanding of the complicated relationship between the "real" and the "ideal." This same tension runs through his representation of the body, which is rooted not in the sublimation of that body but in its very corporeality. In Baudelaire's poetry, the body is required to signify simultaneously as physical object and as immaterial art; the body's "meaning" is substantiated in the aesthetics of a "real" physicality.[8] An artistic project so based in the reality of a sexualized female body, however, was profoundly problematic, and all the more so after the arrival of photographic representation. In what follows, I will reexamine poems from *Les Fleurs du mal* in dialogue with Baudelaire's critical works to argue that Baudelaire's own attacks on photography were a reaction not merely to the indexical realism of photography but more particularly to the threat of nude photography. Baudelaire's reaction against nude photography in turn points to a new reading of his poetics of the body. This rereading is not meant as an apology for his frequently violent and misogynistic representations of women. It reveals, however, that the aesthetic of Baudelaire's bodies is antiobscene rather than obscene, a deliberate rejection of a photographic mode of representation that transformed the real body, worthy itself of art, into the natural body, object only of the basest desires. Unlike the poet's heart, the body was not to be laid bare, but adorned, re-covered, and protected against a new kind of image that, for Baudelaire, threatened to eliminate the possibility for the body to signify at all, and thus to be art.

Baudelaire's objection to photography was not moral but artistic. Consequently, it is worthwhile to reiterate some of the principles of Baudelaire's theorization of art in relation to both literature and painting in order to clarify his assessment of the threat posed by photography and then, more specifically, by obscene or nude photography. Critics agree that Baudelaire's artistic allegiances are basically unclassifiable according to the contemporary camps of Realism and Idealism, the one with its commitment to an art rooted in reality and the other with its commitment to an art unfettered by reality.[9] The best-known version of his unconventional compromise between the two is his famous description of the "double composition" of beauty and its pairing of "an eternal, invariable element" and "a relative, circumstantial element" in the 1859 essay *Le Peintre de la vie moderne.*[10] But this formulation of a real-ideal art, one that exists somewhere between reality and sentiment, between eternal and contingent, between the actual objects perceived and the manner of their perception, takes many forms in Baudelaire's writing. As early as his *Salon de 1846,* Baudelaire wrote, "All kinds of beauty contain, like all possible phenomena, something eternal and something transitory."[11] And elsewhere he explored the ramifications of this tension between the real and ideal in other terms. In 1855, for instance, at the end of an unpublished essay entitled "Puisque réalisme il y a . . .," Baudelaire declared that "Poetry is that which is most real, it is that which is not completely true except in *another world.* This world here, hieroglyphic dictionary."[12] Art is not ideal, it is real, but its reality is not indexical. It renders the world as a set of hieroglyphs that reveal in reality a truth that is something more than reality. In another unfinished essay from the 1850s, "L'Art philosophique," Baudelaire once more reiterated the same definition of art, asking his reader rhetorically, "What is pure art according to the modern conception? It is to create a suggestive magic containing at once the object and the subject, the world exterior to the artist and the artist himself."[13] And again in 1855, praising Delacroix, Baudelaire clarifies and expands the role of the senses in the artistic imagination: "Who has not known those admirable hours, veritable celebrations of the mind, when the senses, more attentive, perceive more resounding sensations, when the sky, of a more transparent blue, sinks away like a more infinite abyss, when sounds ring musically, when colors speak, when perfumes tell of worlds of ideas? Well, Delacroix's painting seems to me to be the translation of these beautiful days of the spirit. It is cloaked in intensity and its splendor is privileged. Like nature perceived by ultra-sensitive nerves, it reveals supernaturalism."[14] Baudelaire's art is the reality of the senses as configured by the artistic imagination, not the natural or the ideal but the "supernatural," a mystical combination of the real world and the particular capacities of the artist to perceive and render that world uniquely, universally, and transcendently. This idea of the "supernatural" is also immediately recognizable as the germ of synesthesia, so famously expressed in his "Correspondances," and his poetics of a metaphysical truth accessed through our synesthetic experience of physical reality.[15] In his appreciation of the visual arts and in his own work, Baudelaire prized and strove toward a unique balance of the real and the ideal.

No subject demanded this delicate balance more compellingly than did the human form, which Baudelaire addresses in revelatory terms in a section of the *Salon de 1846* entitled "De l'idéal et du modèle." Baudelaire here triangulates reality and artistic vision around the body of the model, illuminating the precise balance to be struck between the artist's uniquely "idealizing" eye and the "real" details of the body. He insists that the artist's first task is "the slow and sincere study of the model," so as to acquaint himself with the physical reality of the model's body, and to intuit the model's character—but only inasmuch as this then enables him to exaggerate and manipulate those details "to augment [the model's] physiognomy and render [the model's] expression more clearly."[16] For Baudelaire, the artist is never to copy reality but rather to interpret it: "drawing is a fight between nature and the artist, where the artist will triumph all the more easily the better he understands nature's intentions. It does not consist for him of copying, but of interpreting nature in a simpler and more luminous language."[17] Nature, that is, the visual object untouched by the painter's eye or tools, is at odds with art but still serves as its substance, just so long as that substance is suitably transfigured by artistry. That transfiguration is undeniably a process of idealization in simplification; as he says, "the sublime must flee the details," for these details constitute neither the essence of real existence nor a suitable basis for art.[18] Baudelaire effectively advocates for a kind of airbrushing, in which the overwhelming jumble of meaningless visual information in front of the artist is reduced into the clearest and most pristine reinterpretation of itself, with anything too natural (like a woman's sex) conveniently dispensed with in a suggestive line or two. Still, Baudelaire does not argue for a body that is *too* ideal. His conception of the ideal is the product of two very contingent ingredients—reality and the painter's individual subjectivity—and is therefore in total opposition to the abstract perfection generally associated with idealism: "The ideal is not that vague thing, that tiring impalpable dream that swims on the ceiling above académies; an ideal is the individual redressed by the individual, reconstructed and rendered by the paintbrush or the chisel in the brilliant truth of his native harmony."[19] Reality does not just gesture toward the ideal, it determines the ideal, so that even the ideal never achieves a perfect theoretical form; instead, it takes as many mutable and variable forms as the real body. It is found by way of each individual artist's tools and vision, whose unique renderings of the physical universe make the truth of its "native harmony" shine all the more dazzlingly.

Already in this formulation of artistic creativity, there are hints of why photography—particularly of the body—might be unacceptable to Baudelaire. Yet such a conception of art was in no way threatened by the occasional lubricious drawing. In the same *Salon de 1846*, Baudelaire devoted a section of his study to erotic subjects, focusing on the work of Octave Tassaert, a strange salon artist who took on religious and libertine subjects with equal ease. Tassaert also produced some particularly risqué lithographs in the 1830s and 1840s, to which it is quite possible that Baudelaire refers in his opening of the section "Des sujets amoureux et de M. Tassaert:"[20]

> Has it ever happened to you, as to me, to fall into a great melancholy, after having passed long hours leafing through libertine prints? Have you asked yourself the reason for the charm that one sometimes finds in rifling through these annals of sexual tastes, hidden away in libraries or lost in shopkeepers' cartons, and sometimes also of the bad humor they give you? Pleasure and pain intermixed, bitterness for which the lips are always thirsty! —The pleasure is in seeing represented in all of its forms the most important sentiment of nature, —and the anger, in finding it often so badly imitated or so stupidly slandered. Whether by the fireside during interminable winter evenings or during the heavy leisure of a heat wave, in the corner of the glaziers shop, the sight of these drawings has sent me on the path of immense reveries, more or less as an obscene book thrusts us toward the mystical oceans of the blue. Many times have I been caught desiring, in front of these innumerable samples of each of their senti-

ments, that the poet, the curious, the philosopher could grant themselves the pleasure [*jouissance*] of a museum of love, where everything would have its place, from the unapplied tenderness of Saint Theresa to the serious debauchery of the bored centuries. Without a doubt the distance is immense that separates *Le Départ ou L'Île de Cythère* from the miserable colorings suspended in girls' bedrooms, above a cracked jug and a shaky console; but in such an important subject, nothing is to be neglected. And then genius sanctifies all things [*le génie sanctifie toutes choses*], and if these subjects were treated with the necessary care and reverence, they would not at all be sullied by that revolting obscenity, that is more boasting than truth.[21]

Love, the erotic, and the female body here appear in all the complexities of their position within Baudelaire's real-ideal poetics. As an erotic subject, the body is essentially physical and natural, yet this nature is not the abominable thing of later Baudelaire. Natural love is, in fact, so important, so central to art, that in all of its forms, "nothing is to be neglected." To this end, Baudelaire imagines a strange museum of love, where it is to be displayed in all of its widely variable iterations, from the pure, objectless love of saints down to the cynical "debauchery of the bored centuries." Indeed, for Baudelaire, even the portrayal of such debaucheries is not obscene if portrayed by a real artist, for "genius sanctifies all things" (alas, on this last point, Baudelaire would discover that the French State vehemently begged to disagree). At the end of the section, a large part of which is devoted not to Tassaert's salon paintings but to the racy lithographs of which Baudelaire is reminded by Tassaert's paintings, Baudelaire grants Tassaert's love paintings the highest praise, describing him as "an eminent artist whom only *flâneurs* appreciate and the public does not know well enough."[22] The "libertine prints" with which he opens his musings on Tassaert are not yet this kind of art, but they still pose no threat to it; rather, they open up a new space for art in its quest to portray all aspects of the erotic. If true artists choose to explore these themes, what might otherwise be obscene could instead be art. In fact, the essay essentially implies that the substance of Tassaert's high art lies in his mastery of the low art of erotic lithography, which is precisely the kind of street-object the flâneur would appreciate. The section on Tassaert indicates many themes that will be essential in evaluating Baudelaire's artistic reaction to nude photography: that the natural female body is actually of the utmost importance to art, that art has a particular relationship to obscenity that necessitates at once an engagement with and a transcendence of that mode of representation, and that both of these characteristics of art are fundamentally related to the artist's dual responsibility both to the reality of human existence and to the transformative powers of his own imagination.

By 1859, however, Baudelaire would espouse an entirely different position with regard to obscene images, a shift explicitly linked to the indexical properties of the photograph. The second part of Baudelaire's *Salon de 1859*, "Le Public moderne et la photographie," is devoted to one of the most famous antiphotographic diatribes of the nineteenth century. In the contemporary debate over whether this new mechanism for reproducing reality should be considered an art form at all, Baudelaire came down firmly against photography's right to artistic recognition. He dismissed the new medium as "the refuge of all failed painters, too lacking in talent or too lazy to finish their studies."[23] And he wrote bleakly of the consequences of confusing the new medium with art, saying, "If photography is permitted to replace art in some its functions, it [photography] will soon have supplanted or completely corrupted art, thanks to the natural alliance photography will find in the stupidity of the masses. It is necessary, therefore, that photography return to its true task, which is to be the servant of the arts and sciences, but the very humble servant."[24] Baudelaire, who was good friends with the photographer Nadar, had no objection to photography as such, even appealing from Honfleur to Nadar for photographic prints for him of Goya's *Duchess of Alba* just as he was writing the *Salon*.[25] He did believe that photography was the handmaiden to art, a handmaiden he would not hesitate to use when one could not, as he also jokingly encourages Nadar to do, purchase a Goya painting. But photography already had threatening aspirations to be something more. As he continues on to say in the *Salon de 1859*, "Let it rapidly enrich the voyager's album, [...] let it adorn the library of the naturalist, [...] let it be, finally, the secretary and the note-keeper for whomever needs in his profession an absolute material exactitude, up to that, so much the better. Let it save tilting ruins, books, prints and manuscripts that time is devouring from oblivion, [...] it will be thanked and applauded. But if it is permitted to encroach upon the domain of the impalpable and the imaginary, above all that which has a value only because man has added some of his soul to them, well then, woe betide us."[26] Photography was a dangerous handmaiden, for when it outstepped its bounds, it threatened to upset the delicate balance between the real and the imaginary so vital to art.[27]

At the same time, in the *Salon de 1859*, Baudelaire's rhetoric on the imagination undergoes a seismic shift, from emphasizing artistic production as a product of supersensory, but nevertheless sensory capabilities—"Like nature perceived by ultra-sensitive nerves, it reveals supernaturalism"—to one predominantly governed by the imagination. The imagination was crowned as "the queen of the faculties" and received an entire section of the *Salon de 1859* devoted to her praise (probably not coincidently, this is also the period when Baudelaire championed "art for art's sake" in his article on Gautier). In the wake of photography, the "real" had become an enemy. As Baudelaire describes it, the people had recently taken up a new ideal, "worthy of it and appropriate to its nature," and that dangerous idol was the real itself, art as a mere copy of nature. Photography appeared as if by an act of God to these foolish masses, and they saw in its realism the culmination of art's imperative: "A vengeful God has granted the wishes of this multitude. Daguerre was his messiah. And then they said to themselves 'Since photography gives us all the desirable guaranties of exactitude (they believe that, the madmen!), art is photography.'"[28] Against this terrible primacy of the real, the imagination had to assert herself in a new way. No longer could the senses of the artist perceive the "supernatural" qualities of the universe; instead, the imagination had to create that universe: "It is the imagination who taught man the moral sense of color, of contour, of sound and of scent. She created, at the beginning of the world, analogy and metaphor. She breaks down all of creation, and, with the material amassed and arranged according to rules whose origin cannot be found but in the deepest recesses of the soul, she creates a new world."[29] No solution remained in a photographic world but to wrest art away almost entirely from the domain of the real.[30]

Despite the shock of its first appearance in the Salon, however, photography alone could not have been responsible for the virulence of Baudelaire's attack; it had already been flourishing in France for two decades without receiving much attention from Baudelaire other than a brief reference in 1846.[31] Rather, what becomes clear in "Le Public moderne et la photographie" is that photography merited reconsideration because it had embroiled itself in the representation of the female body. Unlike the lithographs of 1846, the newer genre of nude photography had no place in the realm of art. Baudelaire's diatribe against photography in the *Salon* happens to contain one of the most explicit references to the ubiquity of nude images under the Second Empire, one that has been essential to art historians looking to establish and explore the social and cultural presence of those images:

A vengeful God has granted the wishes of this multitude. Daguerre was his messiah. And then they said to themselves "Since photography gives us all the desirable guaranties of exactitude (they believe that, the madmen!), art is photography." From that moment, our filthy society rushed, like one Narcissus, to contemplate its trivial image on the metal plate [. . .] A short time later, thousands of avid eyes stared into the peepholes of the stereoscope as though they were windows onto the infinite. The love of obscenity, which is as strong in the natural heart of man as his love of himself, did not allow such a beautiful opportunity to satisfy itself slip away. And let us not say that it is only students on the way home from school who take pleasure from these stupidities; they are society's infatuation. I heard a beautiful woman, a woman of good society, not of my own, respond to those who were discretely hiding such images from her, charging themselves with having some modesty for her: "Give them to me anyway; there is nothing too strong for me."[32]

Baudelaire's newly moralistic language about obscenity reflects an unsettling reality determined by the cultural presence of a very specific kind of photography. By 1859, obscene photography truly had become ubiquitous. Its meteoric rise reframed the terms of the debate about art's aesthetic imperative and what kind of erotic representation that imperative permitted. While the very pair of Goya images that Baudelaire jokingly requested from Nadar included a nude whose subject Baudelaire crudely described as "a *bizarre fuckery*," he recoiled against what he perceived as a national peepshow inaugurated by the photograph.[33]

In addition to its sexual fear centered on the woman who takes pleasure in looking at an obscene photograph, Baudelaire's response is not without an element of snobbery. After all, lithography had been used for centuries for similar purposes. Why shouldn't the photograph have a chance to be considered art, even if it was available for the masses? What's more, as Susan Blood points out, Baudelaire projects a certain moralistic pedantry inconsistent with his stance that art is not a moral question; it almost seems as though Baudelaire has acquired a social conscience and "collapse[d] aesthetic issues into questions of public morality."[34] Perhaps there is an elitist tone to Baudelaire's condemnation; nevertheless, the substance of his objection has little to do with "popular" art, or even with obscenity as such, but is about art, plain and simple. Art, for Baudelaire, had never been a question of pure realism. Whatever the subject, the artist achieves the sublime only through elimination of inconsequential and distracting details, through a certain distance from the real. This distance from the real, however, is particularly important in the case of representations of the body. As a medium, lithography is far less realistic than photography, and even erotic lithographs still had the benefit of an artist to do the work of eliding undesirable details. As Baudelaire had said of Tassaert, "genius sanctifies all things."[35] Erotic lithography might then still have passed for art, even if it was low art. Photographs, on the other hand, had neither distance from reality nor genius in their favor. Photography was the project of failed painters operating under the destructive misconception that perfect verisimilitude was art. It provided the opposite of sublimity, a mess of perfectly accurate details, which was particularly dangerous in the case of the body. The "love of obscenity" fostered by photography fundamentally undermined the potential for artistic representation of the body. Unlike the dirty engravings, which still required someone's imagination and might still "flee the details," a dirty photograph was nothing more than that, a dirty photograph of a dirty reality.

The mix of the human taste for obscenity and photography's unrelenting realism together threatened to have wide-reaching aesthetic consequences. Already, the influence of photography could be seen on the visual media that Baudelaire actually considered to be art. As he lamented, in a photographic world, "art has diminishing respect for itself, prostrates itself to exterior reality," and "the painter is becoming more and more inclined to paint, not what he dreams, but what he sees."[36] In such a context, it was impossible not to fear that aesthetic perception was being fundamentally altered by photography. Baudelaire concludes "Le Public moderne et la photographie" by incredulously asking his reader, "Is it possible to suppose that a people whose eyes become accustomed to consider the results of material science as products of the beautiful, have not, after a certain time, singularly diminished the faculty to judge and to sense what there is that is most ethereal and immaterial?"[37] Photographic representation threatened to irrevocably alter the viewer's conception of the beautiful. Again, this would nowhere be more troublesome than in the case of the body, where the proliferation of photographic images did not merely encourage viewers and artists to see mere exactitude as art but (as Baudelaire implies when he invokes the "love of obscenity") to seek and see only *obscene* exactitude instead of art.[38] Moreover, this danger was not limited to the visual arts. In the opening of his section on the imagination, which follows this directly, Baudelaire continues his tirade against the world as seen through the photographic lens, lamenting that, "In recent time, we've heard it said in a thousand different ways: 'Copy nature; only copy nature [. . .]' And this doctrine, the enemy of art, aspires to be applied not only to painting, but to all the arts, even to the novel, even to poetry."[39] The taste for copies of nature, and the tendency to interpret art in these literal terms, was fueled by photography, but it even threatened poetry and the novel, with potential consequences that Baudelaire understood only too well. For the poet who had himself (as both Claude Pichois and Elisabeth Ladenson have pointed out) been effectively accused of obscene realism in his 1857 trial, the radical alteration of the aesthetic faculties caused by photography in general, and nude photography in particular, could be understood as the very reason why his own poems were misread.[40] Whether one copied nature or not, that was the standard by which art was being judged, and it left no place for representations of the body that were anything other than obscene.

The traces of Baudelaire's anxiety about photographic representations of the body are not limited to this outburst. In addition to his poetry, portions of Baudelaire's famous article on Constantin Guys, *Le Peintre de la vie moderne*, written in 1859–1860, also take on new significance in the context of nude photography. As Timothy Raser has argued at length, even at times with reference to the burgeoning commerce in obscene photographs, the choice of Guys itself was an intentional rejection of photography, for photography was already in the 1850s the prototypical "modern" medium.[41] Against this photographic context, Baudelaire's discussion of women, his attack on the natural, and his praise of make-up and other artificial supplements to female beauty at the end of *Le Peintre de la vie moderne* all merit reconsideration, particularly in regard to the way that the photograph is implicated in the "natural" woman. *Le Peintre de la vie moderne* does not simply advocate for the importance of Guys' œuvre, it uses Guys' drawings to make a broader theoretical argument about the importance of details of contemporary life as equally important as eternal and universal concepts of "beauty" in art; indeed, it is for this argument that Baudelaire's article is perhaps better known than for his actual discussion of Guys' works. In the essay, Baudelaire insists on the importance of fashion partially because it models how the seemingly opposed contingent and universal concepts of the beautiful interact and are manifested in modern life: fashion changes with time but also, for Baudelaire, manifests an enduring yearning for ideal abstractions of beauty. Baudelaire's defense of the artifice of fashion is, therefore, also a defense of the "supernatural" structure of idealism in the face of the regime of unrelenting realism. This is the underlying reason why women, while they are the beings "for whom, but above all *by whom* artists and poets compose their most delicate jewels," and represent "all the graces of nature," at the same time require both clothing and makeup to fulfill the potential of their natural beauty.[42]

Baudelaire's vindication of the importance of artifice and idealism in contemporary concepts of feminine beauty, however, is also deployed in the service of another agenda. This discussion of women and the "womanly arts" is less virulent than, but nevertheless consistent with, the explicit misogyny of "Woman is natural, that is to say, abominable" of *Mon Cœur mis à nu*. After linking the unadorned female body to nature through numerous metaphors (and phrases like "natural graces"), Baudelaire then denounces nature (and by extension the female body) in the strongest terms. It is nature that "pushes man to kill his fellow creature, to eat him, to imprison him, to torture him."[43] The realm of the virtuous is the realm of the artificial, for "evil is done without effort, *naturally*, inevitably; the good is always the product of an art."[44] Where women are concerned, art translates to the embellishments of nineteenth-century fashion. As a result, even the most naturally beautiful woman, precisely because of her strange and privileged status as "a beautiful animal" that inspires most of male activity, is better when artificially adorned: "Idol, she must adorn herself to be adored. She must therefore borrow from all the arts the means to elevate herself above nature in order to better subjugate hearts and strike the fancy."[45] While Baudelaire here does not explicitly declare woman to be evil and abominable in her natural state, the logical construction—that nature is a malicious force, that a woman's unadorned beauty is natural beauty, ergo, that unadorned woman is both a manifestation of abominable nature and not truly beautiful—appears to corroborate the claim that Baudelaire's natural female body must somehow be inscribed "into form by social and cultural representations."[46] That is to say, without culture's gilding, woman not only is incapable of achieving her full beauty, she literally does not signify.

Baudelaire's acculturation of the female body is so troubling because it seems to be an inexorable necessity demanded by a "naturalness" intrinsic to that body, much like the quality intrinsic to the bodies of photographic models that identified them as prostitutes. This is precisely the language about the "natural" female body that has given Baudelaire his lasting reputation for misogyny. Yet upon closer examination, what first appears as an unchangeable and fundamental quality of the female body itself emerges instead as something far more contingent. In *Le Peintre de la vie moderne*, "naturalness" is a mode of perception more than a state or quality of being—or, at least, a perception in addition to a state of being. Baudelaire does not simply praise makeup and fashion, he insists *emphatically* on its importance, almost as though he is defending Guys not only from those who would attack him for representing prostitutes and painted women but from those who would attack him for leaving clothing *on* these women, rather than removing it altogether. And the logic he uses to justify his valorization of feminine fashions is not that clothing protects the world from the dangerous and natural sight of these women's bodies but rather that it protects these women from the eyes of men who might be interested in their more "natural" assets.

> Woman is, without a doubt, a light, a glance, an invitation to happiness, a word sometimes; but she is above all a general harmony, not only in her allure and the movement of her limbs, but also in the muslins, the gauzes, the vast and shimmering clouds of fabric in which she envelops herself, and which are as the attributes and the pedestal of her divinity; in the metal and the mineral that snake around her arms and her neck, that add their sparks to the fire of her glances, or that babble gently at her ears. What poet would dare, in his painting of the pleasure caused by the apparition of a beauty, separate the woman from her costume? Who is

the man who, in the street, at the theater, at the park, has not enjoyed, in the most disinterested manner, a skillfully composed toilette, and did not take from it an inseparable image of the beauty to whom it belonged, thus making from the two, the woman and the dress, an indivisible totality? This is the place, it seems to me, to return to certain questions relative to fashion and finery, that I only touched upon at the beginning of this study, and to avenge the art of the toilette from the inept slander heaped upon it by certain dubious lovers of nature [amants très-équivoques de la nature].[47]

For Baudelaire, the adorned female body is subject to the same male scrutiny that the nude body would be—that is, a very clearly sexual scrutiny. The clothing he praises as an extension and amplification of inherent female beauty (to a degree that one wonders whether, perhaps, he was trying to convince himself) becomes a kind of protective "idealist" shield against the gaze of those who might want to wallow in the merely real. But it is this gaze, and not some quality of the body itself, whose result is "the natural." And it is this gaze that therefore necessitates clothing. The gauze of female costume operates as did the painter's brush in "De l'idéal et du modèle." It blurs and disguises details, creating "harmony" (here "general harmony," which evokes the "native harmony" of 1846) and abstracting the body just enough to allow it to signify and to protect it from obscenity. It encourages men to "enjoy" ("jouir," which also has the sexual meaning of climaxing) with disinterest, as opposed to the way the body alone might cause a different kind of "pleasure" ("jouissance," again with a sexual connotation); it discourages the lesser "poet" (or more generally, artist) from too eagerly attempting to "paint" an image of the pleasure inspired by the body alone.

Still, the phantom of the peep show lurks in the shadows. As much as Baudelaire advocates for the beauty of costume, he cannot entirely banish the instinct of the male gaze to seek out a different kind of "painting of the pleasure caused by the apparition of a beauty." The passage (and that section of Le Peintre de la vie moderne) ends with exactly those who would want to see this insidious alternative: the "lovers of nature." Strictly speaking, the "lovers of nature" are those who advocate for beauty unaltered by the artifice of makeup and fashion. Yet in the context of Baudelaire's rhetoric on nature, the phrase "lovers of nature" also takes on a more louche and literal meaning, lovers of the female form in its natural, that is, nude, state (nudists are naturistes in French). This reading of their motives is encouraged by Baudelaire's use of the negative dubious ("très-équivoques" in French) to qualify the word "lovers." Indeed, the passage's entire structure, which places women constantly under the eyes of men, while repeatedly emphasizing the importance of hiding the body from these eyes, allies the "nude" or "natural" body with the body as it functions in obscenity, a genre whose power resides precisely in exposing what should be hidden. Obscenity, however, is not some intrinsic quality of the body; it is a representational mode. If, therefore, the natural is the obscene, it, too, is a representation of the body distinct from the body itself. At the same time, Baudelaire's emphasis on the "indivisible totality" of woman's "natural" body and the protective sheen of the artificially constructed ideal (clothing) serves to collapse the two categories, again implying that the category of the natural body is no less constructed than that of the art of costume. Ultimately, the "natural" body consists merely of that which is shielded by the "artificial" and sought by the equivocal gaze of men under those decorative layers. It is not the real body, but the body as perceived and represented through this equivocal gaze. "Naturalness" is therefore the opposed mode of representation to the adorned or artistic body, a representation that probably looks a lot like the realism of the obscene photograph. The female, the abominable, and the natural only truly coexist at the point where obscenity invades art, where the proliferation of extreme realist representation and love of nature necessitate that the body can only mean sex and must be adorned and acculturated to signify anything beyond that.

These consequences of photographic representation of the nude body are never fully developed in *Le Peintre de la vie moderne* or Baudelaire's other prose, but instead become evident through Baudelaire's poetic production. Many critics have argued that Baudelaire's description of Guys is actually a description of his own artistic practice; whether or not this is the case, Baudelaire's poetics, particularly his poetics of the body, very much relies on the same delicate balance of the real and the ideal that he valorizes in his art criticism.[48] And the nude photograph emerges as anathema to this representational paradigm even more strongly in Baudelaire's poetry than in his prose. In *Les Fleurs du mal*, obscene photographic representation of the body invades the text through the most violent moments of death, decay, and their Freudian pairing with sex, against which Baudelaire asserts another reality of the body, one that leads not to obscenity but to art.

The first of these violent incursions is the famous "Une Charogne," a poem strangely overlooked by the censors. Encountering a rotting carcass while out with his beloved, the poet seizes the opportunity to remind her of exactly what her body will become in death: "Flies buzzed on the putrid torso / Whence proceeded black battalions / Of larva, that ran like a thick liquid / Along these rags of flesh."[49] The poem as a whole is a disgusting, putrefied form of the heightened sensual experience of synesthesia and of the Nature of "Correspondances": Along with the repugnant sight and "stench . . . so strong," there's "a strange music." All of these repulsive physical realities, "all that she has joined into a whole," are surveyed by "the great Nature," and at the end, the lover who will become this rotting carcass is also metaphorized into symbols of Nature's beauty: "And yet, you will be like this filth / This horrible infection / Star of my eyes, sun of my nature, / You, my angel and my passion."[50] The poem seems to be a very damning conglomeration of the physicality of the female body, of the most repulsive aspects of a nature toward which Baudelaire was more than slightly ambivalent, of all the sensual aspects of his poetry (sight, sound, smell), and of the sublimation of the whole mess into metaphor.

All this is true, but such a reading ignores certain key details of the poem. In the middle of the putrefaction, the poet has a strange transcendent moment:

> And this world made a strange music,
>   Like running water and the wind,
> Or grain that the winnower, in rhythmic movement,
>   Agitates and turns in his basket.
>
> The forms faded and were nothing more than a dream,
>   A sketch slow to appear
> On a forgotten canvas that the artist completes
>   Only from memory.[51]

Out of this world of decay surges a metatextual scene of the artistic processes as theorized by Baudelaire that has not yet turned into a naturalist nightmare but that is nonetheless ephemeral and endangered: metaphoric correspondences become sketches of forms achieved through memory, which have already almost faded away into a dream. (In 1846, Baudelaire would write in the *Salon*, "art is a mnemotechnique of the beautiful"; while I do not discuss it here, memory was another essential Baudelairian creative force).[52] Something more is at stake than the horror of the female body established in the prevailing metaphor, "your beautiful body is like a rotting carcass." Art is threatened by this decomposing flesh, and there is the possibility that it will not be able to transcend it.

The exact nature of this threat is clarified by the poem's opening lines, the very lines that establish the parallel between the corpse and a woman's body. To describe the carrion, Baudelaire writes, "An infamous corpse / On a bed strewn with stones / Its legs in the air, like a lubricious woman / Burning and oozing poisons / Exposed, with a nonchalant and cynical air / Its effluvious womb [*ventre plein d'exhalaisons*]."[53] This carcass isn't just like any body, it's like the body of a woman with her legs splayed out on the bed in a lubricious position, a woman who is not absorbed by her position but is nonchalant and cynical. This position is exactly that popularized by the "beaver shot" and, indeed, more generally, by

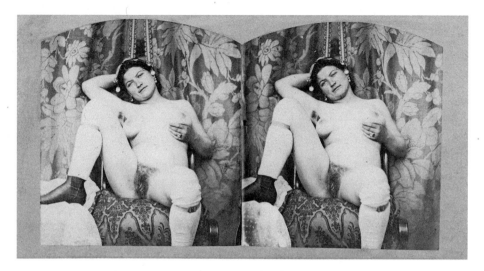

[FIGURE 40]
Anonymous, Second Empire.
Photographic print on stereo card.
Bibliothèque nationale de France.

many obscene photographs, which are full of cynical and nonchalant women exposing their "effluvious wombs" for the eyes of desiring men (Figure 40). And much like in those images, it is as if the woman's sexual organs take over the entire poem. They are the source of the rot, the stench, the decay, because this is *all* that we can see, all that is there. Not just any female body threatens art and signification, but one particular representation of the female body. The threat of the natural woman is located not only specifically in female genitalia (the most natural site of femininity) but in a certain realist portrayal of those organs, one in which all the rest of the woman simply vanishes into her sex. Obscene photographs are the putrid carcass that makes Baudelaire's correspondences rot and the art of memory fade into a dream.

The violence of the obscene photograph is even more graphically rendered in another poem from the 1857 edition of *Fleurs du Mal*, "Une Martyre." Buried three stanzas into an overheated, voluptuous, and perfumed bedroom is a decapitated woman. As though she has been interrupted in a last amorous encounter (the nature of which becomes the source of much speculation in the poem), her headless cadaver lies on display for all to see:

> On the bed, the naked torso shamelessly flaunts
> With the most complete abandon
> The secret splendor and fatal beauty
> Bestowed on her by nature.

On her leg, a rosy stocking with golden trim
    Clings like a memory;
The garter, like a secret gleaming eye,
    Darts a jeweled glance.[54]

Once again, the woman's sexual organs are on photographic display in an explicit pose, "shamelessly" and "with the most complete abandon." Not far from her body is her missing head, which "On the night table, like a ranunculus / Reposes; and emptied of thoughts, /A look, vague and pale as dusk / Escapes from her rolled-back eyes."[55] Like the metaphoric lubricious woman of "Carrion," this woman's regard is significantly empty, vacant, devoid of meaning. She, too, has been severed (quite literally) of all meaning that comes from anywhere other than her sexual organs, for although they are not the site of her fatal injury (presumably the decapitation is), they take on all the weight of signification in the poem's staging of her body. Again, this obscene scene is also one of gruesome death. Again, this morbid sexual display is directly connected to nature, the source of the "fatal beauty" that not only is laid out in front of the viewer in death but seems to blossom in that death like a cut flower in the boudoir. Again, there is an invocation of the failure of memory, that force so important to Baudelaire's art—the stockings left on her legs like a memory do little to conceal the body that has been so violently revealed. This time, however, the effect is amplified, for this woman is not linked to death metaphorically (your body is *like* a rotting carcass); she is herself dead (she *is* a rotting carcass), and dead in the pose of an obscene photograph.

One of the ways that "Une Martyre" engages more directly than "Une Charogne" with the problem of obscene photographic representation is through sight and the gaze. In this iteration, the woman's face (with all its larger significance of volition, thought, identity) does not simply disappear in the background to the foreground of her sex. It has been eliminated entirely. Interestingly, in those "beaver shot" photographs where women do not return the viewer's gaze with cynical nonchalance, they are often decapitated, either by the frame, by their clothes, or because they turn and hide their faces (see, e.g., Figures 18 and 41). In the poem, Baudelaire transforms this into a literal decapitation, leaving the viewer with only the body's "trunk." As a result of this decapitation, the eyes must be relocated elsewhere. Staring back at whomsoever would dare to observe this obscene image doing its violence against art is the garter, another essential prop in the lexicon of nineteenth-century nude photography. Although she does not discuss them, garters certainly participate in the erotics of the stockinged leg identified by Solomon-Godeau. Sitting at the top of women's stockings, the gar-

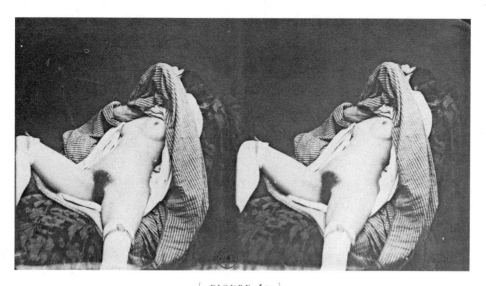

[FIGURE 41]

Anonymous, Second Empire.
Photographic print on stereo card.
Bibliothèque nationale de France.

ter acts as a marker of the "last stop" on the body before gratification in many photographs (see, e.g., Figures 6, 18, 29, 33, 40, and 41).[56] In Baudelaire's poem, it also acts as a metonymic substitute for that far more disturbing "secret gleaming eye," the woman's sex, becoming a symbol more generally of the confusion of sexual gratification and visual stimulation at work in the consumption of sexually explicit photographs. The compulsion to look consequently takes over the poem in a way that it does not in "Une Charogne." The reader is complicit in this voyeurism, providing another pair of the "provocative eyes" that wonder about the "tenebrous love" that preceded this woman's death. Indeed, just as the poem wanders off toward postulating the "guilty joy" and "infernal kisses" of the dead woman, it stops itself again, returning to "the elegant gauntness / of the shoulder's harsh contours, / the slightly pointed haunches and the trim waist."[57] Any time the reader's gaze wanders, the poem brutally compels it to return to the body and the cruelties inflicted on it. We, too, in a sense, become consumers of obscenity, forced to see this corpse as a sexual object that, even in death, awakens "lost and errant desires."[58]

Unlike "Une Charogne," "Une Martyre" offers no glimpse of the redemptive power of art, no hint of the body's inherent beauty, only a more complete metaphor for the damage inflicted by the realism of photographic nudity. Having already established the obscene staging of the body as a consequence of a brutal murder, the poem also links this murder not only to sexualized looking but to a disturbed sexual desire that can be satisfied only by necrophiliac rape. Baude-laire asks the cadaver whether "The vindictive man that you could not, while living / Despite so much love, satisfy / Will he heap onto your inert and obliging flesh / The immensity of his desire?"[59] The poem reenacts photographic obscen-ity as not one but two of the most devastating assaults on the body, murder and rape, both abominably spawned of a lust that is quite literally insatiable in life (there is, of course, no living woman when one looks at explicit photographs). When the female body is truly "flaunted" for all eyes to see, this is the gruesome result. Whatever the content of an individual photograph, photographic obscen-ity metaphorically effects this deadly sexualized violence on the female body and, by extension, art itself in every image.

Against this horrifying threat of nonsignification, many poems of the collec-tion strive to protect the body by clothing it, insisting on signification through adornment in much the same way as Baudelaire does in *Le Peintre de la vie mod-erne*. They rectify the wrongs done by realism to the body by re-dressing and re-covering that body. This covering of the body often looks something like ide-alization and sublimation: denying the materiality of the female body, repressing the natural to make woman signify. In the gruesome "À une Madonne," bodily adornments are expressions of the poet's violent sentiments that commandeer the body's meaning. Addressing a former love, the poet says, "With my polished verses, a trellis of pure metal / Adroitly constellated with crystal rhymes / I will make an enormous Crown for your head."[60] His jealousy will become a coat, "lined with suspicion" and embroidered with his tears, to "enclose your charms."[61] And most importantly, "your dress will be my Desire, quivering, / Undulating, my Desire that rises and falls."[62] In "À une mendiante rousse," on the other hand, the poet's fantasies are more anodyne, as he dreams of granting new meaning to a young beggar's beautiful body by readorning her in clothes that suit her beauty. She wears her rags "more gallantly / Than a queen from a novel," so he rejects the reality of her poverty and evokes the great beauty revealed if "instead of too-short rags / Let a superb courtly habit / Trail its long and rustling pleats / Across your heels."[63] Violent or admiring, both poems seem to reinforce the idea that the female body must disappear under layers of clothing signifiers in order to bear poetic meaning.

Yet here and elsewhere, such attempts to clothe the body into signification fall short. Clothes can be cast off; the ravaged body of "Une Martyre" is embed-ded "Amongst flasks, gilded cloth / And voluptuous furniture / Marbles, paintings and perfumed dresses / Trailing their sumptuous pleats," and her severed head still has earrings in its ears.[64] Indeed, by the end of "À une mendiante rousse," the poet actually seems to take some delight at the idea that instead of being adorned, the beautiful body of the beggar girl might stand alone in proof of its own beauty, "without other ornament / Perfume, pearls, or diamonds / Than your emaciated nudity / O my beauty."[65] "Un Fantôme," a multipart poem explicitly concerned with the artistic value of the female body, is even more insistent that the body itself should be art, not merely the clothed body. The third part, "Le cadre," proposes a different conception of the relationship of the body to its adornments.

> As a beautiful frame adds to a painting,
> Even if it is of a much-vaunted brush,
> An indefinable strangeness and enchantment
> By isolating it from immense nature,
>
> Thus jewels, furniture, metals, gilding,
> Adapted exactly to suit her rare beauty;
> Nothing offended her perfect clarity,
> And all seemed to serve as her frame.[66]

Even though "jewels" and "gilding" adapt themselves to the body, they do not themselves make that body art. They act only as the frame that distinguishes the body from nature, without acting on it in any way that might offend the "perfect clarity" of the female form. This poem completes Baudelaire's portrait of the difference between the artistic and the obscene body, between the real body and the natural body. The real body, the body itself, has a beauty that alone is art, and for which all signs of culture are a mere frame, a finishing touch.

The task of Baudelaire's poetry, then, is not to adorn the body into signification but to negotiate its own way of making art of the unadorned body without either idealizing away that body's physical beauty or falling into the trap of obscene naturalism. His solution points to the very foundation of his own poetics, that is, metaphor. The famous synesthesia and correspondences of "Correspondances" are effectively metaphors for metaphoric representation.[67] Synesthesia is physical metaphor, the coordination of the senses so that they refer to each other; a correspondence is a symbolic metaphor, one that establishes a connection between reality and the metaphysical realm. Metaphor is the means by which Baudelaire navigates his precarious relationship between the ideal and the real, allowing the hieroglyphs of the ideal to appear within and beyond physical reality at the same time. It also allows him to represent nudity that is not indecent nakedness. If one approaches the female body as a metaphor for *other ideas*, these divisions between real and ideal seem to be inscribed on that body, along with many other dualities, turning the body into little more than, as Richard Burton notes, "passports to something beyond themselves—nature, spirit, or, most frequently, the 'monde autre' of art."[68] When woman is read as nothing but a metaphor for art, her real body becomes the cause and site of a troubling conflict between, as Sanyal puts it, woman as "regressive materiality and meaningful sign."[69] However, if one considers metaphor as it serves to depict the body rather than as it turns that body into a sign for something else, it becomes clear that metaphor does not work to sublimate the body but instead protects it from being naturalized into mere obscenity or idealized into mere form. Baudelaire's use of metaphor to represent the body returns the trope to its most fundamental rhetorical functions. Thinkers from Aristotle, who first remarked that "a good metaphor implies an intuitive perception of the similarity in dissimilars," through to Roman Jakobson, who millennia later argued that the principal of metaphoric similarity underlies poetry itself, have understood metaphor as a mediator of similarity and difference.[70] To escape from the twin traps of obscenity and idealism, Baudelaire's poetry exploits precisely metaphor's unique power to illuminate uncanny qualities of likeness in difference. He festoons the body with linguistic forms that are drawn from a basic "sameness" with that body and reveal qualities inherent to it, rather than merely covering it up. Baudelaire's use of metaphor allows the body to remain naked in front of the viewer's eye while shielding it in a layer of meaning that is not alien to that body but fundamentally rooted in it.

Although it was among the condemned poems, this is precisely how Baudelaire depicts the female subject of his poem "Les Bijoux." In it, the poet's beloved is naked except for her jewels. Enraptured by her beauty, he watches her as "she tried different poses, / And candor united with lubricity / Granted her metamorphoses a fresh charm."[71] The poem is infused with palpable erotic longing, yet neither her body—the object of that longing—nor even the jewels that adorn it are ever clearly visible to the reader. The poem's most graphic description of her physical endowments is almost entirely obscured by figurative language: "And her arm and her leg, and her thigh and her loins, / Polished like oil, sinuous as a swan, / Passed in front of my clairvoyant and serene eyes; / And her belly and her breasts, these grapes of my vine."[72] The lines of the woman's body are transformed into a swan, her breasts become symbols of plentitude; we perceive both the physical shape and the meaning of the woman's body only through metaphor. This does not mean that the poem is exactly prudish. Two stanzas later, Baudelaire compares "the dearly beloved" to a hybrid creature made of "the haunches of Antiope with the bust of a boy / So much did her trim waist accentuate her loins"; here as in a few other places, the description has an obvious sexual significance and lacks the subtlety of the swan metaphor.[73] But nothing in this poem is graphic in the mode of "Une Charogne" and "Une Martyre," with their emphasis on the stink, the blood, and the fatality of the female sexual organs. There is no question here of a natural sex that consumes and destroys all meaning other than death, even as the body is omnipresent, uniting the poem's many metaphors into an image of itself.

Another striking example of the simultaneously real and symbolic body is "La Chevelure," a poem added to the *Fleurs du mal* for the second edition.[74] As Hélène Pinet has noted (with reference to one of Baudelaire's prose poems, "Une Hémisphere dans une chevelure"), there existed in the nineteenth century an entire subgenre of nude photography (legal and illegal) of naked women with their hair cascading down, released from its usual pinnings and trappings (Figure 42).[75] "La Chevelure" is both the fullest example of how Baudelaire uses metaphor against obscenity and the only example where his poem seems to do so in

[FIGURE 42]

Anonymous, Second Empire.
Carte-de-visite.
Les Archives d'Eros, Paris.

direct engagement with the visual tropes of nude photography, acting out poetry's triumph over the photograph. Already in the first stanza of the poem, the erotically charged hair brings the poet to ecstasy with its "perfume laden with nonchalance" and is, at the same time, metaphorically resonant, becoming a "sheepy fleece," a "handkerchief," and the site of "the obscure alcove / of sleeping memories."[76] This hair is then transformed into an imaginative geography of the world, both real and figurative: "Languorous Asia and burning Africa / An entire distant, absent, almost-defunct world, / Lives in your depths, aromatic forest! / As other spirits sail on music / Mine, oh my love! swims in your perfume."[77] All of Baudelaire's symbolist and sensual themes are reunited in "La Chevelure" — *luxe, calme et volupté* are in correspondence with metaphysical experience. Notably, however, the hair's texture and scent are foregrounded even as they are transformed into an "aromatic forest" reminiscent of the forest of "Correspondances," and then, in turn, into "a sensational port where my soul can drink / Streams of perfume, sound and color."[78] The poem continually valorizes the physical experience and beauty of the women's hair through figures that place the real body in a larger matrix of metaphoric relations. The "blue hair" is a "pavillon of tender shadows," and their color evokes "the azure of an immense and rounded sky," yet at the same time, the poet is still present, plunging his face into the "tangled tresses" and inhaling their "confused scents / Of coconut oil, musk and tar."[79] In the last stanza, after having wandered throughout the fantastic universe created out of the hair, the poem insists yet again on the real hair that "represents" all these things, by juxtaposing it directly with the metaphors it has inspired: "A long while! forever! my hand, in your heavy mane, / Will sow rubies, pearls and sapphires, / So that you will never be deaf to my desire / Are you not the oasis where I dream, and the gourd / Whence I inhale long draughts of the wine of memory?"[80] Unlike photographs, in which (for Baudelaire) hair is nothing but hair, and mere idealism, in which hair is nothing but an oasis, this hair is itself and an oasis, all at once. This is how the female body can signify in its nudity without being obscenity.[81]

In 1846, in a section of his *Salon* entitled "De l'héroïsme de la vie moderne," Baudelaire makes almost the same argument as that which he would later develop in *Le Peintre de la vie moderne* about the importance of the contingent details of contemporary reality for art. The difference is that in 1846, Baudelaire actively advocates for the modern nude, proclaiming "The *nude*, that subject so dear to artists, that element so necessary for success, is as frequent and as necessary as in ancient life: in bed, in the bath, at the amphitheater. The means and motifs of painting are equally abundant and varied; but there is a new element, which is modern beauty."[82] In this earlier formulation, the naked and the natural body have not been collapsed. Yes, the nude body is to be rendered by an artist, but Baudelaire argues for no other cultural adornments; indeed, he argues against them. The only requirement is the particular element of "modern beauty," located in the body itself. In his way, Baudelaire was painting his own modern nudes with his poetry, nudes of modern women and modern situations, nudes that were most modern in that they revealed more about modernity than they revealed of the body. As modern as his nudes were, however, Baudelaire rejected the most modern mode of representation—photography—because of his perception of its threat to replace the nude with the natural body. Ironically, he was accused of obscenity precisely for expressing the same misgivings about nude photography shared by many of his contemporaries, even those who believed in photography as an art. Attempting to balance delicately between the idealism required to transcend obscenity and the beauty of the body itself, Baudelaire's poetry was, like the modern nude, caught in the confusion of the desire to "lay everything bare" and the desire instead to reveal the fundamental beauty of the human form.

⚞ CHAPTER 4 ⚟

Manette Salomon and Anti-Modernity

Unlike many of their contemporaries, the Goncourt brothers did not accuse Baudelaire of obscenity. They, too, had been charged with affront to public decency early in their career, and in a moment of sympathy they wrote in their journal in December 1860, "It is rather peculiar that it should be the three most righteous men of this time in any profession, the three quills the most dedicated to art, that have been arraigned under this regime on the benches of the criminal court: Flaubert, Baudelaire and us."[1] The Goncourts recognized in Baudelaire's total devotion to his art a kindred spirit and a fellow victim of a government whose aesthetic standards were absolute and arbitrary. This commiseration did not last, however. By the time Baudelaire died, it had given way to scorn for a poet they described as "a bourgeois who tormented himself his entire life to give himself the elegance of appearing to be mad."[2] Yet short lived though it was, their support for Baudelaire points to fundamental connections between the realist novelists and the poet. They, too, reacted fiercely against nude photography because of its insalubrious influence on artistic representation. They, too, explored the larger aesthetic repercussions of these images through their literary production and reflections on the "modern artist." And though they disdained the poet, they grappled with these aesthetic issues in terms taken directly from Baudelaire himself.

The Goncourts' ambivalent relationship to Baudelaire's aesthetic theories and the importance of these theories to their confrontation with nude photography both crystallize in the pages of the 1867 novel *Manette Salomon*. The book follows a group of young artists in the 1850s, focusing on two painters and close friends, Anatole Bazoche and Naz de Coriolis. Bazoche introduces Coriolis to the novel's eponymous model Manette just as Coriolis is attempting to complete his great masterpiece, a large orientalist nude called *Le Bain Turc*. Soon, Manette becomes Coriolis' model and lover.[3] Their artistic relationship embodies Baudelaire's conceptions of the modern artist, caught between his obligation to portray the ideal and eternal form of Beauty through the contingent details of modern life. Moreover, throughout the novel, the character Chassagnol (considered by critics to be the *porte-parole* of the Goncourt brothers) echoes Baudelaire's famous essay, *Le Peintre de la vie moderne*, and various Salons.[4] Yet even as the novel's inquiry into the nature of artistic creativity relies heavily on Baudelaire's ideas, it also questions them, using a nude photograph of Manette to do so. Manette's photographic nude is essential to her place in a text that often seems unaware of why she serves as its title and is at the heart of the novel's critique of the very ideas underpinning its philosophical structure. In *Manette Salomon*, this photograph exposes the failure of Baudelaire's modernity to mitigate the artistic danger posed by photography. By means of Manette's painted body, *Manette Salomon* attempts to demonstrate the perfect "modern" relationship between the painter's individual talent, the real model he represents, and the ideal categories of beauty to which art must aspire, all in Baudelairian terms. By means of Manette's photographed body, however, the novel suggests that the categories employed by Baudelaire (and Chassagnol) to validate modern art are ultimately insufficient. After photography, art must move beyond modernity.

⚜ Realism, Genius, and Photography in the Goncourt Journals ⚜

The aesthetic preoccupations of *Manette Salomon* are grounded in discussions about art, realism, and photography that first appear in Jules and Edmond's journals. By the time that they began writing *Manette Salomon* in 1865, the two were ardent realists. They embraced their obligation to render the real world in their art and bristled at the suggestion that aesthetic or moral concerns might entail alterations of that reality. In 1864, when their publisher asked them to modify passages of *Germinie Lacerteux*, the brothers stridently defended its ugly verisimilitude: "At the place where she says that upon arriving in Paris, she was covered in lice, Charpentier tells us that we must write: 'pests,' for the sake of the public. Yet, who is this king, the public, from whom we must hide the truth and rawness of everything? [. . .] What right has he that the novel should lie to him and veil from him all the ugliness of life?"[5] They expressed the same sentiment when, in 1865, as they were hard at work on *Manette Salomon*, they wrote in their journals that the pursuit of truth had led them to turn from writing history to writing novels and had sustained them in their artistic endeavors: "As of now, there is only one great interest in our life, the feeling of the study of truth. Without this, ennui and the void. Of course, we galvanized history as much as possible—and galvanized it with a truth more truthful than that of others, in sincere reality. Well then, now this defunct truth no longer speaks to us! We have the feeling of a man accustomed to drawing from wax figures, to whom is suddenly revealed a living académie or more accurately life itself, with its warm, restless entrails and its pulsating innards."[6] Their commitment to reality is so strong, in fact, that despite having tried to "galvanize" their nonfiction historical writings with real detail, they decide to abandon them completely for fiction that is more real than fact, fiction that is alive with the violent abjection of the real.

Yet these two militant declarations about realism are nonetheless tempered by a pervasive ambivalence about other realist artists, one that then reflects back on their own work. Even while continuing to rank "truth" above all other artistic qualities, the Goncourts also express doubts about whether merely copying reality actually constitutes art. These fears surface most explicitly in their musings on Flaubert's novel *Madame Bovary*. Their reaction to the novel is tinged with resentment, and some of its criticism is clearly driven by an unwillingness to acknowledge their friend's achievement. This seeming resentment, however, is grounded in a fundamental uncertainty about what realism is and what relationship "great art" has to reality:

> Truth is the core of all art, its foundation and its conscience. But why then is the soul of the mind not completely satisfied by it? Must there be some sort of alloy of falseness so that a work of art continues on as a masterpiece for posterity? Who decides that *Paul et Virginie*—a fanciful novel, in which I sense no truth, but sense at every moment the characters are imagined, personalities are dreamt—will remain an immortal masterpiece, while *Madame Bovary*, a stronger book with all the strength of maturity as compared with youth, observation compared with imagination, a study from life and from nature compared to poetic composition, *Madame Bovary*, I believe, will remain a prodigious effort and will never be such a book, a kind of bible of the human imagination? Is it because it lacks this grain of falseness [*grain de faux*], which is perhaps the ideal of a work of art? And then, what truth is there? Is there truth at all? What is more true than one of Hoffmann's fantastic tales? Alas, do the beautiful, the good and the observable in literature have not some absolute? The more we write, the more worry grows. We slip in our principles; we grope around in the dark more than ever. One day, we say to ourselves: "there is only observation." And then, the day after, observation seems insufficient. One has to mix in a je ne sais quoi, that should be to the work of art like the bouquet to wine. And the more we are conscious of it, the more we have doubt and anxiety.[7]

Something in the perfect realism of Flaubert's novel made the brothers question the artistic project of a fictional world constructed as a simulacrum of the real one. These doubts are ultimately not about *Madame Bovary* but about their own literary output. The claim that Flaubert's novel was too replete with real details to convey a larger emotional truth is a deflection of the gnawing concern, voiced at the end of the passage, that perhaps their own pursuit of "the true" might ultimately be insufficient. Truth is a slippery concept for an artist; in a work of fiction, emotional truth can be totally divorced from (and far stronger than) reality. More troublesome still for the champions of a brutal and often ugly realism, this artistic truth is, above all else, beautiful. In this passage, they acknowledge that art's truth-telling imperative is tempered by its imperative to create, or, at the very least, to locate, the beautiful and the good in the real world. The "je ne sais quoi," the "bouquet" that the Goncourts fret about in their own literary production may be a "grain of falseness," it might be a dash of idealism; most generally, what the Goncourts are describing is an awareness that the artist must add something of his own genius to the world to transform it into art. Only this indefinable quality of the artist distinguishes between mere copies of reality and artistic representation of reality; the problem is they are not entirely confident that they themselves possess it.

These anxieties about realism and talent coalesce around photography. The Goncourt brothers, like Baudelaire, had little good to say about the medium, but as a bête noire it was nonetheless essential to their attempts to define their artistic project. In 1856, for instance, during an appreciative discussion of Clodion's sculpture, they abruptly turn to photography, hypothesizing that "realism is born and bursts out when the daguerreotype and photography demonstrate how much art differs from the truth."[8] Though brief, this early reference to photography is emblematic of the medium's role throughout their work. Like many at the time, the Goncourt brothers equate photography with absolute representational truth. But instead of drawing a parallel between the project of realism and photography, as critics of realism would for the rest of the century, they assert realism against photography. Realism is the artist's final attempt to claim some kind of hold over the real world in the face of photography's perfect accuracy. No matter, therefore, how realistic art might strive to be, precisely because it is art, and not a photographic representation of reality, its relationship with reality cannot be one of simple indexicality. In the age of photography, art, even realist art, must be more than the real. The Goncourt brothers did not mention the "grain de faux" until years later, but already in 1856, their reaction to photography laid the groundwork for it. This falseness, the mark of the artist's humanity, is exactly what sets realism apart from a photograph.

Unsurprisingly, the Goncourts often use photography to censure artistic output that is too true, so perfectly rendered as to lack individual marks of the artist's genius. In fact, just before their reflection on the "grain de faux" and the failures of *Madame Bovary* in 1860, they compare the novel to photography: "Deep down, and in truth, *Madame Bovary* — a masterpiece of its genre, the last word of truth in the novel — represents a very material side of art and thought. Accessories are as alive and almost on the same plane as people. The material environment is thrown into such relief around the sentiments and passion that it nearly suffocates them. It is a work that paints for the eyes more than it speaks to the soul. The most noble and compelling part of the novel is taken more from painting than literature. It is the stereoscope pushed to its final illusion."[9] While they acknowledge that the best parts of Flaubert's novel are worthy of the art of painting, the Goncourts ultimately condemn its materialism by way of the stereoscope, the viewing apparatus for hyperrealistic, three-dimensional photographic cards. In Flaubert's cold reproduction of a world of things, individual objects crowd out the emotional content just as the mechanical verisimilitude of photography might. The novel's tendency to speak thus to the eyes rather than to sentiment is precisely what forces them to acknowledge the importance of the "grain de faux" in artistic truth. Ironically, of course, by parroting the critics of Flaubert who compared his realism to photography, they cast doubt on their own project. The more they emphasize the need for art to be something more than a copy of reality, the more they are consumed by anxiety and self-doubt; it is clear that they fear that they, too, might not produce anything more than "the stereoscope pushed to its final illusion."

This deployment of photography against art is not limited to discussions of Flaubert or realism. The Goncourts use the adjective "photographic" to signal any art that lacks the mark of individual genius, even against artists who predate photography by centuries. They criticize, for example, ancient sculpture for the same materiality as *Madame Bovary*, writing in their journals that, "Greek art is too much a photographic deification of the human body, too much the perception of completely materialistic civilization" and deploring the absence of even "a grain of genius."[10] Here and elsewhere, photography becomes a rhetorical device signifying everything that the Goncourt brothers hoped to avoid in their own literary production and art collecting: coldly perfect reproductions of reality without the individualizing (and humanizing) mark of genius. Indeed, in some cases, the photograph indicates not merely a lack of individuality in the reproduction of material reality but the absence of talent altogether. As a consequence, even if the photograph complicates the relationship between art and reality, it nonetheless helps to fix the Goncourt brothers' notion of what artistic genius is and should do. Photographic verisimilitude forces them to reexamine the artist's role in the creative process, diminishing the importance of truthfulness relative to that of the talents and perspective of the artist.

The photograph also has a similar role in precipitating a change in their stance on beauty. For Edmond and Jules, the photograph is fundamentally ugly. It captures an essentially unpleasant reality with a harsh accuracy and black-and-white contrast that amplifies that unpleasantness: "Everything in this century is becoming black: photography is like the black frockcoat of things," they complained in 1857, and their aesthetic assessment would only harshen over time.[11] By 1867, they would dismiss photography out of hand with a depressive complaint about life more generally, saying, "Here, the world is as ugly as its photograph."[12] Photography cast a pall on everything. Grim as the real world was, photography had the uncanny ability to make it even more unattractive while seeming simply to copy it. And despite protesting in 1864 about their own right to a depiction of reality that was harsh and crude, ultimately the Goncourt brothers do *not* want realism to be code for mere ugliness. Art based on observation is still supposed to be a rare thing of beauty in an unsightly world. It should not be "Ugliness, always ugliness! And ugliness without its greatest quality, ugliness without the beauty of ugliness!"[13] In this case, they are complaining about Courbet's version of realist painting, but they might as well have been yelling about photography, which they saw as truly the incarnation of ugliness unattenuated by the peculiar beauty of genius.

For the Goncourt brothers, then, photography is associated with two of the most troubling problems of contemporary artistic production, the conflict between truth and beauty (or between mere reality and realist art) and the artist's role in navigating these oppositions. If these theoretical issues plague the medium as a whole, they only become more pronounced in the case of the body. The Goncourt brothers were fascinated by the new genre of nude photography, opining on all of its variations from the academic to the obscene. They were willing to allow, like their friend the artist Paul Gavarni, that photographic studies of the body might have a limited artistic role; Gavarni consigns photography to the role of documentary tool, a means of producing "completely drawn *académies*" for the true artists who paint and draw from them.[14] When it came to nonacademic forms of nude photography, however, the Goncourts had equal scorn for images and consumers alike. They sneered at wildly popular photographs of the cancan dancer Rigolboche wherein she "shows her legs in all their positions" (Figure 22).[15] They called these kinds of photographs "petty [*petit*] genteel obscenities," decrying the taste for them among the "better" classes (to the detriment of real artistic appreciation).[16] They mocked their friend Aurélien Scholl, a consummate womanizer whose apartment was "cluttered with nudities, photographs of actresses."[17] And they smirked at the scandal after the death of the duc de Morny (illegitimate half-brother to Napoléon III) when the duke's friends were put out by the disappearance of "a certain little coffer, that Morny always kept close to his nightstand, containing the portraits of all his conquests from every social rank, photographs, nudes, with, typically, flowers covering their genitals."[18] Scholl's nudities and Morny's trophies were risibly pathetic.

Yet if photographic nudity was a laughing matter when it embarrassed their acquaintances, it also had real artistic consequences. For the Goncourt brothers, even the most academic photographs of the body revealed the medium's fundamental tendency to descend into obscenity and voyeurism. Visiting Gavarni's studio in October 1859, the brothers examined an example of photographic "documents for painting" depicting the underside of a woman's foot.[19] They were repulsed by its "terrifying reality, with its homely web of ticklish wrinkles," which revealed the unappealing starkness that they remark on as a characteristic of photography more generally. But there was something else about the foot, a strange sexualized violence, that was far more upsetting. It was, to them, "similar to the foot that Mercier saw, during the Terror, sticking out from a cartload of warm cadavers, dead and voluptuous."[20] This is not to say that the foot itself was fundamentally sexual (although their reaction has the hallmarks of a Freudian fetish). It was, instead, something in the very nature of photography, in its uncanny ability to capture and expose details that either were unremarkable to the naked eye except at very close range or were simply best (and most often) left covered, and, therefore, only to be seen in the most intimate settings, that rendered this body "voluptuous" and morbid. In unearthing this hidden physical reality, the photographic medium itself became obscene.

In this encounter, the foot metonymically represents the entire body inappropriately exposed to the scrutiny of the camera; their reaction to it likewise encapsulates the Goncourts' response to the genre of nude photography as a whole. The same sense of the morbid voluptuousness of photography's attention to that which is better left unseen reappears and is developed in other journal entries. Recounting a performance of "Ne bougeons plus!" from Cogniard and Clairville's *Revue de l'année 1860* (see Chapter 2), the Goncourts describe the production in terms of this very photographic obscenity: "The play is only a pretext to stage, in every act, a brothel parlor. Nothing else but the coyness of actresses undressed by a snip of the scissors, in short petticoats and flimsy corsets. The censor permitted them to produce all of photography's petty [*petit*] obscenities in tableaux vivants. Even the photographs of laundresses, where one can see the breasts—of the ones who iron while bending down—as if one were holding them."[21] Again the modifier "petit" appears, designating not explicit nudity, but the tantalizing display of corsets, bare arms, and half-exposed breasts epitomized by the laundresses of Lamy or other producers of Second Empire erotica (see, e.g., Figures 26–29). Like the photograph of the bare foot, these images of domestic tasks conducted in semiundress imply a disconcerting intimacy and grant a false sense of possession to the viewer, experienced by the Goncourts as a confusion of sight and touch. However "petty" these obscenities were, they were photographic. And as the phrasing "photography's petty obscenities" suggests, as a consequence simply of being photographic, they had certain unique qualities. The dominant quality for the Goncourt brothers was a troublingly tactile eroticism that made the medium necessarily indecent when it represented the body.

In the eyes of the Goncourts, these traces of obscenity clinging to the photograph in turn magnify the medium's other negative qualities—its cold and mechanical impersonality—exponentially. This is evident from their description of a visit to the sculptor Jean-Pierre Dantan. After briefly examining some of Dantan's own sculptures, they are escorted (along with Flaubert) on a tour of another collection.

> He leads us to his pornographic crypt, signaled on the door with a little *gaudriole* of a woman lifting her skirt up to the small of her back. A sort of tawdry chapel of the phallus, adorned with trophies of winged penises and garlands of molded genitals. There are dildos, libertine drawings, Aretine poses, ithyphallic china and tea sets, watercolors, gouaches, hermaphrodite prints, playing cards, brothel addresses, legions of nude photographs, 74 rulers on the wall, similar to baker's sizes, 74 *culimètres*, measuring the mouth and the cunt [*cul*] of specific women, collected by Sauvageot; and then there are the daguerreotype cunts, wide open sixteen-year-old cunts like the cunt of a mare. After some time, a wave of disgust washes over you, like a horror and a fear of coitus. The stomach turns before these instruments of love, so crude, so ugly, so repugnant, so anatomical, so rightly made to be concealed by love, and the sight of which drives you towards all which isn't *that* in love. This is where one sees what a poet is man and what a crude and material laborer of pleasure and creation was God.[22]

Dantan has a veritable private museum of all of the different apparatus of modern pornography: dildos, statues, drawings, playing cards, and "scientific" tools for measuring, classifying, collecting, and commemorating the female sex. For sheer numbers, however, Dantan's collection is strongest in photographs. He has amassed not only "legions" of nude photographs but also daguerreotypes that the Goncourts refuse to even classify as "nudities." These "daguerreotyped cunts," likely the same "beaver shot" that invades Baudelaire's poems, are deeply disturbing even to Dantan's cynical guests. The women in them become nothing but animals, revolting the two brothers. The photographs are obscenity in its purest form, the female body reduced to nothing but its physical and reproductive properties. Forced to look on these photographs, the Goncourt brothers are seized with the conviction that this terrifying physical locus of sexuality, the "instrument" of love, must not merely be idealized. It must be completely concealed by the emotion of love. Indeed, in this moment, they claim that the very meaning of art, that which is both its inspiration and its precondition, is the imperative to conceal the frightful physical reality of the vagina. "This is where" the great divide separating the beauty of art from the ugliness of reality is most apparent, "this is where" we finally comprehend just how great man's creative powers are, even compared to God's. If the woman's sex is indirectly acknowledged in this passage as the ultimate impetus of both society and of art (just as in the title of Courbet's *The Origin of the World*), the Goncourts' reaction against its exposure, their horrified instinct to re-cover it, at the same time reveals just how much of its power is rooted in attempts to disavow its very existence.

Nothing could be more overtly Freudian than the fear of the female sexual organs that emerges in this scene. In his study of the prostitute in nineteenth-century literature, *Figures of Ill Repute*, Charles Bernheimer maintains that precisely this fear is at work in modernist literary production. Bernheimer sees in the pervasive fascination with the prostitute, and more specifically, the prostitute's sex organs, the generative side of repression and the castration complex at work, as writers used their art to "contain, sublimate, or metaphorize the contaminating decomposition of her sexual ferment."[23] Faced with the "pathological erosion" embodied in the physical sexuality of the prostitute, the modernist writer had to "construct art against nature, against woman, against the organic."[24] In other words, what Bernheimer attributes to modernism as a movement, the Goncourt brothers demand of all art: the denial of the ugly physical reality of generative female sexuality. This attitude toward art was not only theoretical but also personal for these two brothers, whose journals and novels betray a deeply engrained misogyny and pathological terror of the opposite sex. They would have made a perfect case study for both Bernheimer and Freud, replete with examples of the repressive psychic and artistic mechanisms deployed against the castration complex.

What is striking about their conception of art for the purposes of this study, however, is not how it lends itself to Freudian analysis, but rather how it turns on photography. The legions of daguerreotyped vulvas in Dantan's crypt are too terrifying to be redeemed by art *because* they are photographs. Where "true" art is predicated on the erasure of the physical reality of the female sex, the photograph is predicated on its exposure. No other medium before photography so completely wallowed in this most dangerous and abject locus of creativity, for no other medium was so defined by the way that it exposed what was best left unseen. In refusing to participate in the primal act of sublimation, the disavowal of the female sex organs, the photograph is transformed from a tawdry and talentless copy of reality into something distinctly more sinister. In Dantan's crypt, the obscene photograph becomes a coded object whose stark depiction of female sexuality symbolizes not just the hazards of the medium but also the potential obliteration of artistic signification altogether.

⚐ Baudelaire, Beauty, and the Modern Painter in *Manette Salomon* ⚐

The problem of realist representation follows nude photography from the journals into the pages of the *Manette Salomon*, mediated by Baudelaire. The reader, however, would be forgiven for overlooking the importance of photography—or even for wondering what the novel actually *is* about, given how scattered and wide ranging it is.[25] Manette makes her appearance exceedingly late in the text that bears her name (Chapter 48); it turns out hers was the third choice for the title, after *Les Artistes* and *L'Atelier Langibout*.[26] The significance of Manette and Coriolis' ill-fated liaison is equally unclear. It looks like a variation on the old story of the artist destroyed by his lover, a plot repeated three times in Goncourt novels and mirrored in their own disdain for the attractions of the fairer sex.[27] Coriolis' painting of Manette establishes his artistic reputation, but once she becomes the mother of their child, Manette transforms from muse to harpy. Coriolis ends the book a broken man, misunderstood and abused by critics, crushed by Manette's greedy Jewish opportunism, and without even art to sustain him. The novel's philosophical language, however, abstracts this story of artist-destroyed-by-lover into an allegory for the vexed relationship of the artist to the real bodies he paints and to his own aesthetic ideals, precisely the same set of issues embodied for the Goncourt brothers by the nude photograph. Among many possible readings of the novel, mine will focus on these philosophical concerns and the novel's failed attempt to use Baudelairian aesthetics to recuperate realist art from (nude) photography.

True to the novel's diffuse style, Coriolis' story truly begins only on his return from the Orient, more than a hundred pages in. He brings back an entirely new kind of Orientalist vision—"fine, nuanced, vaporous, evanesced, subtle"—and "a talent whose originality, then completely new, caused a sensation amongst the small circle of friends that frequented the studio on the Rue de Vaugirard."[28] Soon, Coriolis' theoretical preoccupations broaden from the representation of the Orient to representation more generally. Coriolis' early Orientalism is so different precisely because it is, in its nuance and subtlety, "realist" and observational. Unlike other painters, Coriolis claims he himself arrived "brand new before the oriental light" and observed without any "parti pris."[29] As his career advances, Coriolis turns to a larger project, one that mirrors very closely that undertaken by the Goncourt brothers. He spends much of the novel striving to create a "new realism," a realism "sought beyond the idiocy of the daguerreotype, the charlatanry of the ugly, and working to draw from the typical, selected, forms, expressive of contemporary images, the contemporary style."[30] Just like the Goncourt brothers, Coriolis perceives that the photograph complicates the task of the realist artist, necessitating that representations of reality distinguish themselves from photography if they are to be art. His artistic identity depends on creating a realism that has nothing to do with the unsatisfying copies of reality generated by photography.

The theoretical structure of Coriolis' quest to reinvent realism "beyond the idiocy of the daguerreotype" is provided by Chassagnol, the novel's philosopher and Baudelairian interlocutor. In a long tirade toward the end of the novel, he uses Baudelaire's figure of the modern painter to rouse Coriolis out of inactivity and inspire him to start painting again after a long series of disappointments. Although it appears late in the text, I begin with Chassagnol's discourse because it reveals the framework for the novel's engagement with realism and the theoretical basis for Manette and Coriolis' relationship, and it is, therefore, essential to understanding the role of the photographic nude. Coriolis has already by this time taken up with his model and begun to waste his talents. Disappointed in Coriolis' neglect of his art, Chassagnol commands him to reevaluate his work. If he is really seeking an alternative to "this caricature of the Truth of our time, a bourgeois stupefaction: realism!" which is more or less "a parlor religion of stupid ugliness, of poorly collected, undiscerning vulgarity," he must commit to being a truly modern painter. Above all, in his search for this modern style, he must look at "his own time in front of him" and not elsewhere to find the supreme, eternal, and abstract Beauty sought by artists:[31]

> Do not all painters, the great painters of all time, extract the Beautiful from their own era? Do you believe that the beautiful is given only to a certain epoch or select people? But every era contains the Beautiful within, some Beautiful or another, more or less at ground level, graspable

and exploitable. . . . It is simply a question of excavation. . . . It is possible that the Beautiful of today is enveloped, buried, concentrated. . . . Perhaps, to find it requires analysis, a magnifying glass, myopic eyes, new physiological processes. . . . Hey, what about Balzac? Did Balzac not discover the grandeur in money, in housework, in the filth of modern things?[32]

Chassagnol's alternative to bourgeois realism is not academic abstraction or a return to classical subjects, but an art of the contemporary against presumed critics who would declare this an unfit subject. He argues that the ideal category of "the Beautiful" is variable and to be found in more than one epoch. As such, it must be possible to find and convey the beauty inherent in modern life. Modernity per se does not preclude an abstract and ideal category of the Beautiful; it simply requires the right gaze to find the beautiful in "the filth of modern things." No detail is so mundane, no aspect of contemporary dress and street life so unappealing that it could not be, in the right hands, inspiration for art and, therefore, in its way, a manifestation of the Beautiful. The true artist, presented with the seemingly ugly and banal details of contemporary reality, renders them in such a way that this beauty is made visible in all its glory.

Readers of Baudelaire will immediately recognize echoes of *Le Peintre de la vie moderne*, wherein Baudelaire reconciles the artist's conflicting obligations both to render contemporary reality and to attend to abstract aesthetic categories by locating the eternal category of the Beautiful in the ephemeral details of modern life.[33] The language used by Chassagnol, however, is perhaps even closer to the section of the *Salon de 1846* (discussed in the last chapter) entitled "De l'héroïsme de la vie moderne." In it, Baudelaire rejects the notion that only ancient subjects are sufficiently full of "majestic attitudes" and "sublime motifs" to nourish the arts.[34] Instead of looking backward in time, he urges painters to look for the Beautiful in the variety of individual contemporary beauty around them, in a concise summary of the ideas subsequently explored at length in his essay on Guys:

> Before turning to what might be the epic side of modern life, and proving by examples that our epoch is not less fecund than the ancients in sublime motifs, we can affirm that, since all centuries and all peoples have had their beauty, we inevitably have ours. It is in the order of things.
>
> All beauties contain, like all possible phenomena, something eternal and something transitory, — something absolute and something particular. Absolute and eternal beauty does not exist, or rather is only an abstraction skimmed from the general surface of the diverse beauties. The particular element of each beauty comes from the passions, and as we all have our particular passions, we have our beauty.[35]

Like Chassagnol, Baudelaire, too, argues that modern life is the appropriate subject for modern painters, that the abstraction of the Beautiful must always come from the details of one's own time, that, despite appearances, there is such a thing as modern beauty, and finally, that this beauty, while rooted in reality (and therefore endlessly variable), constitutes something more than an array of beautiful objects: it constitutes the Beautiful itself. This would later become Baudelaire's more famous formula in *Le Peintre de la vie moderne* of the "eternal, invariable element" and the "relative, circumstantial element" that together make up the Beautiful.[36] And out of this formula emerged the best-known articulation of Baudelairian modernity, which valorizes the contingent and real components of beauty: "Modernity is the transitory, the fugitive, the contingent half of art, of which the other half is the eternal and the immutable."[37] Lest there be any doubt of Baudelaire's influence, just one week after finishing *Manette Salomon* the Goncourt brothers wrote about this very idea of art as a mediation between the eternal and the particular in their journals. On 29 August 1866, they note that "Art is the eternalization, the binding into a supreme, absolute and definitive form of a moment, of a fleetingness, of a human particularity."[38] Baudelaire's theories underpin the fundamental philosophical problem of *Manette Salomon*, the same one the Goncourt brothers puzzled over in their journal: How do we understand art's—and the artist's—relationship to reality?

⊴ Manette, Coriolis, and the Rejection of Baudelaire ⊵

Chassagnol's redux of Baudelaire's *Salon de 1846* is so closely aligned with the original that it even includes many of the poet's distinctive arguments (such as a defense of the *habit noir* and the choice of Balzac as a model for modern visual art, despite the fact that he was a writer).[39] Yet at the same time, Chassagnol also plants the seed of a total repudiation of the poet's aesthetic theories. Dorian Bell argues that both the novel's echoes and its critique of Baudelaire are directed at pre-Baudelairian philosophical categories of the real and ideal; I will argue instead that it is directed very pointedly at Baudelaire's use of them to define modern art and the modern artist in the context of photography.[40] More particularly, it is directed at the mechanics of the delicate partnership Baudelaire ultimately forges between the real and the ideal in art by way of the Beautiful. Caught between realism and idealism, over a period of almost twenty years, Baudelaire laid out an aesthetic taxonomy that distinguishes an idea of beauty from the transitory beauty of modern life while simultaneously insisting that the ideal can only be deduced *from* the real. His writings variously entangle the two categories. In

1846, Baudelaire proclaims that the category of the Beautiful only actually exists as a kind of cream skimmed from the milk of life, rooting the eternal solidly in ephemeral physical reality. The difference between the two is more pronounced in *Le Peintre de la vie moderne*, where Baudelaire's language more explicitly invokes the Aristotelian categories of form and matter in order to clarify further the way in which the two kinds of beauty exist in relation to each other; even then, however, they remain mutually dependent: "The duality of art is a fatal consequence of the duality of man. Consider, if it pleases you, the eternally subsistent element as the soul of art, and the variable element as its body."[41] By 1863, the Beautiful had ascended to the realm of the immaterial, but the widening gulf between real and ideal beauty did not mean that material reality was any less essential to art. For Baudelaire, even if art is irrevocably divided, the two categories of beauty nevertheless exist in a necessary and mutually sustainable relationship. The soul needs the body to manifest itself in the contingent universe as much as the body needs the soul to exist.

Despite his debt to Baudelaire, Chassagnol's is a murkier and far more pessimistic conception of the relationship between ideal categories and real incarnations of beauty. Chassagnol does not in his first outburst speak of timelessness and purity, he merely gestures at a Platonic ideal of beauty by capitalizing "Beautiful" and allowing it to stand as the representative of that category. Moreover, whatever his protests against "bourgeois realism," and his pain that his contemporaries' ateliers are built on the "cemetery of the Ideal" (an echo of Baudelaire's "grave of the ideal" from "Laquelle est la vraie" perhaps?), his beautiful is tethered far more tightly to reality.[42] Baudelaire continually invokes an eternal category that necessarily exists in relation to the contingent reality below, but Chassagnol's contingent beauty is not just *of* this earth, it may even be buried *beneath* the earth, hidden in it, "enveloped, buried, concentrated." Consequently, where Baudelaire accepts the concurrent existence of the two kinds of beauties and their necessary relationship to each other, so that the real is always glorified and is necessarily worthy of exaltation, Chassagnol is unclear whether the Beautiful is to be found in reality or is instead obstructed by that reality. Chassagnol's ideas suggest the troubling possibility that reality *isn't* the source of ideal Beauty at all but is, instead, a fundamental obstacle to it; for the Goncourt brothers, this is precisely the intractable problem exposed by the photograph.

In *Manette Salomon*, this ambivalence develops into an outright rejection of Baudelaire expressed via the relationship between Coriolis and the nude body of his model, Manette. Like the rest of the novel's conceptualizing of modern art, this use of the nude to explore the complex triangulation of the real, the ideal, and the artist also has a precedent in Baudelaire. In the last chapter, I discussed at length Baudelaire's section of the *Salon de 1846*, "De l'idéal et du modèle," wherein Baudelaire extends his discussion from "De l'héroïsme de la vie moderne" to the nude. In it, Baudelaire continues to distinguish between the reality of the model's body and an ideal form of beauty, while simultaneously insisting on the necessity of both. His analysis relies on a total confidence in the painter's eye as a force of art, which he situates as a conduit directly between the two; it is the painter's talent that is worthy of being an idealizing force because only the painter's eye has the ability to reconstruct the real body "in the brilliant truth of its native harmony."[43] Baudelaire even goes so far as to argue that the artist's role is precisely to create the ideal from the real body in front of him. Throughout the novel, the relationship between Manette and Coriolis is described in language that clearly places it in dialogue with these same Baudelairian terms. However, in their pairing of artist and model, the Goncourt brothers betray their ambivalence about not only the relationship between the real and ideal but also the role the artist plays in mediating between the two in his art.

At its inception, Coriolis' collaboration with Manette looks like a perfect example of Baudelaire's modern artist at work, mediating the Beautiful through the body of his model. In their description of her first modeling session for *Le Bain Turc*, the Goncourts write,

> Nature is an unequal artist [. . .] From time to time, in the midst of all the junk of humanity, she chooses a being at random, as if to prevent the example of the Beautiful from dying. She takes a body that she polishes and finishes with love, with pride. And it is then a veritable and divine being of art who steps out of the artistic hands of Nature.
>
> Manette's body was one of these bodies: in the studio, her nudity had suddenly taken on the radiance of a work of art.[44]

Manette is beauty incarnate, the eternal and the contingent in a single human form. Hers is that rare body that is itself art; in her nudity there is no sign of nakedness, only the brilliance of a future masterpiece. Yet make no mistake; she is not *only* some mythical ideal, she is also a product of Nature, a real physical woman who will need to be faithfully rendered for the artist to find artistic success. She is the perfect modern model, the stuff of modern art. Along with Manette's body, moreover, Coriolis' particularly modern talent is also on display. For two full pages of the novel, "his eyes were lost in the coloration so rich and so fine, in those tonal movements so soft, so variable, so nuanced, that many painters express and believe they are idealizing with a banal and flat pink; they embraced those fugitive transparencies, that tenderness and warmth of color that is barely color, [. . .] all the delicious je ne sais quoi of the feminine epidermis."[45]

Coriolis and Manette here embody a perfect collaboration between artist and model, in which the unique aura of Manette's body is absorbed and rendered by the individual eye of the artist. As the painter works, his model responds in kind to his progress, sharing "the annoyed air" of his painting during difficult moments and then, as the artist achieves success, "one might have said that her skin was ecstatic."[46] In this seemingly flawless pairing of artist and model, the two are so close that Coriolis can even see the marks of the painting on her body, and her body responds to the movement of his brush: "I saw the reflection of my canvas on her body, and it seemed to me that she was tickled everywhere that I placed my paintbrush. . . . It was something bizarre like magnetism, the current of a caress from portrait to figure."[47] This mutual relationship of artist and model, in which reality becomes an incarnation of the Beautiful, more or less reenacts for the reader Baudelaire's ideas from "De l'idéal et du modèle."

Their untainted collaboration, however, is short lived. Even in its early days, it is plagued by the same doubts about realist observation and artistic talent that pepper the Goncourt brothers' journals. On the one hand, the text stridently asserts the importance of Manette's physical body as a transformative artistic force. Before Manette appears, Coriolis is almost at the end of his patience with *Le Bain turc*, telling Anatole that the nude figure is "stupid like an académie of a Parisienne."[48] The first model's real body ruins the painting. It is overdetermined by the contingent, by quirks that locate her in space and time as a "Parisienne." Manette's body produces an entirely different result. She is a work of art on her own, a "veritable and divine being of art who steps out of the artistic hands of Nature," chosen by chance to stand out from others, to keep the Beautiful alive and present.[49] Her body alone changes the painting, because it manages to be real and transcendent at once. It seems that the "je ne sais quoi" of art might be bestowed directly onto her fleshly self, and Coriolis is less talented than lucky to have stumbled across the perfect model. On the other hand, the text is never quite clear if the ideal form of the Beautiful *is* actually incarnated in Manette's physical body or emerges from Coriolis' perception of that body. Manette models for many painters, not all of whose paintings achieve the quality of Coriolis' work. Moreover, the text makes just as much of Coriolis' eye, and the symbiotic relationship between that eye and the body, as it does of the body alone. Beautiful though she is, Manette only incarnates the Beautiful inasmuch as she is "an inspiration and a revelation of his talent," raw material waiting to become a masterpiece.[50] If she attains immortality through the canvas, it is because Coriolis put her there. She must be seen and painted in order to become what nature has already made her. And yet, even then, Coriolis doesn't *make* this ideal through his painting as Baudelaire's painter does; instead, he recognizes it, transforming the pure materiality of Manette in that moment of recognition. What, then, is his relationship to Manette? Does he single-handedly bestow meaning onto Manette's body or merely recognize and fulfill the potential of that body in his art? All of this tension bubbles to the surface when Coriolis mocks Manette for the pride she takes in her body, saying to Anatole, "Oh! A real vanity. . . . It is comical. [. . .] She is persuaded that her body makes the paintings."[51] Given Coriolis' rapid fall into mediocrity after *Le Bain turc*, his dismissal of the importance of Manette's body is hubristically ironic. Still, the novel continually equivocates on the issue of who does "make" the paintings. The real body before the artist's eyes is nothing without his talent, but his talent, as the novel makes perfectly clear, is nothing without that body.

The Photography Effect: The Failure of the Modern Artist

Even at their best, then, Manette and Coriolis never quite fulfill the promise of Baudelaire's modern painter. And as their relationship disintegrates and Coriolis' once bright prospects dim, a shadow is cast on Baudelaire's artistic paradigm as well. There is, moreover, a very particular catalyst that sets Coriolis' fall in motion: photography. Photography is just as problematic in the pages of the novel as it is in the Goncourt brothers' journals. Recall that Coriolis himself defines his own realist project—like the Goncourt brothers themselves—in opposition to photography, in opposition to the "idiocy of the daguerreotype, the charlatanry of the ugly."[52] Chassagnol, meanwhile, likens Ingres' lack of individual genius to the harsh realism of color photography. Comparing Ingres to ancient sculpture, he declares that the "beautiful objects" of antiquity "have a modeled air; this seems to be truth and reality itself, but this is reality envisioned by the personality of genius. . . . In Ingres' work? There is nothing of the sort. . . . I will tell you what he is: the nineteenth century inventor of color photography for the reproduction of Perugino and Raphaël, that's it."[53] Garnotelle, the novel's fictional embodiment of a critically acclaimed salon painter, is likewise dismissed by the novel's narrator via a photographic metaphor. His painting is described as "freezing the human face with rigid graphic lines like the trace of a sketch, reducing the skin's coloring to the dead tones of an old daguerreotype, colored, back in the day, for ten francs."[54] Whereas in the attack on Ingres, color enhances the photographic reality effect to bolster the argument that his art is so perfect as to signal a fundamental lack of talent, in Garnotelle's painting, color is a marker of the photograph's distorting and inherent ugliness. The garish colors he uses, reminiscent of cheap daguerreotypes, are a false note that nevertheless fails to redeem the photographic quality of his work, instead magnifying its deathly ugliness. Whether the Goncourts describe real painters or fictionalized ones, whether in the pages of the novel or outside of it, "photography" is code for talentless hack.

The medium quickly casts a pall over Coriolis and Manette. One night, soon after their artistic relationship has become a sexual one, Coriolis returns home to his model-turned-lover in a mute rage. Grabbing a chair as though to beat the sleeping Manette, he pauses to contemplate her body in front of him.

> Her body could be divined under the sheets, obscure and charming, as well as her face, round, veiled and soft, all gathered together and curled up in her nocturnal grace, as if it was still posing in sleep. . .
>
> Before this bed, this woman, Coriolis stood speechless; then, his hand let go of the chair and the dowel that he had held fell broken on the carpet.
>
> The next day, rummaging through the clothes of Coriolis, who was not yet awakened, Manette found a photograph of a naked woman—who was her—a card she had allowed to be made, believing that Coriolis would never know anything of it. She understood her lover's rage, replaced the card, and waited, prepared for anything. She began, so as to be ready to leave, to secretly gather her laundry, her things.[55]

The discovery of Manette's photographic infidelity is a pivotal scene in the novel. In it, Coriolis' gaze, once a metonymy for his unique talent, is transformed and corrupted by a photographically inspired fury. Manette is so much his model that even in sleep she seems to be "posing" for him still. Yet rather than contemplate the clarity and illumination of Manette's physical form in the joy of creation, Coriolis is confronted with a form that, while still seductive to his eye, is instead "obscure" and "curled up," closed off from him. In his hand, the paintbrush that was formerly animated by an otherworldly synergy of painter and model has been replaced by a broken chair he might have used to destroy Manette's beauty forever. The discovery of this single photograph has transformed light, creativity, and imagination into destruction, darkness, and frustration.

Coriolis is half mad with artistic jealousy throughout the novel. He is already at this point so obsessed with Manette that he spends his time dissecting the nudes of other artists for signs that she has posed for someone else behind his back. By the time Coriolis discovers her photograph, Manette's body has become a talisman reassuring him of his artistic abilities. Any attempt to pose for another artist would constitute a betrayal. The violence of this scene, however, is determined by the medium of her artistic infidelity. Manette hasn't deserted Coriolis for another painter's superior genius, but for photography, the anti-art, the embodiment of the endless indignities faced by the modern painter. This nude image, then, is entangled with the central puzzle of the novel: whether observation of reality or individual genius, Manette's body or Coriolis' talent, constitutes the power of art. To surpass the photograph in rendering reality, Coriolis must necessarily have talent, but what if he doesn't, or that isn't enough? What if Manette's nude body, staring back at him in the harsh ugliness of the photographic form, is more beautiful than any painted version of it? Or, to rephrase these anxieties more broadly, the photograph is attended by the most fundamental questions of all: What is the artist? What is art? And where do they exist in relation to reality? Photography not only complicates these questions, it may even foreclose the very possibility of realism as an art form. It is, after all, the precise representational form against which Coriolis' artistic project is conceived. By participating in the photography's assault on painting, Manette has betrayed not only the artist but art itself.

The photograph's implied sexual content only amplifies its negative implications in the text. While Edmond Goncourt's 1896 theatrical version of *Manette Salomon* specifies that Manette's photograph is an académie promised to a rival painter before she had met Coriolis, the original text is vague about its content.[56] A "card" could signify any kind of image at all, but it is more commonly used to designate a small carte-de-visite or a stereograph card than a true academic study. It opens the possibility that Manette's photograph was explicitly erotic rather than artistic, transforming it into the embodiment of the most dangerous kind of photography in the Goncourts' antiphotographic discourse, the obscene nude image. Photography intrudes into the text at its most abject, representing precisely that which the Goncourt brothers believe art must *never* show: the physical locus of sexual desire. Before our eyes, Manette the muse, the source of artistic creativity, is turned into Manette the temptress, little better than one of the women on display in Dantan's crypt, an object of sexual pleasure whose body has no potential for signification beyond the sex organs spread out for the camera and whose exposure in this manner signifies the terrifying prospect of the end of art.

Manette's photographic nudity, thus ambiguously sexualized, has the further role of tying together the novel's philosophic preoccupations with its other plot about the dangers of mixing sexual and artistic partnerships. Even before discovering the photograph, Coriolis' belief that "celibacy was the only state that left the artist his liberty, his strength, his brain, his conscience" was already threatened by his affair with Manette.[57] And, indeed, her artistic hold over him only deepens with their sexual entanglement as, "With his love was mixed the love of his life, his art. The artist loved alongside the man."⁵⁸ Coriolis' jealousy over the photograph is clearly the product of both passions. The novel's vagueness about the content of this photograph further insinuates sexual jealousy into his artistic fury. By obfuscating the distinction between erotic and artistic photographic nudity, the text enacts within the content of the photograph the same blurring of erotic and artistic relationships that will destroy Coriolis. Photography, already its own formidable threat to art, thus also implicates itself in the destruction of the artist by women and by sexual desire as well. In this sense, the nude photograph becomes the structural center of the novel, uniting the text's preoccupation with postphotographic realist representation and its misogynistic allegory of the artist undone by sex in a single object.

The photograph's role in precipitating Coriolis' downward spiral in the novel confirms this dark reading. As a result of the discovery of the photograph, Coriolis finds among Manette's possessions a gold coin he had given to her many years before when she was a young girl. The "divine will" perceived by Manette in this bond from their past ultimately leads to her pregnancy and the complete disintegration of their once-fruitful model-artist relationship. ⁵⁹ After the birth of their child, "the model had been killed suddenly, it had died in her."⁶⁰ With Manette the model replaced by Manette the human, Manette the (obscene) photograph, Manette the sexually reproductive mate and mother, Coriolis' doom is sealed. The destruction begun by Manette's photograph reaches its culmination in Coriolis' artistic breakdown at the end of the novel, a scene that works in counterpoint to that of the photograph's discovery. Again, Coriolis lashes out at Manette, saying,

> "Do you know what you have made of me? A working man, a hand-to-mouth painting maker, a servant to fashion, to merchants, and the public! . . . a wretch! [. . .] Ah! What I would be today with the paintings you prevented me from making! . . . and the money that you would have made, you! . . . You don't know anything about money. [. . .] Ah! you have utterly depleted the artist! . . . I hate you, don't you see, I hate you. . . . And do you know what else! There are days . . . ," and his slow voice took on a homicidal sweetness, "some days . . . where an idea comes to me, a very serious idea, to begin with you, and finish with myself, to put an end to this life!"⁶¹

This second scene of confrontation between Coriolis and his model doubles the first and completes it. The first time, Coriolis is silent; the second time, he teems with verbalized rage. Again, but even more so, his creative urge has been converted into one that is completely destructive, wherein his vision of Manette is totally altered. Once again, money (the recurring symbol of the Jewish Manette as woman and wife who slowly comes to overwhelm the model Manette) is invoked. This time, however, Coriolis will finish what was begun with the discovery of Manette's photograph. Gathering all of his paintings together, Coriolis sets them on fire in front of his wife. When he has finished, he extracts a morsel of silver from the burnt ruins of his art and throws it at Manette (in addition to denoting coinage, silver was essential to certain early photographic processes). Where the gold coin fatally bound them together, setting Coriolis' decline in motion, the silver finally ends all that was formerly creative or affectionate in the liaison:

> "There you go! Here's an ingot worth one hundred thousand francs!" he said to her.
>
> "Ah!" exclaimed Manette, with a leap of terror that made the ingot slip to the bottom of her burnt dress. "Burn me! . . . He wanted to burn me!"
>
> "Now," Coriolis said to her, "You are free to leave. . . . I no longer need you."[62]

After discovering the photograph, Coriolis only threatens to destroy the body that first inspired his art and then impeded it; with the end of his hopes, he follows through. In a heavily symbolic substitution, real body and painted body are exchanged, so that even as the "real" Manette is hardly touched, Manette the model, the art object, the subject of the many paintings, is burned to ashes; with her painted self goes, at long last, all in Coriolis that still could create art. Where the Goncourt journals threaten the end of art after nude photography, the novel enacts the violence of this end.

⚜ Baudelaire, Nude Photography, and the End of Modern Art ⚜

Baudelaire's theorization of the modern painter does not emerge from this mess unscathed. As nude photography destroys the novel's "modern artist," Baudelairian aesthetics do nothing to save him. Baudelaire's theories, as embodied by Coriolis and Manette at the start of their partnership, crumble in the face of photography along with Coriolis' prospects. Indeed, the text ultimately indicts both Baudelaire's conceptualization of the modern artist and (nude) photography for Coriolis' ruin. This indictment is expressed by way of the critical reaction to the paintings Coriolis produces in response to Chassagnol's scoldings about modernity. These paintings should be the culmination of Coriolis' career. They are meant to exemplify his antiphotographic and modern realism, the quest for which has occupied the entire novel. When the paintings are displayed at the 1855 Exposition universelle, however, they are met with near-universal opprobrium:

There was held against his paintings the general idea, the set opinion, that the question of the representation of the modern in painting of another artist, raised by essays brazen to the point of scandal, was definitively decided. Critics did not want to revisit it; and between them and the public there was a tacit preconceived understanding not to credit Coriolis with the new realism that he was inaugurating, a realism sought beyond the idiocy of the daguerreotype, the charlatanry of the ugly, and that worked to draw from the typical chosen expressive form of contemporary imagery, the contemporary style.[63]

The very moment when the novel explicitly situates Coriolis' realism in opposition to photography is the moment of his greatest failure. He has attempted to produce modern painting, he has rejected the ugly realism of the photograph, he has sought the beautiful in the mundane of modern life, but to no avail. His talent goes unrecognized, his Baudelairian quest for modern art is willfully misunderstood and dismissed by critics. The very debates about "modern painting" that inspired his work here become the instruments of his destruction; having declared these questions "definitively decided," the critics resent Coriolis for reopening the issue. Of course, the novel has made it clear by this point that Coriolis is meant to incarnate the "modern" painter, and the reader knows better than to put any stock in the critics' abuse. Indeed, we are meant to blame those critics (and the public) for their small-mindedness. Still, the fact that critics could find a foothold at all in the same ideas about modernity that guided Coriolis' work reveals a fundamental limitation of these ideas. What good are theories about modern painting if the painter who embodies them can be undone by their critical misappropriation?

Not only do these critics use theories about modern painting against the modern painter, they also use the photograph against a painter who has spent the novel struggling to create a representational form that transcends photography. With biting irony, these same critics demand to know how Coriolis could have dared to produce such regrettable paintings:

> How did the creator of these two poor and unfortunate canvases, a *Conseil de révision* and a *Messe de mariage*, not understand that great painting was incompatible with vulgarity, with the common reality of the modern? How did he not understand that it is practically blasphemy to want to make a nude, a divine nude, a sacred nude, from the nudity [*nu*] of a conscript? How did he not understand that dress needs to lose its contemporaneity and frivolity in the character of eternal and permanent nobility that only masters know how to attribute to it? [. . .] To paint such subjects is to miss

the lofty and original purpose of painting, it is to debase art to the level of news photography. To what abysmal depths of the so-called "contemporary truth" are we to be dragged?[64]

Coriolis' realism is transformed by his reviewers into the worst kind of common vulgarity and photographic verisimilitude. Notably, not just any aspect of Coriolis' painting inspires this virulent backlash, but the specific case, once more, of the nude body. In his *Conseil de révision*, Coriolis depicts the scene of new conscripts into the army undergoing physical examinations; the centerpiece of the painting is a male nude being inspected by the army doctor. Here, again, the critics deliberately and maliciously misread Coriolis' work, denouncing his painted bodies as tainted by that same horrific apparatus of "the contemporary truth" and of popular modernity that is destroying art. Although this model is male and the vast majority of the figures in both photographic studies were female (including, of course, Manette herself), it is important that the degrading mark of photography manifests itself once again in a body; as in the Goncourts' journals, the photographic perspective is most evident and most dangerous when it captures the body, no matter its gender. The critics, of course, are just as misguided about Coriolis and photography as they are about Coriolis and modernity, but they nevertheless confirm the significance of Manette's photograph. After the invention of photography, artists can no longer simply devote themselves to rendering reality. They will always operate in photography's distorting shadow. Even the paradigmatic modern artist, one who defines realism against photography, will be compromised by its preponderance.

The novel's cautionary tale, then, is perhaps less about nude photography as such and more about a mode of theorizing art that cannot account for nude photography's traumatic incursion. When Coriolis' critics use Baudelaire's "modern art" against Coriolis, they reveal that contemporary aesthetic discourse has not simply failed to account for photography, it has betrayed that which it was meant to defend. The language of beauty, of reality, of individual talent, and of modernity, invoked by the text to shape its painter, fails to rescue him. Sick and dejected, Coriolis denounces modernity completely: "I thought I had found the *modern*," he says, but "presently, I no longer see in it what I saw, and perhaps it is not there."[65] The modern is a phantom, a theoretical construction offering no solace to the real artist. The only path left to art is to move beyond it, to seek out an entirely new means of representing and theorizing art's relationship to the world. By the end of the novel, both Coriolis and his friend Anatole are so crushed by their accumulated failures that they abandon representation altogether for a total communion with reality through immediate experience. This turn to experience is expressed as Anatole's strange vision of "the primitive home of humanity" among the animal menagerie of the Jardin des Plantes.[66] In the darkness of the novel's prophesy about the end of art, its final scene offers a glimmer of hope that somewhere in this antimodern "felicity of the first man in the face of virgin Nature" are the seeds of a new kind of art nowhere promised by the text, and everywhere longed for, one so far removed from modernity that photography will have no means of spoiling it.[67]

PART II

The Third Republic

CHAPTER 5

The Rise of an International Industry: 1870–1900

The political and economic turmoil of the Franco-Prussian war and the collapse of the Empire meant a significant, if brief, interruption in the distribution of nude photography in the French capital.[1] By March 1871, however, an irate reader of the *Journal des débats* wrote to the newspaper to complain that the respite had ended. "For the entire duration of the siege," he exclaimed, "licentious drawings or photographs had disappeared from display. They are reappearing."[2] The photographs returning to streets and shop windows were part of an industry that was not entirely different from before and yet was also rapidly changing. Many of the structures of production and distribution carried over from the Empire. Indeed, until 1881, when sweeping new laws on the press were passed, photographs were still subject to the 1852 censorship law, and the government still had a role in regulating the production of certain forms of photographic nudity. At the same time, the first decades of the Third Republic saw technological advancements, international expansion, and, after 1881, the end of censorship, which, in turn, meant new forms and greater quantities of photographic nudity, new methods of distribution, and changing legal structures governing an increasingly anonymous and international industry.

This chapter continues where the opening chapter left off to lay out the history of photographic nudity from 1870 to 1900, again focusing on Paris. In the wake of the upheaval of 1870–1871, the task of writing that history became considerably more difficult than it was for the Second Empire. Even before the censorship law was repealed, many fewer photographers and editors submitted images for authorization. After 1881, when it became entirely voluntary to register images for the Dépôt légal, the ranks of those seeking authorization dwindled even further. Government policing and record keeping became far less intensive just as photographic production exploded. No archives exist from the Third Republic that contain the same wealth of information as the BB3 and the Dépôt légal of the Empire. In the Third Republic, the history of the photographic nude must be gleaned from print sources rather than pulled from government registers.

These changes to policing and legal enforcement were not merely impediments to future historians, they also reflected one of the most significant developments of the Third Republic: the redefinition of legal and illegal nudity after the repeal of the censorship law in 1881. The old categories of authorized and unauthorized nudity, always somewhat nebulous, began to disintegrate entirely as the government abdicated its role in assessing and categorizing nudity. Against this background, and in concert with the other radical changes to the industry, the language about photographic nudity shifted as well. With the rise of social reform movements of the fin de siècle, discourse about nudes focused on their nefarious social effects to the complete exclusion of questions of art. Despite a revival of the nude led by the Pictorialist photographers in the 1890s, by the end of the century, nude photography was no longer treated as a problematic genre that hovered at the border of art and obscenity. Instead, it had become one among many social ills plaguing fin-de-siècle France.

⟋ Legal History ⟍

Already by the 1860s, the imperial government was no longer pursuing producers of obscene photography with the same zeal as it once had. The records in the BB3 become sparser and sparser until finally ceasing altogether in 1868. In that year, Napoléon III reversed one of the key provisions of the decree of 17 February 1852, allowing print publications to be sold without prior authorization. This was followed by another series of legal changes. In 1870, the new government moved to do away with censorship of the press, as well as to grant cases of affront to public decency a jury trial rather than a trial in the *tribunaux correctionnels*. Images, however, did not benefit from these liberalizing tendencies; they were governed by the 1852 censorship decree until 1881 and were not granted jury trials for cases of indecency.[3] Only with the passage of the landmark press laws in July 1881 was the decree of 1852 finally fully overturned, releasing photographers from the legal obligation to submit images for authorization. From that point forward, those photographs that were submitted to the Dépôt légal were granted only copyright privileges, not protection from prosecution. The 1881 law also abrogated the statute of 1819, with a clause governing affront to public decency, *outrage aux bonnes mœurs*, by means of the sale, exhibition, or distribution of visual materials.[4] Even then, however, images prosecuted for affront to public decency were not tried by a jury;

this remained the case through the end of the century, as the laws of the 1870s and 1880s enshrined a rift between the legal status of images and that of texts.[5]

The Legal Académie

The Endurance of the Genre

In the early days of the Third Republic, much about the legal académie remained the same, including the photographers themselves. Some Second Empire photographers died, gave up their business, or vanished form the historical record around 1870.[6] However, some producers of legal and illegal nudity registered photographs (nudes or otherwise) after 1870.[7] Indeed, sometimes the very same photographs from the 1850s reappeared. For instance, in 1876, the photographer Welling submitted for authorization stereoscopic images that must have been taken in the 1850s, for they use the same model who appears in Figure 1 and in many other photographs from the early 1850s.[8] Until 1881, moreover, conditions were still placed on the authorization of many images, such as restrictions on display and place of sale or authorization for export only.[9] Indeed, even after the last Second Empire photographers disappeared from Dépôt légal rolls and the censorship law had been repealed, the structures of authorization remained.

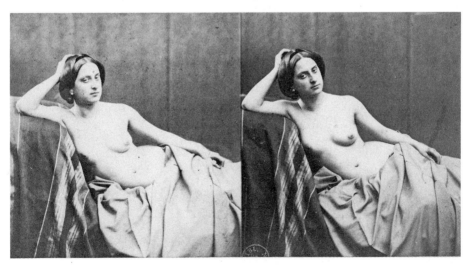

[FIGURE 43]

Anonymous, Second Empire.
Registered by Welling, 1876.
Photographic print on stereo card.
Bibliothèque nationale de France.

Photographers did continue to submit images to the government, if only for copyright protection. The number of nudes submitted for the Dépôt légal declined dramatically in proportion to the total number of nude images in circulation, but the *idea* of the legal art nude and some of the government apparatus around it endured well into the 1880s and 1890s.

Many of the académie's aesthetic conventions also persisted. Authorized photographs from the 1870s and 1880s employ the same kind of visual vocabulary as Second Empire academic nudes. The models' legs usually remain tightly clasped,

[FIGURE 44]
Louis Bonnard, 1881.
Albumen print from glass collodion negative.
Bibliothèque nationale de France.

their bodies arranged in flattened, stylized poses, their gaze either distant or averted, as is the case in the four hundred or so nude studies deposited by Louis Bonnard and Henri Vargenau in the early 1880s (Figures 44 and 45). Cascading hair, gauze, and other early visual motifs endure as well (Figure 46). The images also fall into similar categories as their earlier counterparts, which include stark depictions of unadorned nudity, studies that use draperies and simple props, and scènes de genre. More complex scenes continued to use painted backdrops and elaborate staging to evoke different settings and justifications for the nudity

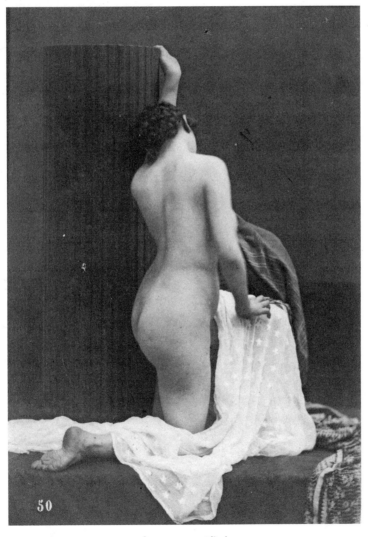

[FIGURE 45]

Henri Vargenau, 1883.
Albumen print from glass collodion negative.
Bibliothèque nationale de France.

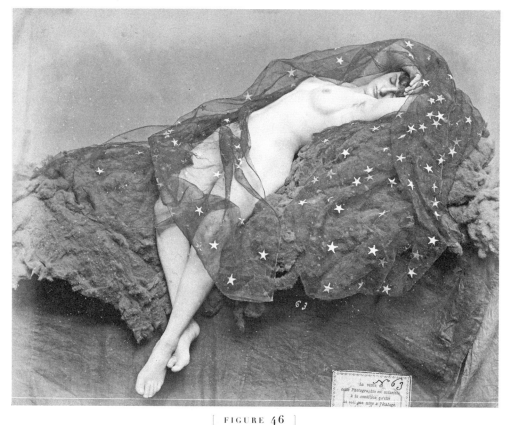

[FIGURE 46]

Jacques Edmond Lecadre, 1881.
Albumen print from glass collodion negative,
mounted on cardboard.
Bibliothèque nationale de France.

of the model, including exotic, antique, boudoir, and natural settings (Figure 47).
At the end of the nineteenth century, many photographers were looking backward in their académies.

Additionally, the académie continued to coexist with other photographic nudity that was not always entirely artistic and yet was nevertheless tolerated by the
government. Just as they had during the Second Empire, these photographs included portraits of actresses and dancers and other scantily clad women, some of
whom were depicted in flesh-colored, formfitting maillots.[10] Photographers, too,
continued to work across genres and on both sides of the law. Although it is likely
that many photographers did so, because of the increasing anonymity of the industry in the 1870s and 1880s, we know the name of only one.[11] In January 1892, a
man identified as "Kirchner" was arrested for producing illegal nudity.[12] Nearly at
the same time, the newspapers reported on the extradition from Brussels of one

[FIGURE 47]

Grisart, 1882. Cabinet card.
Bibliothèque nationale de France.

"Kirschener Lear," who was wanted for the production of "a certain number of
obscene photographs."[13] A photographer by the name of "Léar" was also producing legal artist's nudes from a studio located at 50 rue Saint Lazare in Paris, five of
which were registered with the government in 1884 (Figure 48).[14] Meanwhile, one
Albert Kirchner, who also used the professional name "Léar," was acting as the

[FIGURE 48]

Léar, 1884. Cabinet card.
Bibliothèque nationale de France.

cameraman for what is considered to be the first pornographic film, *Le coucher de la mariée*, featuring the actress Louise Willy taking off her clothes.[15] All of these different Kirchners and Léars were likely one man who registered legal photographs even as he was producing illicit photos and movies.

Change and Decline

The académie, however, was far from immune to change, the most basic and fundamental of which was technological. Gelatin dry plates, which came into general use after 1880, allowed for faster exposure times and clearer images; coupled with advances in camera technology, they made it possible for photography to capture images in just fractions of seconds for the first time.[16] In comparison to their predecessors, photographs from the later nineteenth century look more like twentieth-century snapshots, conveying more of a sense of motion and instantaneity. And while some of the photographs submitted for authorization were still the large-format prints of the 1850s, many were four-by-six-inch cardboard-backed cabinet card photographs (precursors to the picture postcard of the 1890s) produced in exponentially larger runs of one hundred to one thousand prints per image (see, e.g., Figures 47, 48, 53, 54, 56, and 58).[17] From the 1880s through the end of the century, the publishing house Calavas produced nudes in another new format, offering a series of small poses on a single album page (Figure 49). And just after the turn of the twentieth century, thanks to developments in photogravure printing, a flurry of "art" periodicals purporting to contain nudes for artists distributed these photographs in magazine form (Figure 50).[18]

The conventions of the académie also evolved, at least partially as a result of photography's technological evolution. Faster exposures allowed for more athletic and contorted poses (Figure 51). New props and set pieces that required more strength and dexterity appeared, such as swings, or archer's bows (Figure 52). The visual effects of advances in the photographic process are particularly pronounced in the scènes de genre, which display more sophisticated integration of foreground and background than they previously had (Figure 53). Technology aside, some new props appeared that likely reflected changing cultural fascinations, such as the hammock as a signifier of exoticism, or photographs of women stepping into and out of bathtubs (Figure 54). The visual language of the académie was also shifting in more significant ways. Although it had long been the case that the government authorized images that pushed at the boundaries of artistry, many more académies from the 1880s and 1890s undermine the conventions of propriety that governed the genre. They often do so via subtle shifts in pose, perspective, and camera angle. Some photographs, for instance, compress the distance between the model and the camera, bringing the viewer within a few feet or even inches of the model, as in a series by Bonnard (Figure 55). Increasingly, models' poses break the single visual plane, foregrounding certain (usually erotically charged) parts of the body. In an académie by David, the model's backside is prioritized in a pose that recalls illegal imagery of the Sec-

[FIGURE 49]
Calavas, éditeur, 1880.
Albumen print from glass collodion negative.
Collection of the author.

39. MES MODÈLES

En adoptant une formule présentant le modèle nu et habillé,
nous avons seulement voulu montrer les déformations
provoquées par les artifices de la toilette. (Modèle 24 ans.)

[FIGURE 50]

Page from *Mes Modèles*, 30 May 1905.
Bibliothèque nationale de France.

[FIGURE 51]
Henri Vargenau, 1882.
Albumen print from glass collodion negative.
Bibliothèque nationale de France.

[FIGURE 52]

Louis Bonnard, 1881.
Albumen print from glass collodion negative.
Bibliothèque nationale de France.

[FIGURE 53]

Jacques Edmond Lecadre,
Étude no. 6, 1881. Cabinet card.
Bibliothèque nationale de France.

[FIGURE 54]

Jacques Edmond Lecadre,
Étude no. 10, 1881. Cabinet card.
Bibliothèque nationale de France.

[FIGURE 55]

Louis Bonnard, 1881.
Albumen print from glass collodion negative.
Bibliothèque nationale de France.

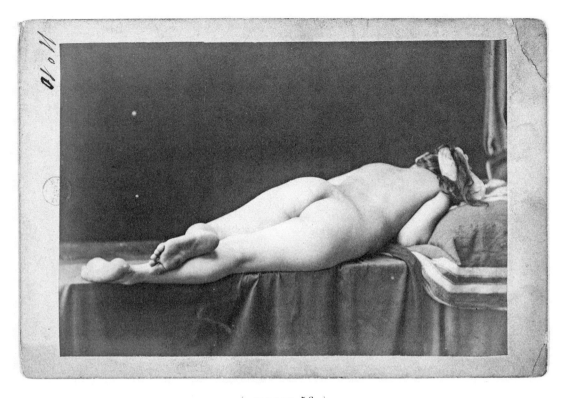

[FIGURE 56]

David, 1880s. Cabinet card.
Bibliothèque nationale de France.

ond Empire (Figure 56). Various académies from the 1880s by Vargenau, on the other hand, reorient the lower part of the models' bodies toward the viewer, posing her with her legs crossed only just enough to conceal what the académie was never to reveal (Figure 57). In one particularly damning series of photographs by Klotz, the models—many of whom appear to be adolescents—thrust hips or breasts toward the camera, opening their legs or raising them up. This series also includes a reclining nude in which the camera looks almost directly between the model's legs (Figure 58). In these photographs, the styling of illegal imagery invades the space of the academic nude.

The photographs in the magazines and compilations of art nudes printed just after the turn of the century are even more confounding. To avoid prosecution, these publications were sold without nudity on the cover and with large notices that said that they were to be displayed *sous bande* (closed with a paper band) only. As to the pictures inside, it is often hard to tell whether they were governed by any artistic motivations at all. When an antiobscenity campaigner declared in

[FIGURE 57]
Henri Vargenau, 1882.
Albumen print from glass collodion negative.
Bibliothèque nationale de France.

1905 that the photographs in such publications were "less preoccupied with expressing the harmony of forms and lines than with representing the most intimate details, such as body hair," he was not without reason.[19] The publication *Le
Stéréo-nu*, for instance, sold only nude stereographs (the format of which already
suggests that they were not really intended for an artistic audience). Its photographs included time-tested tropes like gauzy boudoir scenes, mirrors, scènes de
genre, and implied lesbianism, as well as newer settings and props like open-air
scenes and live animals (Figures 59 and 60). Some of the stereographs are quite
explicitly erotic, and a troubling number of images feature adolescent and even
prepubescent models.[20] Meanwhile, the boring and repetitive photographs of the
magazine *Mes Modèles*, while decidedly unerotic, read more like a mail-order
catalog for naked women than a compendium of artist's studies (see again Figure
50).[21] And yet, we know that Matisse worked extensively from its pages.[22] Finally,
and perhaps most troubling, is *Le Nu académique*. In its first issue, while lament-

[FIGURE 58]

Klotz, 1884. Cabinet card.
Bibliothèque nationale de France.

ing the expense of paying live models in the age of women's emancipation (!), the
editor presents the magazine as a solution for poor starving artists. At the same
time, he explicitly addresses himself "to all those who worship and respect the
beauty of women."[23] The photographs reflect this split identity. Occasionally, *Le
Nu académique* printed remarkable photographs, as in the case of one reclining
nude that evokes those of Quinet and Belloc a half century earlier (Figure 61; see
also Figures 13 and 30). However, it also contains photographs of prepubescent
girls and women opening their legs for the camera (Figure 62).

Photogravure printing also facilitated the production of other kinds of nudity
that, while usually not as explicit as these "artistic" compilations might be, further muddled the definition of an art nude. Seminude illustrations began to
appear in the photo-illustrated magazine *La Grande Vie* (then *La Vie de Paris* and
La Nouvelle Vie de Paris); they might or might not be justified by such accompanying articles as "Les dessous de la parisienne" (Figure 63). Publishers also began to exploit photographic illustrations for works of fiction. From 1897 to 1908,
the publishing houses of Per Lamm Nilsson and Offenstadt Frères released a

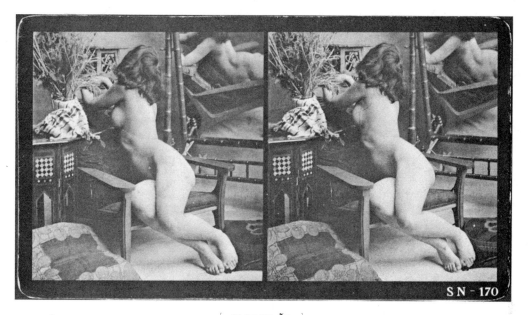

[FIGURE 59]

Le Stéréo-nu, 1905.
Photographic print on stereo card.
Collection of the author.

[FIGURE 60]

Le Stéréo-Nu, 1905.
Photographic print on stereo card.
Bibliothèque nationale de France.

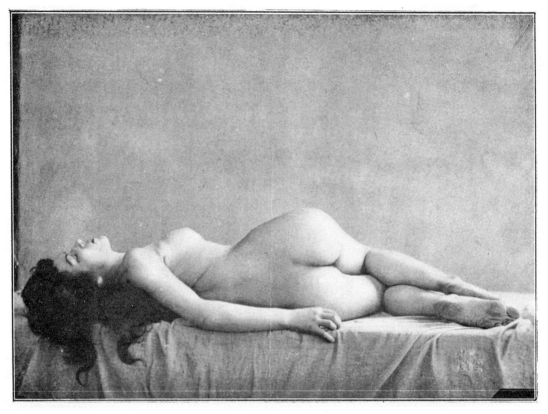

[FIGURE 61]

Plate from *Le Nu académique*,
15 September 1905.
Bibliothèque nationale de France.

series of photo-illustrated novels, often including nudes among their illustrations (Figure 64).[24] (The photo-novels of René Maizeroy are the topic of Chapter 8.) Nude photographs also began to appear in even more disreputable books.
The suggestively titled *Encyclopédie amoureuse*, for instance, is littered with bare
shoulders, buttocks, and airbrushed breasts, and a 1904 guidebook by Victor
Leca entitled *Pour s'amuser: Guide du viveur à Paris* (essentially, a guide to Parisian
prostitution) also included several nudes (Figures 65 and 66). These kinds of illustrations are not sexually explicit and were contained within books that were
registered for copyright purposes and, as far as we know, allowed to circulate.
Indeed, some of the illustrations of photo-novels may well have been considered
"artistic." Yet the spread of nudity into every possible print medium did not necessarily advance its artistic reputation.

[FIGURE 62]
Plate from *Le Nu académique*,
1 June 1906.
Bibliothèque nationale de France.

Perhaps not surprisingly, whereas during the Second Empire the académie had been a source of confusion and concern about the definition and meaning of art, during the Third Republic it was merely a source of exasperation. News-papers had, of course, long complained about stores where "under the pretext of the sale of 'artistic photographs,' obscene engravings or photographic cards rep-

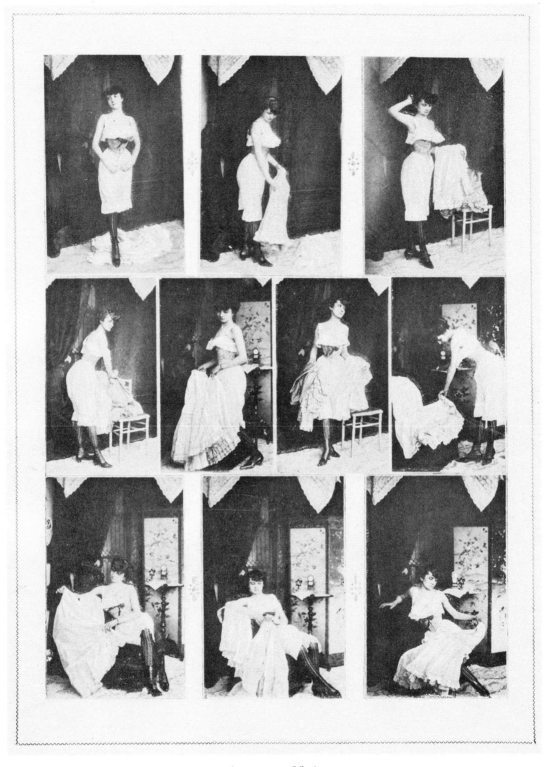

[FIGURE 63]

"Le Jupon," *La Nouvelle Vie de Paris*, 1903.
Bibliothèque nationale de France.

Collection
" La Voie Merveilleuse "

Jean LORRAIN

LA DAME TURQUE

ILLUSTRÉ PAR LA PHOTOGRAPHIE

D'APRÈS NATURE

Paris
Librairie NILSSON. — PER LAMM, Succʳ
338, rue St-Honoré

[FIGURE 64]

Title Page, Jean Lorrain, *La Dame Turque*.
Collection of the author.

resenting nudities that were scarcely artistic were offered to amateurs."[25] Treatment of académies, however, was increasingly negative. Gone were the raptures in
photographic publications over the beauty and value of the nude. Instead, newspapers gleefully reported cases such as that of one Dame Lafontaine, who had
stocked thousands of "art" nudes in her Paris shop that she sold not to artists but
to "everyone who asked her for them," including to clients who had requested
"frankly erotic" images.[26] The growing cynicism about académies likely stemmed
in part from the mix of images circulating in the guise of art studies, but it probably also had to do with the new legal reality. After 1881, registration with the
government did not confer any particular legitimacy on an image. Any photo-

226   ENCYCLOPÉDIE AMOUREUSE.

Graisser les joues de vaseline.

Les saupoudrer de poudre de riz et ensuite avec une patte de lapin prendre le fard, l'étendre légèrement sur les joues en ayant soin de bien le fondre, c'est-à-dire d'en mettre un peu plus aux pommettes qu'au bas des joues.

[FIGURE 65]

Page from *Encyclopédie amoureuse*, 1901.

QUELQUES DAMES GALANTES 12

Tout à fait mignonne, blonde grassouillette, aimant les bavardages et les lectures pironesques.

Collectionne les cartes postales illustrées et se donne toute pour un spécimen qui lui plaît.
(Née à Paris.)

[FIGURE 66]

Page from Victor Leca,
Pour s'amuser: Guide de viveur à Paris, 1904.
Bibliothèque nationale de France.

graph might claim to be an académie unless it was prosecuted for indecency; indeed, even then, its meaning might be unclear. The courts, for instance, disagreed about the artistry of Dame Lafontaine's merchandise. She was acquitted by the eleventh chamber of the *tribunal correctionnel* but ultimately convicted by the ninth chamber, less because of the content of the photographs than because of incriminating letters from her clients.[27] During the Third Republic, a category that had previously been nebulous but somewhat bounded by the law instead became totally amorphous and nearly impossible in many cases to differentiate from other commercially distributed nudity. And the more the académie was subsumed by the other kinds of nudity in circulation, the less artistic it might seem, even when it perfectly respected the bounds of artistry and decency.

Whatever the reason, by the end of the century cynicism about the académie was so entrenched that the less scrupulous openly exploited the genre to other ends. The 1905 *Guide complet des plaisirs mondains et des plaisirs secrets* (another guide to Parisian prostitution) includes a section on artists' models that is little more than an advertisement for prostitution and photographic obscenity. The sales pitch for nude photographs assures the reader they satisfy "the most rigorous laws of aesthetics and the most minute demands of the most refined taste," but the subsequent enumeration of body parts depicted therein (lips, hair, shoulders, legs, breasts) leaves little doubt as to what was really being sold. To conclude, the author informs the reader that "The set of these photographs is like a poem that woman might sing, from the first smile, still modest and discrete, through awakening desire, to the dazzling swoon of triumphant love. Nota — For the sum of *three francs* we mail our luxuriously artistic catalog, ornamented with ninety specimens of reduced size and one print in album format 13x18."[28] The académie had been reduced to three-franc catalogs of naked women, a pretense by which no one even feigned to be deceived.

⚔ Unauthorized Nudes ⚔

Early Continuity

Meanwhile, unauthorized nudity was similarly caught between continuity and change. During the 1870s, the censorship law remained in effect. The old legal category of the "unauthorized image" persisted, and some vestiges of the police surveillance that went with it also endured, as the Paris police continued keeping limited records in a small register known as the BB6. Entries on nude photographs are few, scattered among many other crimes, and contain no information about models, photographers, sentencing, recidivism, quantities of images, or what images looked like. Yet despite these limitations, in concert with contemporary print sources, the BB6 indicates that in the first years of the Third Republic the commerce in illicit nude photographs remained very similar to what had come before. Although the police did not leave behind examples of photographs from raids and seizures, extant examples in private collections likewise indicate that the range of poses and many of the formats remained the same.[29] Many illicit images in the 1870s were probably cartes-de-visite or stereographs that skirted the edge of decency. Some of them likely looked very much like académies, particularly after 1881, as the new laws meant that images that *looked like* académies could realistically avoid prosecution. At the other end of the spectrum, explicit obscenity also abounded. Both the photographic and the written record testify to the endurance of explicit sexual iconography of the Empire, including "lesbian" images, masturbation, and images of coitus. A reference to the "beaver shot" photographs examined by Tardieu in Louis Fiaux's 1892 treatise on prostitution indicates that those images also remained popular.[30] And, just as during the Second Empire, even the most explicit images continued to influence other art forms; the monotypes of Degas, for instance, allude to some tropes of illicit nude photography.[31]

The system of production and distribution also shared much with that of the Second Empire. Some photographers were professionals, but many were still amateurs, such as one photographer who was also a doctor, a coachman-photographer working with a wine merchant accomplice, an electrician and mechanic (and eventual murderer), and a photographer's assistant (and anarchist) who took up nude photography.[32] As to models, the most important accomplice, they were still actively pursued by the courts.[33] Newspapers indicate that models were often as unprofessional as their Second Empire predecessors, plied many of the same trades, and were similarly recruited off the streets and at balls, although the price for the most risqué poses allegedly rose to twenty francs.[34] Prostitutes also continued to work as models; indeed, production of photographic obscenity became even more closely integrated into the business of prostitution during the final decades of the nineteenth century (see Chapter 6).[35]

Many book, photography, and print shops continued to display and sell unregistered nudity. Newspapers reported that these sites of illicit commerce were spread all over Paris, from the Quartier de Grenelle to the Passage Jouffroy, and along the arcades, passages, and side streets of the Rue de Rivoli and the Palais Royal.[36] The same mixture of mere naughtiness and outright obscenity continued to adorn window displays with what seems to have been increasing brazenness and corresponding dismay.[37] Police raids, threats from the ministry of the interior, and the concerted effort of the chief prosecutor did little to control shop displays, which continued to be a problem through the turn of the century.[38] Starting in the 1880s, commercial sites of distribution also included kiosks and *tabacs* selling various print materials; the operators of these shops had government authorization to operate, and by 1905, the government was threatening to revoke the authorization of those who sold licentious postcards along with cigarettes and newspapers.[39] As had always been the case, nudity might also be found in some surprising commercial establishments. Dealers included the proprietors of a stationary store, a bicycle shop, and a store selling "surprise gift boxes."[40] One notorious Lucie Haussmann sold photographs out of her glove shop; she was apparently not alone in keeping "boutiques of gloves [*ganterie*] and back-boutiques of gallantry [*galanterie*]."[41] Images were often sold out of wine shops, and in 1882, *Gil Blas* complained that they were primarily responsible for the distribution of nude photographs in certain Paris neighborhoods.[42]

Street sales also continued during this period. Vendors were arrested all over Paris, from Montmartre, along the Grand Boulevards eastward, along the Rue de Rivoli, in the Place du Théâtre Français, in front of Saint Eustache, down the Avenue de l'Opéra, on the Champs-Élysées, and even along the banks of the Seine.[43] As had always been the case, the ranks of people selling nude photographs (particularly on the streets) still included many people who weren't merchants or peddlers. Along with the ever-ubiquitous commercial courier, those arrested on suspicion of distribution included a paper maker, a female card reader, a watercolorist, a Florentine shoemaker, a hairdresser, a jewelry designer, a medical bandage specialist (he may have been a customer), and the head vendor of the newspaper *L'Assemblée nationale*.[44] In 1878, the police discovered a large cache of obscene photographs in the home of one Eugène Laroque, whom they suspected of being a dealer. He was released because he was "under the protection of very influential persons," and he is perhaps the same well-to-do businessman whose portrait now hangs in the Musée Bonat in Bayonne.[45] Many of these part-time dealers had fallen on varying degrees of bad luck. Some had long been homeless, while others had more recently descended from loftier positions, such as a former government *attaché* peddling photographs on the Champs-Élysées or a wealthy law student from the countryside who tried to pay for a beer with a nude photograph after losing all his money gambling.[46]

Finally, as before, possession remained legal, and there was a varied market for nude images.[47] In *L'Orgie parisienne*, Aurélien Scholl wrote that "the delicacy and the grace with which these intoxicating productions are executed, their great number and their low price prove that all classes of citizens share the same taste and encourage this use of talent."[48] What we know of his own taste for nudity from the Goncourt brothers tends to corroborate this assessment, but there are few concrete historical examples from the period. Contemporary fiction, particularly the work of René Maizeroy, provides the best glimpse of consumers. Photographic nudity, much of it illicit, is ubiquitous in Maizeroy's novels and is consumed by characters at all levels of society (see Chapter 8). Indeed, the variety of people and businesses implicated in the industry over the last three decades of the nineteenth century suggests that the early "networks of complicity" not only had remained intact but had grown and spread.

International Expansion

Like the académie, however, much about illicit image making also changed drastically in the last decades of the nineteenth century, beginning with its legal definition. After the end of censorship in 1881, authorization no longer had the same power to define an image's legal status. The old category of "unauthorized" imagery gave way to a broader, more nebulous class of photographs produced without any form of government intervention. Since no photographs legally had to be registered, the "unauthorized nude" grew to include nearly all of the nude photographs produced in the 1880s and 1890s, the vast majority of which likely would not have been registered with the government whether they truly were artistic or not. The end of censorship reshaped the boundaries of legality, further breaking down distinctions between art and obscenity that had always been difficult to define and enforce.

As the category of illicit nudity expanded to encompass more kinds of images, advancing technologies also brought new formats, just as they had done for academic nudity. One of the earliest, and strangest, developments was the increasing popularity of altered photographs, wherein photographers pasted heads—often of celebrities—onto anonymous naked bodies, a famous example of which involved Sarah Bernhardt.[49] Starting in the 1880s, invisible photographs that appeared on paper when exposed to flames were popular in cigar boxes, as were packages for rolling papers adorned with nude lithographs or photographs.[50] In 1896, the invention of the picture postcard transformed the industry (Figure 67).[51] Postcards were produced in such massive numbers that they should be the subject of their own book. Suffice it to say that they ran the gamut from art nudes to explicit obscenity, and they quickly replaced stereographs as the format of choice for nudes and the primary target of antiobscenity campaigners, who by 1905 were calling them "the greatest pornographic danger."[52]

Not only was the category of unsanctioned nudity more inclusive than it had been during the Empire, it was also quantitatively larger. Even before the arrival of the postcard, one of the most significant changes of the last decades of the nineteenth century was what one contemporary legal commentator described as

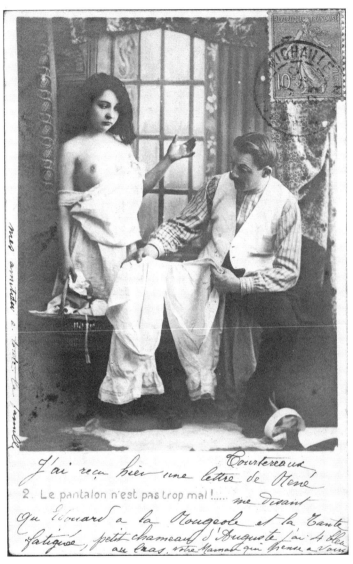

[FIGURE 67]

Postcard, ca. 1900. Stamped and dated 1904.
Collection of the author.

a "prodigious" increase in production.[53] During the debates on the press laws in 1881, the government complained that images accused of indecency should not be tried by a jury because there were "so many cases of affront to public decency by obscene drawings and images, that to send such cases in front of the assizes would render repression almost impossible."[54] Around the same time, *Le Figaro* claimed in 1881 that almost daily raids were being conducted on photography shops.[55] These raids yielded unprecedented quantities of images. The police seized some two thousand photographs from Dame Lafontaine in 1883.[56] In 1895, nearly five thousand photographs were discovered in an apartment on Avenue Parmentier.[57] In 1900, the police reported seizing fifty thousand "pornographic photographs" in one raid, all supposedly imported from Germany.[58] These numbers, however, did not even approach the output of Kirchner—alias Léar—and his accomplice, Mathieu Grand. In less than three years, the two allegedly produced eight hundred thousand images at a profit of eighty thousand francs.[59] The quantity of photographs in circulation probably totaled in the many millions by 1900. As their numbers exploded, nude photographs had an increasing public presence in the streets of Paris. By the end of the century, one reformer described their ubiquity in Paris' shops and streets as a scandal that "strikes the eyes and exceeds all bounds."[60] The presence of nude photography in the insalubrious streets of the capital would become a major preoccupation of fin-de-siècle discourse, all but replacing the model in the public imagination (see Chapter 6).

These images were being produced in larger and larger quantities by photographers who were increasingly anonymous even as they had become astoundingly productive. One reason for this anonymity was the end of censorship (and with it the intensive police surveillance of the industry). Kirchner exemplifies another reason for it: he was not French. During the early Third Republic, photographic nudity became a truly international enterprise. Many European countries produced their own nudes, which were then exported to other countries (including France).[61] Obscene photographs had made their way to the farthest reaches of the world, including Afghanistan and Tahiti.[62] By the early 1890s, sales often involved complicated multinational schemes: Kirchner was a German who worked in France, exported to England, fled to Belgium to avoid arrest, and was finally extradited back to France to face charges.[63] Other newspaper reports refer to an Italian operating out of Switzerland and a Dutchman operating out of Belgium after expulsion from the Netherlands, both exporting to France.[64] The same photographs might be found in many different European countries, making it nearly impossible to identify the photographer, the model, or even the geographical source of an image. This international anonymity made it so difficult to pursue those involved that it may also partially explain why older concerns about the identity of particular models gave way to concerns about the street distribution of nudity during this period.[65] International production structures masked the identities of everyone involved.

The new international models of distribution also further complicated questions of legal jurisdiction that had never been simple. Legal precedent indicated that French law applied to exports out of the country when France was the point of origin for the transaction.[66] But which laws applied to photographers exporting images to France from other countries (France or the country of origin) depended on the law in those other countries. In 1892, these jurisdictional issues came to a diplomatic head, as Switzerland complained that France, unlike its other neighbors, was refusing to take appropriate action against newspaper ads for dubious products.[67] As the *Journal des débats* remarked in 1893, precisely these complicated legal questions incentivized international commerce; those profiting from obscenity made sure, "in order to escape the full rigor of the law, only to operate from abroad."[68] Indeed, international sales employed new distributional methods that posed still other legal problems. In 1882, as they amended the 1881 press laws, legislators inadvertently modified the original language of the law so that it became unclear whether the clauses governing outrage aux bonnes mœurs applied only to *public* display and sale or all sales regardless of publicity.[69] The courts later ruled that sales did not have to be public to violate the law, but vendors of nude photographs and other illicit wares increasingly sought to avoid prosecution by selling their wares "privately." Some advertised euphemistically in newspapers, inviting people to apply by post for the desired merchandise.[70] Others sent unsolicited "prospectuses" (mail-order catalogs) for various goods or services directly to people's homes.[71] By 1894, legislators had begun to target this form of distribution.[72] In 1895, members of the government themselves received prospectuses in the mail from Amsterdam advertising obscene books and photographs.[73] Finally, in 1898—with specific reference to the events of 1895—the law criminalized "home distribution" and "unsealed distribution by the post" and eliminated the requirement of publicity for cases involving minors.[74] By 1908, language about publicity was removed altogether.[75]

The Social Menace

In the face of the perceived onslaught of nude photographic images overwhelming France from home and abroad, discussions of photographic nudity were dominated by impassioned denunciations of its corrupting social influence. During the 1870s and 1880s, much of the language sounds very similar to that of the Second Empire, but with a darker tone. Already in 1871, a letter to the editor of the *Journal des débats* raised the alarm about the return of the briefly banished menace in familiar yet amplified terms. The author, one Legouvé, wrote,

> Therein lies a real peril for the Republic, whose mortal enemy, in morality as in politics, is license [*licence*]. With a nervous, ardent, feverish population such as ours, all that touches the senses soon overwhelms the entire being.
>
> Do you see these men of every age, of every condition, their faces pressed against these shop windows filled with obscene images; it is poison that they drink through their eyes. Sometimes, an encounter with one of these ignoble exhibitions suffices to destroy the entire life of a young man. You need, against such vileness, radical, absolute, implacable censorship, at once preventative and repressive; I demand it in the name of all fathers of families.[76]

Where Pélin cried "Ruffiano!" and Prud'homme limited himself to insinuation about prostitutes, Legouvé instead warned of the complete dissolution of French society. In the wake of the Commune, according to Legouvé, the situation had gone from troublesome to dire. Public displays of obscenity placed the entire population of France in imminent peril. It was no longer enough to demand that the shop displays be cleaned up; Legouvé demanded absolute censorship (and the paper indicated support for his position in its framing of the letter). He transforms Pélin's apoplectic horror into apocalyptic fear.

As nude photography became increasingly common, its reputation only diminished. Increasingly sensational newspaper coverage of photographic nudity in the columns of the *faits divers* (salacious anecdotes printed in the back pages of the newspapers) added to the growing anxiety about these images.[77] This reporting emphasized the most insalubrious characters involved with the industry, including an anarchist, a murderer, a fraudster, a man who (along with his family) beat his neighbor to death, a man who used his daughter as his nude model, three-card-monte hustlers, a con artist posing as a Finnish diplomat, a thief, a man sexually abusing his sister, an illegal bookmaker, a man wanted in the disappearance of a ten-year-old girl, pimps and *proxénètes* (female procurers) trafficking underage girls, and a doctor who beat his wife.[78] Sensational though this reporting was, the government and various reforming organizations shared the attitude that nude photography was solely the purview of the lowest members of society. At the end of the century, as he pushed for ever-stricter laws against public indecency, the senator René Bérenger expanded on Legouvé's language of degeneration and social disaster, figuring the fight to remove these images (and other immoral objects) from the street as a fight for the national character of France against forces of decline that "debase the character, degrade the mind, abase the moral and intellectual level of a people" to the point where France's very existence was at stake (again, see Chapter 6).[79]

The New Amateur Photography

From Lovers' Portraits to Pictorialism

As the two old categories of unauthorized and authorized nudity were fundamentally changing in the face of new laws and patterns of international commercial distribution, the fin de siècle also saw the creation of a new category of nude imagery defined by its remove from the commercial sphere. In 1888, Kodak released the first "personal" camera, creating an entirely new kind of amateur photographer.[80] The realm of photography opened up to include anyone who could afford a camera. Like the very first photographers, these new amateurs immediately took up the nude. Many of these nudes were probably private objects that have long since been lost or destroyed. A few such personal nudes, however, were preserved because the photographers were more famous. Émile Zola, for instance, took many seminude photographs of his mistress, Jeanne Rozerot. The photographs are disconcertingly—if chastely—intimate, focusing closely on Jeanne's hair or shoulders or the nape of her neck (Figure 68). On the other hand, the decadent author Pierre Louÿs was an avid producer and consumer of photographic obscenity. He posed for explicit images, took photographs of his lovers, and amassed a large collection of nude photographs.[81] Even his more personal images tended to the hardcore. An album recently acquired by the Bibliothèque nationale includes not only images of his lover, Zohra Ben Brahim, but also pornographic images of underage girls with whom he was likely sexually involved.[82] Explicit or not, these kinds of amateur photographs were largely treated with a smirk. Newspapers gleefully published stories of such photographs falling into the wrong hands and being used to blackmail erstwhile lovers.[83] A 1903 story in *La Nouvelle Vie de Paris* called "Photographe amateur" perfectly epitomizes the contemporary attitude, mocking a fictional Monsieur Courmelon whose angry wife exclaims, "Since you've been doing photography— bad photography—I only find prints of nude women."[84]

Gisèle Freund has argued that the rise of amateur photography contributed to the decline of art photography at the end of the nineteenth century.[85] Yet as photographic equipment became cheaper and easier to use, visual artists could produce their own photographic studies, turning "professional" painters or

[FIGURE 68]
Émile Zola, late 1890s.
Modern print from glass gelatin bromide negative.
Ministère de la Culture/Médiathèque
de l'architecture et du patrimoine, France.

sculptors into "amateur" photographers. Alexandre Falguière, Gustave Moreau, Bonnard, and Degas (to name only a few) all took their own nudes.[86] In Degas' most famous photograph, probably used as a study for his 1896 painting *After the Bath*, the model twists to the side to dry herself, an active position that would have been completely impossible to capture in the early days of photography when exposure times were longer (Figure 69). Degas' photograph is more than a simple figure study. It grants the photograph the same texture and depth as the pastel drawings and paintings based on it. These amateur photographs are one space where the nude photograph flourished as art.

Only in the last years of the nineteenth century did the art nude see a true revival, thanks to Pictorialism. The anticommercial Pictorialist movement worked to rehabilitate the photographic nude as part of its goal of elevating the photo-

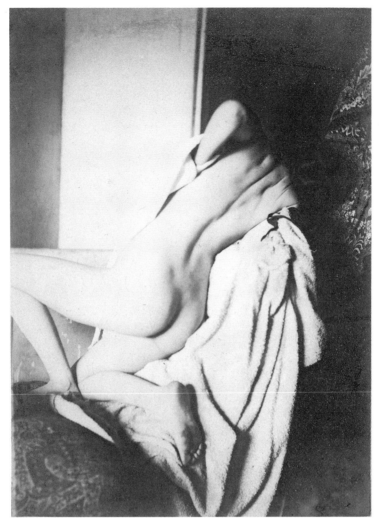

[FIGURE 69]

Edgar Degas, *After the Bath,*
Woman Drying Her Back, 1896.
Gelatin silver print.
J. Paul Getty Museum, Los Angeles.

graphic medium to the status of painting via visual effects that softened and
"idealized" it (Figure 70).[87] A series of exhibitions organized by the Photo-club de
Paris in the 1890s showcased the artistic possibilities of the new approach for all
photographic genres, explicitly including the nude.[88] In 1898, Paul Bergon and
René Le Bègue, the "uncontested masters" of the Pictorialist open-air photographic nude, published a slim manifesto entitled *Art photographique: Le Nu et le*
drapé en plein air (Figure 71).[89] The text advocates broadly for Pictorialist aesthet-

[FIGURE 70]
René Le Bègue, *Magdeleine*,
from *L'Épreuve photographique*, 1904.
Chalk-manner etching from photographic print.
J. Paul Getty Museum, Los Angeles.

ics: natural posing, loose drapery, outdoor settings, hazy focus, and retouching, all of which abound in the accompanying nude illustrations. Bergon and Le Bègue justify their choice of "a bit brazen" of a subject by situating it as the basis of all other figure photography, the "primordial study for every open air composition."[90] Echoing the first defenders of photographic artistry, they describe their book as a humble attempt to "aid photography [. . .] to broaden its field of operations and penetrate into the domain until now reserved for drawing and paint-

— 42 —

utilisés ; mais ils feront bien plus souvent le bonheur des professionnels et des amateurs débutants, heureux d'obtenir facilement et en quantité des épreuves bien propres et bien nettes, que des artistes véritables.

Le papier au platine est froid. Il est pourtant recommandable et peut donner de très belles épreuves en teintes noires ou sépia.

Les papiers au gélatino-bromure d'argent ont des avantages nombreux. Ils se prêtent aux agrandissements directs, aux manipulations intelligentes dans le développement; leur teinte désagréable, grise et plate, peut être modifiée dans des bains divers. On en tirera souvent de bons effets.

Les papiers au charbon, avec leurs gammes de teintes, leur finesse, leur inaltérabilité, sont des plus recommandables et, pour les études agrandies faites en plein air, ils sont précieux.

Enfin, avec l'héliogravure qui donne des reproductions très artistiques, et la photocollographie dont le tirage demande beaucoup de soins, il y a encore le procédé à la gomme bichromatée, fort à la mode en ce moment. Il a des avantages uniques. Il permet une interprétation personnelle de l'image, une retouche souple, intelligente, importante ou légère ; il laisse à l'artiste le choix du papier et

[FIGURE 71]

Page from Paul Bergon and René Le Bègue,
Art photographique: Le Nu et le drapé en plein air, 1898.
Bibliothèque nationale de France.

ing," placing the nude squarely back into debates about the art status of photography.[91] The text's impassioned conclusion likewise speaks to art photography as a general discipline rather than to the nude in particular. It decries the "vulgar commercial print" of contemporary photography but also excoriates those whose well-merited "profound scorn" for commercial photography blinds them to photography's true potential, exclaiming, "Art is not a monopoly, and painted works are not all, and the only, art objects, just because they are painted. [. . .] Believe us, that in everything, art is something rare, precious, and difficult, and that one can hardly purport to reel it off like a ribbon, under the pretext of exercising one's profession."[92] Bergon and Le Bègue attempted to revive the art nude using Pictorialism's distinctive aesthetics and a return to language about art central to discussions of photography at the medium's invention.

◁ The End of the Art Nude? ▷

Pictorialism, however, was no panacea. Its aesthetics were coopted by any number of publications with more or less explicitly dubious intentions. *Le Stéréo-nu*, for instance, often included quasi-Pictorialist open-air nudity. Various books containing extensive photographic illustration and long essays arguing for the moral and artistic value of photographic nudity parroted Pictorialist arguments for the nude along with their aesthetics, their excessive enthusiasm exposing their bad faith.[93] Meanwhile, members of the Pictorialist movement themselves argued against the very idea of the photographic art nude.[94] Of course, this complicated and ambivalent attitude toward the académie was not new. What was new, however, was that by the end of the century, even the great practitioners and defenders of the nude manifested a decided ambivalence about it. In their introduction, Bergon and Le Bègue write, "The nude treated by photography, despite the scabrous appearance that it can take on in inexperienced hands, does not therefore appear impossible to us."[95] The same tone dominates even the most positive reviews of nudes in the exhibitions of the various international photoclubs. They describe the nude as a "delicate question," "difficult to render [. . .] chaste in photography," a subject that "often only produces a vulgar obscenity" and at best "demands much tact not to fall into vulgarity."[96] At their most positive, they describe nudes as "irreproachable" or "chaste."[97] There are no exuberant advocates like Lacan or Wey describing the nude in clearly positive and artistic terms. In 1896, one reviewer simply described a group of nudes as "of a character not to shock anyone," as if that was the highest standard to which such photographs could aspire.[98]

By the turn of the century, however, the photographic nude received little better praise, the victim of a number of other concurrent social and historical trends. The end of the nineteenth century in France was a period of larger anxiety about moral decline and collapse. Numerous "leagues" of citizens sprang up to assist the government as it attempted to address different social ills.[99] As nude photography came to be increasingly closely associated with others of these social ills in the space of the street (discussed in Chapter 6), it, too, was seen as a moral danger. The days had long passed since the newspapers, as they reported on models arriving before the magistrate, paused to reflect on the harm to photography's artistic reputation. At the fin de siècle, the nude photograph became another sordid detail in the numerous tales of murder, incest, and adultery of the faits divers. The tepid defense of the genre offered by Pictorialist publications was drowned out by the antinudity stance of social reformers. The result was not merely that fewer people were advocating for the art value of the photographic nude—even in the early days, there were few such staunch advocates—but that the question of artistry disappeared entirely. While Bérenger and others raged against photographic nudity in reactionary and incendiary language, Zola and Maizeroy took up the social problem of the nude and refigured it in terms of complex issues of sex, gender, economics, and agency that remain familiar to us today. As the twentieth century began, the debate about photographic nudity had shifted so as to displace debates about art in favor of debates about the place of nude photography within a disintegrating social fabric, pushing the genre ever more definitively into the realm of obscenity in the process.

⚔ CHAPTER 6 ⚔

The Dangerous Streets

In 1891, the Paris Observatory concluded an unprecedented four-year project in collaboration with other observatories around the world: the *carte du ciel*, a map of the heavens, undertaken for the first time with the aid of photography. To commemorate this accomplishment, *Gil Blas* printed a satirical article that cast the sky as a recalcitrant old man who had long resisted this portrait. With tongue fully in cheek, the newspaper lamented that the map was "due to an unspeakable abuse of force: it is by violence that the sky was photographed, without its consent, and in a way, *manu militari*."[1] The act of photographing the sky without its consent is described with a language of coercion and violence that, humor notwithstanding, suggests nothing good about photography. The conclusion goes further still: "Unfortunately not all photographers work for science, and without a doubt after those of the Observatory other less scrupulous operators will arrive who, without respect for the sky's great age and high situation, will present it in obscene poses, cynically entangled with some can-can dancer of the Moulin Rouge, and before long, on the grand boulevards at nightfall the peaceable pedestrian will doubtless be accosted by hucksters who will whisper in his ear, 'The card of the sky [*carte du ciel*] for fifty cents! It's transparent.'"[2] Substitute a venerable male public figure for the sky, and suddenly it is clear that the joke is not about the nature of scientific progress at all but about the unscrupulous photographers who were already rushing to profit from "obscene" and "cynical" nudity along the Parisian boulevards.

Astronomical advancements aside, the sky's unfortunate fate illustrates a fundamental shift in attitudes toward nude photography. In the 1850s and 1860s, the model dominated discourse about nude photography, only to disappear almost entirely by the end of the century. As the controversies over the model-accomplice and the attendant debates about art value faded from public consciousness, a new site of meaning and a new set of terms took her place. This new site of meaning was the public space of the street, *la rue*, the very place where sleazy dealers of cartes du ciel were found. The streets were, as Vanessa Schwartz has argued, a privileged social space at the fin de siècle, their cafés, theaters, department stores, and crowds at the center of a new spectacular concept of modern life.[3] But if the streets had become the center of a particular concept of urban modernity, they had also become the nexus of clandestine commerce and of worries about the darker side of that urban modernity. This commerce, and these worries, prominently featured nude photography. As nude photography was increasingly associated with the streets, it was bound together geographically and conceptually with a larger set of vices to be targeted for eradication, their meaning determined by the urban space they shared.

Two of these street vices in particular, prostitution and pornography, came to figure centrally in nude photography's changing cultural and artistic status. Prostitution and nude photography had long been linked via the body of the model, but in the context of the street, the terms of that association changed. By the end of the century, a web of practical and economic ties bound the industries together, in turn shifting attention away from the activities of particular models to the way that nude photography and prostitution both functioned in an economy of the sexualized body. Meanwhile, in 1880, France was hit by a "pornography crisis." An explosion of obscene publications (or so it felt at the time) overwhelmed the French capital. In response, the French press repurposed the academic and infrequently used word "pornography" to denote the offending publications, granting it a new and unprecedented cultural currency as well as accelerating a shift in its meaning. After the initial panic subsided, pornography nevertheless remained one of the defining social issues of the fin de siècle. The association between nude photography and the new genre of pornography was key to the process by which the word "pornography" was reimagined in the early 1880s. At the same time, this association reveals the degree to which photography's reputation had been diminished. In its fall into the street, its ever-closer association with the economic structures of prostitution, and its role in the rebranding of the word "pornography" at the end of the century, nude photography lost most of its artistic status. It finished the century firmly fixed in the gutters of Paris, in the hands of peddlers hawking obscene cards that were decidedly *not* of the sky.

✑ Nude Photography in the Street ✐

The public sale of nude photographs had since the late 1840s generated a mix of consternation and hysteria from those who were subjected to their display in shop windows and along the thoroughfares of Paris. The same mix of negative reactions endured during the Third Republic, intensifying with time.[4] In an 1873 description of photographic displays in shop windows, one Gaston Gaillardin lamented, "These displays reflect our mores in their entirety, and no-one is concealing this orgy of undressed women with the coat of Shem. [. . .] Obscene photographs have a prominent place in these exhibitions. By what inexplicable tolerance do we allow these women loose in the streets?"[5] He finished with an appeal to the police to "Remove these gruesome images and throw all this trash in the gutter," but to no avail.[6] Again in 1880, a piece in *La Presse* sarcastically noted that "Naturalism is taking over the displays of photography merchants," going on to specify that it did not mean those photographs that limited themselves to actresses and dancers exploiting "harmless effects of busts and maillots" but that "live models, photographed with the most complete abandon, at least with regards to their torsos, are offered up to the gaze of passersby, behind the magnifying glass of an enormous monoscope."[7] Try as they might, the police simply could not keep nude photographs out of public view; as *Le Figaro* lamented in 1885, "scarcely have licentious photographs been seized when they reappear in displays."[8] Even after more raids, various circulars threatening the proprietors of such shops, and the passage in 1898 of more restrictive laws on the press targeting obscenity, the problem continued unabated.[9] Two government reports from 1903 and 1907 repeat, verbatim, the same description of the continued problem, noting that "In the front windows of stores, in kiosks, and in train station bookshops, one can see absolutely revolting images on display. At every step, children, young women risk stumbling across truly scandalous photographs and engravings."[10]

The problem of shopwindow displays was not new, nor was the language generally used to describe them. However, the same massive increase in production that put more photographs in shop windows also put unprecedented quantities of images in the broader public space of the street. By 1881, the *Parquet* was ordering (in response to yet another arrest) "that the peddlers of these obscenities that abound on our boulevards be arrested as soon as possible," but their efforts could not stem the rising tide of nudity.[11] Between 25 July and 1 September 1889, a group of plainclothes policemen who had mobilized to clear the streets of undesirable activities of all kinds reported the arrest of thirty-three dealers of obscene photographs, an average of one a day.[12] During the first decades of the Third Republic, the problem of photographic nudity was spreading from shop windows onto the public thoroughfares of the city, confounding contemporaries. In his *L'Orgie parisienne*, Aurélien Scholl (the same man who, according to the Goncourt brothers, himself had a youthful taste for "nudities") denounced the boulevards as the public face of a city entirely given over to the search for new "resources of pleasure." While the police managed to "throw a veil [. . .] of decency" over this pervasive vice, the veil concealed little: "It is, in effect, easy to remove this superficial envelope; all one needs to do is to wander the streets, and to see the obscene lithographs and photographs on display everywhere, to know what is the essence of our mores and what the true penchants of the population are; books, engravings, paintings, everything contributes to a general corruption."[13] Nude photography along the streets was seen as a sign of total moral disintegration.

The nude had particularly infiltrated the kinds of public spaces that were the centers of fin-de-siècle modernity: the cafés of the *grands boulevards*. Many snippets of newspaper reportage attest that vendors wandered among the late-night patrons seated outside hoping to attract prospective customers.[14] Of these, Octave Mirbeau's "Nocturne parisien," a tribute to nighttime Paris in all its grit and filth, is the most illuminating. Writing in 1882, he describes the boulevards just after the theater, the opera, and the *café-concerts* have spilled their spectators and revelers out onto the streets:

> Despite the cold wind, despite the menace of the sky laden with large clouds, the terrace of the café teems with people. Not one table is unoccupied. [. . .]
>
> One hears unceasingly the piercing voice of the vendors of pornographic newspapers, who move back and forth, throwing out the name of a well-known woman, the news of a sensational scandal, in the middle of their bawdy sales-pitch, while dissolute and shifty young kids, slip like cats between the tables, offering games of transparent cards and pulling half-concealed obscene photographs out of their jacket pockets, to whip up dormant desire and ignite extinguished curiosity. And young girls, whose precocious vice has already wilted their thin children's faces, come to present bouquets to you, smiling equivocal smiles, and imbuing their glances and gestures with the knowing and hideous impurity of old prostitutes.[15]

Mirbeau's scene is a mixture of reportage and invention (an expanded version of it appeared years later in his collection of stories and essays *Les Grimaces*). He goes on to paint a bleak picture of the Parisian demimonde seated at these cafés, whose brilliant costumes, frenetic activity, and loud laughter hide moral degeneracy, hypocrisy, and profound unhappiness. This opening description of vendors hawking obscenity while young girls sell flowers as a first step towards selling themselves sets the scene for his social commentary. They are all (written obscenity, photographs, prostitution) of a piece, he implies, and tied up in the culture of the boulevards, where people go to see and be seen while hiding secrets as dark as the city's hidden sexual commerce. In this gloomy tableau Mirbeau embeds obscene photography solidly into the social substrata of the dangerous streets.[16]

La Licence des Rues

As Mirbeau's street scene insists, however, photography was not alone in thus polluting the boulevards of fin-de-siècle Paris. According to Scott Haine, although Haussmannization accelerated a shift away from street commerce to shops, this process was partially derailed in the 1880s, when an economic crisis increased the number of street vendors from six thousand to nearly twenty thousand.[17] The end of the nineteenth century saw a flood of illicit commercial activity and other kinds of undesirable public behaviors in the streets that plagued pedestrians and garnered intense attention from reformers and in the press. The article noting the arrest of an average of one street distributor of nude photography per day in September 1889 also reports the arrest of a total of 4,988 individuals for more or less significant infractions at the same time, including peddlers operating without authorization or hawking illicit materials (including obscene photographs), beggars, loiterers, street musicians, fraudsters, gamblers, and the occasional pedestrian accused of seditious language.[18] As it spread onto the streets of Paris, nude photography was integrated into a web of underground commercial activities peopled by a broad cast of unseemly characters, all of whom were viewed as impediments to public propriety.

One of the most complete surveys of the iniquities of the street, and of another place of photographic obscenity within that pantheon of vices, is provided by the former chief of the Sûreté, Gustave Macé, in his memoir *La Police parisienne: Un joli monde.*[19] The streets of Macé's Paris contain a teeming mass of human commercial activity similar to Mirbeau's café scene. They are mobbed with men and women selling wares in costume or displaying advertisements on boards, girls selling flowers, prostitutes and pimps soliciting customers, homeless vagabonds sleeping on benches, and children (goaded by exploitive adults) begging for money in the cafés.[20] According to Macé, most are a menace. His exposé begins with a description of the "the parasites of the Parisian pavement," street peddlers.[21] Some of these people, Macé admits, are simply trying to survive honestly as best they can, but he focuses on the "flotsam of social shipwrecks" whom he describes as the "avant-garde of a veritable army of evil."[22] Trafficking in everything from "fake news [*fausses nouvelles*]" and stolen goods to "photographs of the actresses of Paris in the costume of Eve," these salesman were taking over the public spaces of Paris.[23] They were bolstered by a rear guard consisting of the vagabonds of Paris who swarmed the boulevards. Stealing, begging, and playing three-card monte, these vagabonds formed "the swelling, progressive battalion of this army of evil, which propagates, multiplies, spreads and becomes menacing."[24]

After introducing the "army of evil," Macé turns to prostitution. He finishes his chapter on the topic with a diatribe that enumerates all of the evils of the street, right down to photographs for sale in shop windows. Every evening, he writes,

> You will be able to observe on our most attractive boulevards, the activity exerted by prostitutes and pimps, the presence of vendors of transparent cards, the commerce of the little flower-sellers. [. . .]
>
> On the benches, you see the various prowlers lying down, vagabond ex-convicts, men of little faith, without a domicile, whose language is revolting when they are disturbed and whose apparel even more so if they are forced to get up.
>
> At the edges of cafés, around ever more invasive tables and chairs, swarm couples exploiting children. These poor little creatures, barefoot, ask for alms in a pleading voice while holding out grimy hands containing pencils or writing paper. [. . .]
>
> Evil exists, profound, nobody can deny it; we must fight it, in first bringing a little order and morality to our public thoroughfares, for the decency of the street is disappearing. [. . .]
>
> The displays of little bookstores feature naturalist drawings that explain the innuendos of printed texts, and also photographs of unknown women in primitive costume. Crimes, rapes, attacks on morality have their special illustrators, reproducing the different phases of judicial findings. And it is in front of these horrible black engravings that children gather each morning on the way to school. Young people are thus infiltrated with intellectual poison no less dangerous than food poisoning.[25]

As Macé represents it, the nude photograph was not simply a form of problematic merchandise hawked by various miscreants on the streets of Paris. Instead, it was part of a network of people, objects, and behaviors that had overwhelmed those streets by force—peddling, vagrancy, child poverty and exploitation, prostitution, nude photography, dirty books—all of which were infecting the populace with dissolute ideas that threatened to destroy the future generation before it even had a chance to make its way in the world.

Macé's description of the streets seethes with reactionary terror over the disintegration of social mores on public thoroughfares. This anxiety about the moral implications of photography and the other forms of illicit commerce appears throughout contemporary discussions of city streets, reaching its apex in the various legislative campaigns and organizations led by the senator René Bérenger against the *licence des rues,* or license of the streets. Bérenger was a militant social reformer known for his work on child labor law and penal reform, but his passion was public morality. He was described as "an obscenity maniac" and dubbed by his detractors *Père la Pudeur* or *Bérenger la Pudeur* ("Papa Prude" or "Bérenger the Prude").[26] As a senator, Bérenger pushed for harsher anti-indecency and antiprostitution statutes in 1894 and 1898.[27] He was elected president of the Académie des sciences morales et politiques in 1890. In 1892, he founded a private antivice society (one of many that were springing up around Europe during the 1880s and 1890s) specifically targeting public indecency in the street, the Société de protestation contre la licence des rues (referred to widely as the Ligue contre la licence des rues).[28] Bérenger also headed the umbrella group the Fédération des sociétés contre l'immoralité publique, founded after the success of the first International Congress against Pornography in 1905, and while head of the federation, he published the *Manuel pratique pour la lutte contre la pornographie* in 1910.[29]

As one of the most important public faces of the fin-de-siècle morality leagues, Bérenger provides a paradigmatic example of the discourse surrounding nude photography's classification as part of the problem of the licence des rues and the perceived social and moral consequences of this category as a whole. The passion of Bérenger's career was not merely photographic obscenity, or even visual obscenity, but the much more widespread "perfidious influence exercised on public morality by the licentious exhibitions and excitations of which our streets too often put on a spectacle."[30] He was devoted to fighting these many provocations. In an 1894–1895 legislative effort to pass a law to combat both affronts to public decency and prostitution (it would pass in the senate but die in the chamber of deputies), Bérenger swept together forms of indecency that included everything from obscene "cries," texts, and images to public solicitation by prostitutes. Bérenger targeted all of these behaviors together because they operated together, making the streets impassible for honest and decent French people; as he said, "The street, public spaces, belong to everyone. Their monopolization by a few, to the detriment of all, would be an insufferable tyranny."[31] Indeed, for Bérenger, the state of the streets was more than just an infringement on the liberty of the French people. It signaled a fundamental decline in the French moral character. In the face of this threat, Bérenger argued that the government had not just the right but the responsibility to act. His impassioned remarks opening Senate debate in 1895 describe the grave state of affairs:

> The particular character of the end of this century is the general relaxation of moral standards, the widespread spectacle of licentious exhibitions and excitations of the same nature, in a word the influences that can be so dire for young people. Theater, literature, language itself, even family habits attest to the state of affairs.
>
> Is this not a great danger for a country? Is there not for the morality of youth, and consequently for the future of the nation, a serious peril in this deviation of morals?[32]

Bérenger went on to acknowledge that not all of this national decline could be legislated away, but, he argued, there were some ills that the law could fight. Chief among them were "the licentious manifestations which, taking possession of the street, therein exercise a kind of despotism, presenting themselves with a scandal and an audacity that harms all eyes, revolting modesty and offering young people spectacles which even the most attentive care cannot counteract and which in the long term can exercise the most dangerous and perfidious influence over them."[33] Bérenger does not simply enumerate the dangers of the street as Macé does; he makes clear just what the stakes are: The street was the battleground for the French character, one on which the future of the nation depended. It offered the government the rare possibility to legislate away the moral turpitude of the fin de siècle.

The photograph was just one part of this larger fight, but it was an important part and was targeted specifically by Bérenger and his supporters. The Ligue contre la licence des rues was known for pressuring vendors of objectionable photographs with leaflets and threats that noncompliance would result in prosecution.[34] The language about photography in the laws and reports written by Bérenger indicate that it played a central role in his understanding of the dangers of the street. In the same legislative push of 1894–1895, Bérenger repeatedly invoked photography. One of the most striking cases is in a passage cited from his own manifesto published in 1892 on the occasion of the founding of the Ligue contre la licence des rues, wherein Bérenger conjures up a streetscape pocked by widespread obscenity:

> "The industries that live off debauchery are more audacious than ever. A dangerous license [licence] continues to reign in the streets and in the public spaces of our large cities.

It is impossible to leave home without being offended by those spectacles most suited to demoralize the young. If the walls of Paris heave been more or less purged of the obscenities that have long sullied them, licentious provocations of the most diverse forms have not ceased to solicit passersby. Here, it's a newspaper seller who holds out in front of him a scandalous drawing. There, it's the window of a bookstore or photography shop loaded with titles or images without modesty. Elsewhere, ignoble advertisements are slipped into your hand. The most unsavory broadsheets are offered for free on the public thoroughfare to all who come, often at the doors of schools and high schools.

'It is visual rape [*le viol des yeux*],' a magistrate eloquently said."[35]

Prospectuses, immoral books, and obscene photography were everywhere; to walk the streets of Paris in the 1890s was to submit to visual rape. Photography is, of course, only one of many items invoked by Bérenger, but it is the most graphic and widely distributed of the objects described. It is hard not to see a reference to the most troubling and brutal examples of photographic obscenity in Bérenger's metaphor.

Bérenger's stance on the art value of photography reinforces the notion that nude photography had a uniquely reprehensible visual role in the dangers of the street. His attitude exemplifies a particular stance toward nude photography conditioned by concerns over public morality, one that granted it absolutely no artistic value regardless of content. This attitude is made clear in an earlier (1893) speech Bérenger gave to the senate to promote the work of the newly founded Ligue contre la licence des rues on his usual topic of the unceasing "scandals" of the street.[36] Although his main focus is nudity at "private balls," the speech includes a lengthy discussion of photography paradigmatic of the way that fears about the street were used to renegotiate the meaning of nude photography.[37] First, in addressing public displays of nude drawings, Bérenger argues that the government should not limit itself to targeting obscenity but should also take action against images that while "not being absolutely obscene have a quality of license [*licence*] and indecency of whose danger no-one could be unaware."[38] He then qualifies this declaration by saying that "I am not speaking here of artistic nudity that is the reproduction of an ideal beauty, I am speaking of the vulgar reproduction of the human body presented for the purpose of lubricity in positions and appearance the most capable of exciting the young."[39] Yet despite this lip service to art, Bérenger remains frustratingly vague about what exactly he means by "indecent" images, and his treatment of nude photography does not clarify the matter. He invokes photography as proof of just how bad the problem of public displays of nude imagery has become, using excerpts of letters from angry constituents complaining about the many nude photographs in shop windows around the École des beaux-arts to make his point:

> "Three or four merchants near the École des beaux-arts are displaying at this moment in their windows quantities of nude women photographed from nature in all of the studio poses and with a whole stew of realist details: reclining women, seated women, women raising an arm or a leg.
>
> Naturally, female workers, female apprentices, high schoolers wallow in them. It's a public invitation to debauchery." [. . .]
>
> "You will see in the front window of two photography shops women, doubtless studio models, photographed entirely nude, and in the most cynical poses. Is it admissible, under the pretext of art, and because we are two steps from the school, that such obscenities are exposed to the eyes of passersby, of all of the children in the neighborhood?"[40]

The trouble is, the examples in these letters efface any supposed distinction between those images to be eradicated and the accepted artistic use of photographic nudity. The letter even acknowledges that the models in the photographs are "studio models." Although Bérenger claimed to fight obscenity, and his petitioners use the word, the photographs to which they refer were probably, despite their "cynical poses," just académies. Of course, some purported académies from the period did leave something to be desired. Bérenger, however, does not point out that *some* of these académies were indecent; he dismisses them *all* as a group, pushing the line between art and obscenity so far back into the realm of art as to exclude nudity entirely. For a legislator fighting for the moral character of the nation, it seems, such distinctions were trivial. All photographic nudity was reprehensible.[41]

Bérenger continued his legislative attacks on public impropriety through the 1890s, contributing to government reports on the laws of 1898 and 1908 against indecency.[42] In truth, by 1897, the reality had begun to change. When he again took to the senate floor for two days to speak against the tripartite threat of "the newspaper, the street, the theater" (including prospectuses for nude photographs), other senators responded by noting that the streets had seen remarkable improvement and that private distribution of obscenity by mail was as much of a problem as public display.[43] Moreover, Bérenger was a zealot, and like every zealot, he had his share of vociferous critics.[44] Yet all this having been said, the furor over the licence des rues was fundamental to altering perceptions of nude photography by restricting the possible range of its signification. Nude photography's meaning and value were easily quantified in the street: it was obscenity, of no value at all. Like so much trash, it was to be cleared away at all costs.

⚔ Working the Sidewalk: Photography and Prostitution ⚔

Fears about the street not only generated a new kind of inflammatory rhetoric about nude photography, they also provided the genre with a whole constellation of dubious associates likewise defined by their presence in public spaces. Two of these associates were particularly important to nude photography's evolving meaning. The first of these was prostitution, whose longstanding ties to the genre were strengthened during the Third Republic through their common use of the street as a commercial space. In his study of nineteenth-century prostitution, Alain Corbin describes changes to the prostitution industry—and to the kind of language used to discuss prostitution—that dovetail with the rising anxiety about the street. After 1871, Corbin asserts that there was a perceived increase in street prostitution because of various social changes and changes to the structures of prostitution that brought women out of controlled spaces like the *maisons de tolérance*. He describes outraged complaints about women flooding the boulevards after dark and a pervasive anxiety about social degradation focused particularly on the impassibility of the streets, the same anxiety about the streets that structured reactions to nude photography at this time.[45] Not surprisingly, prostitution and photographic nudity often appear together. In Mirbeau's scene of the Parisian boulevards, dealers in both real and photographic bodies work the same sidewalk cafés. Reformers described both nude photography and prostitution as defiling the street with merchandise for sale. Macé's Paris is both populated by "prostitutes and pimps" and besmirched by "photographs representing unknown women in primitive costume."[46] Bérenger's 1894–1895 legislative push specifically targeted together "the spectacle, so saddening and so widespread today, of prostitution freely displaying its provocations on the public thoroughfare, and the infinite variety of affront to public decency in whatever form in which it is produced," including, of course, photography.[47] This pairing of prostitution and nude photography in the street pointed to more than their common status as moral and social problems. In 1882, for instance, *Le Figaro* reported on various pimps who, their primary source of income limited as they found themselves "tracked on all sides by the Security forces and not knowing what trade to exercise," turned to selling "repugnant" nude photographs in the streets.[48] The theoretical alignment of the two as a public traffic in the body was, by the end of the century, rooted in a very real alignment of the two as interdependent street industries.

These new spatial and commercial connections were in turn cemented by the growing importance of photography to the structures of prostitution off the streets. Indeed, ironically, even as the two were more closely associated by way of

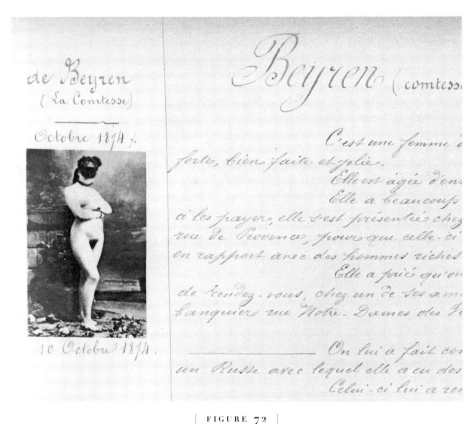

[FIGURE 72]

Entry and photograph from the BB1,
Archives de la Préfecture de police, Paris.

the street, photography was actually helping to move prostitution into private spaces. Photography freed pimps and proxénètes to recruit women from a distance, safely hidden from the reach of law enforcement, and they increasingly took advantage of photography for this reason.[49] Photographs were equally useful for attracting prospective clients, allowing the convenient display of a wide variety of "merchandise" (whether or not it actually represented the women who were available), and additionally allowing women who came from more respectable backgrounds to work more discretely in prostitution.[50] Contemporary accounts do not specify whether the images used were nudes, but one 1874 photograph preserved in the BB1 register of prostitutes suggests that they may well have been (Figure 72). Moreover, photographic nudity was increasingly important to brothel prostitution in other ways. Calling cards featuring obscene photographs were a popular publicity tool for places of prostitution.[51] Pierre Delcourt maintains that prospective clients lured under false pretenses—such as advertisements for sales of art or furniture—might be enticed to buy a very different kind of product after being warmed up with catalogs of obscene photographs instead.[52] Photographic nudity also became one of an arsenal of tools used by sex workers. One large establishment, for instance, allegedly kept a collection of erotic engravings, the novels of Sade, and nude photographs of "gallant celebrities" (the most explicit of which were doctored, with the celebrity's head on another body), along with other more utilitarian paraphernalia like condoms and guides for curing syphilis.[53] Nudes were an important source of income for brothels, which charged clients to look or to buy.[54]

At the same time, brothels became more important for, and integrated into, the photographic business model. Distributors sold directly to brothels, assured of a market.[55] Photographers could safely promote obscenity in brothels, "so sure of impunity that some aren't even uncomfortable leaving their name and address on the back."[56] Indeed, some photographs sold in brothels were commissioned or produced collaboratively by brothels and photographers, particularly when scenes of sexual activity were involved.[57] Brothels were the distribution point of some of the most explicit images, including images of underage girls; according to Louis Fiaux, brothels that engaged in child prostitution were primarily responsible for a rise in child pornography during the period.[58]

The newly integrated economies of prostitution and photographic obscenity generated a new discourse linking the two, even as some of the old rhetoric about the model's body nevertheless persisted. In his 1873 column for *La Presse*, Gaston Gaillardin harkened back to the language of the Empire in denouncing the "low-class Phrynes" hanging in shop windows, and emphasizing the unappetizing models, whom he calls "withered, old, indecent" and "vulgar debauchers, without beauty and without grace."[59] Yet once having described the women in the photographs as faded and unappealing, Gaillardin does not again refer explicitly to prostitution, nor to the bodies of the models. Instead, he suggests a parallel between the women in the photographs and the photographs themselves via their common pronoun, *elle*, and the evil work that they do in society. Without distinguishing which one he means, he writes, "They [*elles*] represent tolerated vice, brazen disgrace, audacious and lucrative scandal, triumphant orgy; they inspire only pity to those of discerning age, but keep an empire of corruption over the young."[60] Prostitutes and photographs were both tolerated vices and lucrative scandals, whatever the bodies involved looked like. Similarly, in 1905, the proceedings of the Congrès national contre la pornographie would trot out old language about the body of the model against one publication purporting to contain "art" nudes only to make an even more remarkable pivot to the consumers of both industries, saying, "The bodies offered as a spectacle for the crowd are ridiculously poorly done: the forms are heavy, pudgy, without muscles, without precise contours; it is evident that the models have been taken from *maisons de tolérance*, among women that debauchery has deformed and only, indeed, the regulars of these establishments could buy these horrors, for one must have tastes depraved by lust to take pleasure in the contemplation of these poor human larvae."[61] The grotesque bodies of both photographs and prostitution are not so much bound by their common ugliness but by the commercial system in which they circulate, the men who are willing to consume both of them, and their consequent role in the decay of French society.

Commercial structures aside, the reality was that the model's body simply could not signify prostitution with its former potency because the ties between the real woman and her photograph had become more tenuous. Not only were models often recruited in other countries, but some of them were not even real women (as in the case of photo collages). The model's body had become something of a distraction from the practical realities of the intertwined businesses of prostitution and photographic obscenity. As these concrete business ties became more evident, a new awareness of the relationship between the two industries emerged. One example of the new way of understanding nude photography and prostitution can be found in the newspaper coverage of one Madame Desmett, proprietress of a photography shop in the Rue Castiglione, who captured public attention in July 1883.[62] Madame Desmett was reported to the police by the scandalized mother of a fourteen-year-old American boy who had gone into her shop to buy photographs of actresses and exited, seventy-five francs poorer, in possession of eight nude photographs that were, in the words of his distraught mother, "dreadful and nasty."[63] Adding insult to injury, the mother alleged that the young lady tending the shop counter sexually assaulted her son and, when she was interrupted by customers, encouraged the young boy to return the next day so that she could teach him "all the secrets of love."[64] At trial, Madame Desmett was convicted of indecency. The employee was acquitted, but an even more sordid tale emerged about Madame Desmett's daughter, who had allegedly been prostituted by her mother before running away.

Newspaper accounts never established the truth of the rumors of prostitution connected to the case. Nevertheless, in an article for *La Presse* entitled "On ne rend pas la monnaie" ("They don't give change"), Madame Desmett became a symbol of how the two forms of fleshly commerce had become a single problem. The main subject of the piece is the brazen impunity of the prostitution industry. The author, however, begins with the story of the Rue Castiglione. Erupting with sarcastic shock, he exclaims, "What a scandal! What, the merchants who sell portraits of Leon XII to the clergy, and that of the obelisk to voyagers in excursion trains [*trains de plaisir*] could be at the same time corruptors of youth, procurers of debauchery at reduced prices, in the obscurity of the back of the shop! What a revelation!"[65] He then turns to prostitution, pointing out that it was no less common nor more concealed, and claiming that if those "paid very well to find the secret houses of naughtiness" would simply hop in a cab with any ordinary Parisian, that person could guide them in a moment to such dens of iniquity. And finally, he uses the case of Madame Desmett to suggest that both thinly veiled sex industries were part of the same problem, one that "what we have agreed to call the justice system" knew about but did not address:

> A seizure was made at a matron's place that proved the crime of sale of obscene photographs but did not demonstrate that of clandestine prostitution. Three thousand raids should be undertaken, this evening, that would put under lock and key three thousand tradeswomen, dressed as shopgirls, of whom a large number sell their own daughters at a reduced price.
>
> You have read, moreover, in the very summary of the trial that now occupies us, that Mme Desmet [sic]—the defendant—had, at another time, in the rue Saint-Marc, a boutique wherein the calves of her own daughter, carefully plumped and put on display, would replace for buyers the seductions of summer sales and of forty-five cent fine-knit socks.
>
> Thus, there is only one of two possibilities: Either the police tolerate the tradeswomen who do not give change, or they want to strike them from the directory forever. In the first case, why bother the lady of the rue Castiglione; in the second, it is indispensable that they start a general search party from this moment forward.[66]

In this denunciation of the two sex industries, the model has vanished because the author is focused almost entirely on the way that they were instead linked through those who profited economically from the exploitation of women's bodies. Madame Desmett got off on the charges of prostitution, he argues, but there are a good many like her who are selling their shopgirls, or their own daughters, using the disguise of a legitimate business (in 1892 Le Figaro would report again on another proprietress of a photography shop using her shop as cover for prostitution).[67] Moreover, whether she was selling obscene photographs or her daughter, she was still one of the many businesswomen who "don't give change." If the police mean to eliminate the practice, they have to go after everyone, photography dealers along with prostitutes and pimps. Indeed, he uses Madame Desmett's case to suggest that the police themselves, despite their lax enforcement, are well aware that the two industries are equally troublesome and closely connected. Although the article then turns almost exclusively to prostitution and white slavery, the specific reference to Madame Desmett at its opening makes clear that for this reporter, whether one sold photographs of young women or the women themselves little mattered. The same kinds of people were profiting from both forms of trafficking, and they both needed to be stamped out.

"On ne rend pas la monnaie" is emblematic of an emerging way of thinking about nude photography and prostitution that was at once revolutionary and reactionary. The author of the article on Madame Desmett is no feminist, and his outrage is motivated less by the harm done to the women involved than fear for the corruption of society. At the same time, this outrage is rooted in the fact that both businesses participated in the same economic exploitation of women's bodies. In this particular case, the focus is on profiteers like Madame Desmett, who furthers the new argument about the relationship between prostitution and nude photographs because she herself dealt in both. But this growing awareness of the sexual economy in which both participated also extended to models. By the end of the century, it would pop up in some unexpected places. For instance, Victor Leca's *Pour s'amuser — Guide du viveur à Paris*, includes a section on "Models" that is devoted to "those [models], absolutely brazen, who pose nude for certain photographers unknown to the public, in the company of men who are also nude—or women—for obscene scenes, printed in profuse numbers."[68] According to Leca, these models were very much prostitutes, even when they didn't prostitute themselves:

> The models who serve for these reproductions are prostitutes, incontestably, even if, apart from their poses, they do not profit from Johns. It would seem that in posing for alcove scenes—the most realist ones— these women make large sums of money, and, in order to procure them (models of this kind), one only needs to publish an advertisement in a newspaper asking for "*photographic models*"; they soon present themselves by the dozens, and one only has to choose the most agreeable persons.
>
> This proves that to live from prostitution, it is not indispensable "*to work the trottoir*"; it is true that, among those who do, many must also be *models* in their spare time.[69]

Certain aspects of this passage are not new to the Third Republic. Leca's claims are based in the old assumption that the women who would take their clothes off for such images were prostitutes because only prostitutes would stoop so low; moreover, he explicitly remarks that many prostitutes likely modeled in their spare time. Leca, however, also points out a structural parallel between prostitution and nude photography that refigures the old use of the body to indict the model as a prostitute. To be photographed naked was to sell one's body, and to sell one's body was prostitution. The bodies do the same work, on or off the trot-toir, and are therefore fundamentally the same, whether or not the models are actually prostitutes. For a sleazy guidebook, this is a remarkable insight. It is more or less the stance that underpins Zola's use of photographic aesthetics in *Nana*, and it is also the argument of some of the twentieth-century feminist crit-ics who have written about nude photography. Still, lest we attribute too much sophistication to Leca, he turns this socioeconomic critique into an advertise-ment for the delights of these models and their photographs. Since obscene photography and prostitution were the same, they were both there for the enjoy-ment of Leca's readers.

⇗ Nude Photography and the Birth of Pornography ⇖

If the nude photograph's ever-closer ties with prostitution illustrate the terms of photography's descent into the street, aligning both industries within the con-temporary sexual economy, its association with another street vice points to the stakes for the reputation of the genre (and the medium). As I noted in the open-ing of the chapter, the period of photography's integration into category of street vice coincided with the rapid rise of another kind of obscene representation that would become one of the primary concerns of fin-de-siècle reformers.[70] During the early 1880s, the streets of Paris were overwhelmed by what was described as an "epidemic" of cheap and bawdy newspapers, full of humorous erotic stories and sexually charged puns.[71] In reaction to their sudden arrival, the French press revived an old word, *pornographie*, redefining it to designate these new publica-tions. In the process, pornography's primary dictionary definition (a treatise on prostitution) was jettisoned in favor of a secondary meaning (obscene represen-tations) that was altered to apply specifically to the bawdy newspapers of the early 1880s and predominantly employed to designate these and other texts with sexual content. The hysteria over these so-called pornographic newspapers in the early 1880s ultimately led to the word pornography's entrance into common usage with the meaning it still has today. All the while, photographic nudity was deployed in the pages of the daily press to cement the transformation of pornog-raphy's linguistic and social meaning. The role of photographic nudity in dis-course about pornography reveals just how much the medium's reputation de-clined as a result of its place in the streets and what the consequences of that decline would be for its artistic prospects.

Like photographic nudity and prostitution, the space of pornography was the space of the contested streets. The pornography epidemic of the 1880s began with the distribution of the various dubious newspapers on the thoroughfares of Paris; not surprisingly, pornography is everywhere in contemporary discussions of the street and is often linked to obscene photography. In Mirbeau's nocturnal cityscape, for instance, "vendors of pornographic newspapers" lurk alongside the children selling nude photographs. According to Macé, the same "army of evil" that flooded the streets of Paris with dirty photographs also dealt in pornography.[72] And above all, the very newspapers that were redefining the word pornography triangulated the new genre with photography in the streets. In October 1880, at the height of the pornography panic, *Le Figaro* dismissively compared the editor of the first and most prominent pornographic newspaper, *L'Événement parisien*, with "the industrial types arrested for selling obscene photographs on the boulevard" as it discussed where he would serve his sentence for indecency.[73] In December 1880, *La Presse* condemned yet another pornographic paper as even worse than *L'Événement parisien*: "*Alphonse et Nana* is an illustrated newspaper that existed for only one day. But in this day, the journal surpassed the filth of all of its peers, even the *Événement parisien*." How did the newspaper sum up the horrors of this new publication? With the revelatory sentence, "It was being sold along the boulevards, with obscene photographs."[74] The obscene photograph and the dangerous space of the boulevards were similarly invoked together by *Le Gaulois* earlier in 1880, when, decrying the state of generalized public immorality, it demanded to know "what ideas of governance the government was obeying in allowing vendors of obscene photography to circulate freely, and in permitting filth to be displayed in *public* rags [*dans des feuilles . . . publiques*]."[75] Once again, the newspaper's outrage is focused on the "free circulation" of vices in the streets; it additionally bundles prostitution with obscene photography and pornography through the use of the phrase "feuilles publiques," a play on *filles publiques*, the term for prostitutes who worked on the street.

Beyond illuminating the place of the street in discourse about pornography and obscene photography, these examples reveal another key aspect of the relationship between the two media in contemporary newspaper reporting. Pornography was an old word being used with a new frequency and in a new way. In the early 1880s, as newspapers were actively regenerating the word's meaning, photographic obscenity was mobilized to bolster claims about pornography's insalubrious influence, as a kind of marker to indicate just how bad this new genre was. That is why, of all the possible ways to describe pornography, newspapers would invoke nude photography. Part of the redefinition of pornography involved its proximity to obscene photography. Newspapers frequently emphasized the similarity between nude photography and pornography even as they, notably, never went so far as to declare them exactly the same. In 1881, an article printed in *Le Gaulois* and *La Presse*, for instance, used the word "pornographer" in its title but then recounted the arrest of someone selling "obscene photographs," without any further reference to pornographic texts as such.[76] *Le Figaro* made an even more explicit equation of the two in 1883, again stopping short of actually describing photographs as "pornographic." Applauding action taken by the parquet to rid shop displays of obscene photographs, the newspaper wrote, "Without being a prude, nudities admittedly took up far too considerable a space in the windows of certain shopkeepers; pornography, chased from the press by way of harsh, but just, condemnations, seems to have taken refuge in the displays of those merchants too inclined to overexcite the unhealthy curiosity of the beautiful youth of Paris."[77] Pornography, something that could be expelled from the press only to reappear in photographic window displays, is *not* obscene photography and yet, at the same time, could inhere in that medium if need be. The two are distinct, but it could be hard to tell exactly where the distinction between pornography and obscene photography lay.

This kind of slippage permitted the substitution of fears about the proliferation of nude photography, which had long had a bad reputation, for that about pornography, whose meaning was still being constructed. Consider coverage of the press laws of 1881 from July of that year in *Le Figaro*. These laws, which granted written texts unprecedented rights and protections, had been written as fears about pornography were growing. Very quickly some averred that they were not harsh enough, and, in 1882, with explicit reference to the onslaught of written pornography, the government went on to pass new laws rescinding some of the protections it had just granted to the daily press the year before.[78] Arguing for these restrictions, the author of a piece in *Le Figaro* wrote in 1881, "It is no longer democracy but filth that will flow abundantly; and if we think that the commerce of books, drawings, and odious photographs is calculated by millions; if we remember that disgusting photographs in particular are the cause of near daily prosecutions, can we not summarize the situation in a single word in saying that the new law will be the triumph of pornography?"[79] In fact, the problem he describes is not that of written pornography but of photography, which was the only kind of obscenity being distributed by anything like the millions at the time. The legal status of the image was not up for debate, and it remained entirely unaffected by the changes that went into law in 1882. Yet to strengthen his argument, the author integrates photography with the category of written pornography so that the millions of photographs can be used to justify an attack on laws that had offered greater freedom to the written press.

Despite the frequent conflation of pornography and photographic obscenity, however, the two were not the same. The pornography crisis in 1880 was only the beginning of a process whereby the question of obscenity took on a new meaning, figured through the word that had been reimagined to denote it. Even after the newspapers from the early 1880s had disappeared, the word pornography remained in the lexicon. As time passed, its meaning referred less specifically to the publications of the early 1880s that had precipitated its jump in popularity, but the lasting effect of the crisis was to usher in pornography as a common signifier for modern obscenity. It was widely used to refer to any object or behavior that might have previously been called "obscene." A favorite target of René Bérenger later in his career, it appeared in many of his legislative reports and proposals and in his 1907 opus, the *Manuel pratique pour la lutte contre la pornographie*, as a signifier for just about everything from naughty songs to contraception.[80] It is hardly strange, then, that nude photography would be closely associated with pornography. What is strange is that even as the two were often linked, photography stubbornly refused incorporation into the broader category of pornography. According to exact phrase searches on Gallica of the major daily newspapers (*La Presse*, *Le Figaro*, *Le Temps*, *Le Journal des débats politiques et littéraires*) from 1870 onward, phrases describing different texts (books, newspapers, or writings) with the adjective "pornographic" yield a total of 249 results. Phrases where the word "pornographic" modifies different visual objects (drawings, engravings, or images) yield 100 results. During this time, the phrase "obscene photographs" in singular and plural forms occurs 175 times (!). The phrase "pornographic photographs," however, appears only 10 times, 9 of which are from the 1890s. It appears once in 1873 in the *Gazette des beaux-arts*, an exceptional use of the term before the early 1880s.[81] Although the slippage between nude photography and pornography was key to establishing pornography as a new social menace, photography was only rarely described as pornographic, even after the word was commonly used as a broad descriptor of sexually explicit representation.

How could it be that the very representational genre exploited to redefine pornography and stoke fears about it was not itself described as pornographic? One particularly virulent denunciation of photographic nudity suggests the significance of the distinction between photography and pornography. Writing for *Le XIXe siècle* in 1892, the antipornography crusader and theater critic Francisque Sarcey explained to his readers the fundamental difference between obscene books and obscene photographs (in one of the few examples of the adjective "pornographic" applied to photography):

> All of you who read my work, do you have among your acquaintances, a gentleman who has assembled in one way or another an album of pornographic photographs? For my part, I do not, and this fantasy, which is not at all artistic, is not in the French character. I know those lovers of books who have, in a secret corner of their libraries, works of this genre for which they have paid quite dearly: but what charms them in these volumes is the beauty of the paper, the grace of the typography, the marvelous execution of the engravings, and sometimes the richness of the bindings, which are themselves alone admirable works of art.

> These books are shown in private circles; and if one looks at the images, I must say that it is not precisely for the subjects that they represent, but for the free touch, full of fire or of charm, of the Eisen who has composed them. But a series of obscene photographs! One looks at them only for their obscenity! I do not want to say that there isn't in France that which excites unhealthy curiosity: I claim only that this is not, strictly speaking, a French vice. We do not esteem, we do not like naughtiness except if it is mixed with a little spice of art. There is not a shadow of art in a collection of cynical photographs. It is pure pornography; it is pornography for the use of the Germans and the English.[82]

Leaving aside Sarcey's strange nationalistic turn and unconvincing naïveté about the French taste for obscenity at the end of a century when France had played a prominent role in bringing photographic nudity into global circulation, the most remarkable aspect of his comparison of the book and the photograph is the way that it nearly perfectly summarizes the attitude toward photography at the end of the century. Like Bérenger, Sarcey allows nude photography only one meaning. Where a book might be both erotic and artful, photography could not be anything other than obscene. Sarcey's argument is, indeed, even more extreme because of his comparison with pornography. In that comparison, it finally becomes clear why photography was not pornographic. It was *more than* pornographic, or at the very least, it was one of the worst forms of pornography. Photographic nudity was the purest form of filth, pornography for the Germans and the English.

In the 1850s and 1860s, proponents of photography fought for its artistic credibility by way of the nude. Yet by the 1890s, the photographic nude was allowed no such pretensions at all. Some of this shift in attitudes was indubitably rooted in the changes outlined in Chapter 5. The growth of the international photographic industry, the increasing numbers of explicit photographs in circulation, the relaxation of censorship, and the corresponding decline of the government-sanctioned art nude all contributed to lowering its reputation. But photography's fall was the result of something more, for the fact also remained that many artists and amateurs were producing nudes with artistic value and intentions. The cultural obsession with the dangerous streets redefined nude photography's social standing and the perception of its artistic value, lowering both to the level of the gutter into which it had been dragged. In 1883, *Le Figaro* lamented the many moral dangers besetting contemporary youth thusly: "And then, there is the street, the modern street, the street as it has been made by contemporary progress; the street where, at every step, are displayed provocative photographs of seminude girls, their skirts hitched up to their thighs, casting over the passing youth knowing glances, languid smiles."[83] In the street, all of the worst kinds of behaviors were permitted, only the dodgiest merchandise was for sale, and photography had taken its place as the ensign of these provocations, advertising them for all to see.

⩕ CHAPTER 7 ⩗

Nana in the Nude

Long before it was first serialized in October 1879, Émile Zola's novel of Parisian prostitution *Nana* was already embroiled in controversy. For months, the newspaper in which it was to appear, *Le Voltaire*, had run a massive publicity campaign announcing its arrival. According to the conservative journalist Armand de Pontmartin, who devoted more than four pages of his invective against the novel to complaining about the deluge of advertisements, the walls of Paris were plastered with posters commanding, "Ask for the *Voltaire*! Read *Nana*! Read Zola!"[1] Pontmartin was one of the novel's most virulent critics, and as such may have exaggerated his poster counts (forty on the Rue de la République alone!), but by the time it was released as a printed volume in February 1880, the novel had already sold an unprecedented fifty-five thousand advance copies.[2] While the general public clamored for *Nana*, however, reviewers like Pontmartin had been sharpening their knives in preparation for its first installment. *Nana* occasioned a critical tempest, as horrified reviews accused Zola of fabricating the particulars of his courtesan's career and of exaggerating all that was most repellent about human existence. In his typical fashion, they complained, Zola forced "the reader to fixate far too long with his eyes, smell and thoughts on hideous, nauseating and revolting objects."[3] Of all these "hideous objects," the most troubling was Nana's naked body. Reviewers grumbled that Zola paraded his heroine around "completely naked, sometimes in her bloomers, sometimes in her undershirt," displaying "her laundry, her bidet, all of her flesh from her neck to her toes, without sparing the reader even a wisp of downy fuzz."[4] The novelist Louis Ulbach cynically suggested that "when the plot falters, suddenly Nana takes off her chemise."[5] What was perhaps worse, Nana's constant nudity was by no means enjoyable for readers; Albert Wolff, the literary critic for *Le Figaro*, lamented that "this girl who wanders around constantly in her undershirt, sometimes, but rarely, in her drawers, is beginning to get on my nerves."[6] As Léon Chapron described it, the novel's eroticism was unappetizing to all but the most debauched or inexperienced: "The book is so radically bad that the obscenities that adorn it obviously have no appeal except to dirty old men and the curious of all ages. It's erotica, and badly done erotica."[7] In short, *Nana* and its rendering of French society were oversexed and decidedly underappealing.

Pontmartin himself was outraged by more than the posters around Paris, and his attack on the novel is representative of the intense reactions to Nana's nudity. In *La Gazette de France*, Pontmartin raged against Zola's slanderous use of the "respectable" world of the theater as the backdrop for the novel's compendium of "details of nudity, crudity, filth, of pimping [*proxénétisme*], of the sale and display of human flesh, of hideous speculation on the most shameful vices, on the most squalid passions of a gangrened and bestialized society."[8] Like almost every other negative reviewer, he attempted to discredit Zola by accusing him of propagating an unpleasant fiction. Yet unsatisfied with accusing Zola of total ignorance, he went so far as to call the novel pornographic:[9] "In these tableaux that take up more space than the story, and wherein M. Emile Zola, on the pretext of moralizing or lecturing us, convokes all of the cantharides of the religion of the *nude* and of pornographic literature, he accumulates, not magnifications, permitted of comedy and even of the novel, but the most enormous misinterpretations."[10] For Pontmartin, Zola was not just an inaccurate realist, grave as that failing was. He was a follower of the religion of the nude, his novel nothing more than an offering to the pornographic deity of lowbrow filth. Pontmartin's criticism is amplified by his use of the word "pornography" rather than "obscenity," which locates Zola's novel directly in the middle of the pornography crisis of 1880 and the ensuing hullabaloo about obscene texts and images proliferating on the streets of fin-de-siècle Paris. It suggests that, like other boulevard pornographers, Zola has no goals other than his own gain, his novel no merit beyond titillation. According to Pontmartin, Zola permits himself gross untruths in a pornographic pursuit thinly veiled (as thinly, indeed, as Nana herself) as a morality tale.

Pontmartin was not alone in levying this accusation at Zola's novel. In thrall to the hysteria over print pornography, which erupted during the novel's serialization, a host of critics accused Zola not only of being a pornographer himself but also of causing the entire pornography epidemic. The accusations were so widespread that in August 1880, in an article called "La Littérature obscène," Zola felt compelled to respond, citing the dozens of articles that accused him "squarely of leading the century astray" and one, in particular, that "says in so many words that I invented pornographic literature."[11] Zola assured the public

that "the year 1880 is not more vicious than any other, that truly obscene literature is not any more on display than in the eighteenth century, for example[. . . .]
All of this kerfuffle is a crisis of ridiculous prudishness that makes me anxious
for the fate of our famous French wit."[12] Alas, his attempt to defend himself had
little effect on either popular or critical opinion, as newspaper articles, carica-
tures, and popular theatrical pieces perpetuated the image of Zola the pornographer throughout the early 1880s.[13]

Of the many accusations of obscenity and pornography, however, there is one
review that stands out. Both remarkably brazen and remarkably astute in his
reading of the novel's aesthetics of the nude body, Ulbach saw a different kind of
erotic object in the pages of *Nana*: "I repeat, one does not make a book exclusively out of salacious bits; one makes a collection serving as commentary for illicit photographs. Naturalism that limits its applications to showing us men and
women playing a comedy *in naturalibus* does not belong to the literary industry,
the police pursue it under another name."[14] The "other name" to which Ulbach
refers is almost certainly obscenity, but he also makes a distinction that is central
to the novel. In Ulbach's opinion, *Nana* is so utterly divorced from the literary
enterprise, so entirely devoid of "morality, sentiment, conscience," that it can
scarcely be called a book at all (and by extension does not deserve the extra legal
protection and leeway accorded to the book under the laws of the Third Republic).[15] It is nothing but a series of nude photographs strung together with the
author's commentary.[16] Ulbach, like many of his contemporaries, uses the photograph to mark out the *definitive* space of obscenity, be it written or visual. Whereas
books are open to different interpretations and cannot be summarily dismissed
as obscene, a photograph cannot hide its meaning. And this novel, according to
Ulbach, was as explicit as a photograph, regardless of whether it actually contained photographic illustrations in its pages.[17]

Ulbach's review highlights an essential problem plaguing his contemporaries, who, like Pontmartin, described Zola's novel as pornographic. *Nana* bears
little resemblance in style or content to contemporary pornographic broadsheets
and newspapers, which were filled with puns and scatological humor.[18] As for the
contemporary pornographic literature, which emphasized specific female sexual
types (to which Nana does not readily conform), orgies, rape, incest, and deflow-
ering of virgins, *Nana* shares only its minor lesbian subplot with these novels and
very little else; these texts make Zola's heroine look like a paragon of virtue by
comparison.[19] On the other hand, *Nana* does have its own peculiarities, one of
which is the constant exhibition of Nana's nude body so oft remarked by irate
reviewers. Ulbach's accusation is scandalous, but it is also illuminating. While
the novel's plot and style distinguish it from contemporary written pornography,

the visual descriptions of Nana's body throughout the novel allude to common motifs of contemporary photographic nudity.[20] The result of Zola's use of photography, however, is not a collection of obscene photographs, but a novel in which both form and content indict a sexual economy, operating from the top of society downward, in which women are dispossessed of their bodies as those same sexualized bodies circulate for sale in myriad forms. By portraying his eponymous courtesan as a photographic pinup, Zola links prostitution and photographic nudity, just as did so many of his contemporaries. But unlike those contemporaries, Zola's novel presents them not merely as two interconnected vices to be eliminated but as components of a larger—and highly problematic—socio-sexual economic system. And while the novel is set in the Second Empire, neither its imagery nor the system it denounces disappeared in 1870. The novel's photographic allusions thus broaden the scope of its critique from the Second Empire to include the Third Republic. Zola lays bare all of society's sexual hypocrisy along with his heroine's body, condemning not so much Nana or the brute sexuality she incarnates, but the wealthy men who consume her.

✒ Photography as a Marker of Socio-sexual Status ✒

The novel contains four explicit references to photographs, which, at first glance, do not necessarily suggest a connection between *Nana* and photographic nudity. Modeling is not among the pantheon of Nana's sins, nor do window displays of scantily clad women ever mar her frequent promenades in the Passage des Variétés (although the window of Nana's dressing room later in the novel does look out over the terrace of a photographer).[21] Indeed, in three cases Nana is not even depicted in the photographs. Photography first appears in the opening chapter, at the height of Nana's acclaim as an actress. Between the two acts of Nana's theatrical debut in *La Blonde Vénus*, the minor male character Hector de la Faloise studies "photographs of actresses, in frames alternating with the mirrors, between the columns" in the Théâtre des Variétés, a gallery of portraits from which Nana's is conspicuously absent.[22] Later, after Nana has run off with the actor Fontan, she and Satin pay a visit to one Madame Robert, a bourgeois and respectable married woman who had refused a dinner invitation from Nana, and Nana examines her photographic portrait with a flash of recognition.[23] Then, when Nana is forced to return to streetwalking and is terrified of arrest, Satin tries to convince her to sleep with police officers to obtain protection, telling her that there are "certain lists of women, accompanied with photographs, that police agents must consult, with a prohibition against ever touching them."[24] Here again, however, Nana's image is also missing; she is a part of this catalog of female flesh (and that in the theater) only by association. In the final instance, Nana herself is finally captured on camera. Having left Fontan and returned to acting, Nana agrees to become Count Muffat's kept woman. Her social profile is elevated immensely: "Her photographs were displayed in shop windows, she was discussed in the newspapers. When she passed in her carriage on the boulevards, the crowd turned around and pronounced her name."[25] Nana's solo photograph, displayed in shop windows for all of Paris to see, signifies the apex of her career as a demimondaine.

None of these photographs is a nude, and only one actually depicts Nana. Yet all four are markers of the changes in Nana's socioeconomic status, which is throughout the novel intimately bound up with her sexual status. The photographs that link the economic and the sexual most directly are, of course, those that exempt prostitutes from prosecution. These photographs directly facilitate the economic exploitation of the sexualized female body. The others, however, are no less tainted. Despite Pontmartin's protestations, the actress's portraits cannot escape an association with prostitution, as the reader is reminded every time the director Bordenave insists on referring to the Variétés as his "brothel."[26] As it turns out, Madame Robert, despite her wealth and respectability, frequents the same lesbian café as Nana and Satin during Nana's nadir as a street prostitute and solicits sex from Satin.[27] And Nana's portrait in the window is even more entangled in the economics of sex, as it is the result (and a reflection) of her success as a courtesan, her ascent to a higher rung on the ladder of prostitution. These photographs may not depict naked bodies, but each one represents a different step in Nana's progress through the many professions that make women's bodies available for sexual pleasure (or, in the case of Madame Robert, points to Nana's lesbianism while also indicting a hypocrisy of which Nana herself is notably innocent). All of the social roles to which these photographs correspond—an actress, a depraved "honest woman," a prostitute, or a demimondaine—function literally and metaphorically through the consumption of the female body by desiring masses, which is precisely what the photograph facilitates when it *is* obscene. These four brief mentions of photography already hint at the link that the novel will forge between photographic representation and sex for sale.

Indeed, on closer examination, three of these photographs are more directly implicated in the commerce of nude photographs than they might otherwise immediately appear to be. Both the portraits of the actresses at the Variétés and Nana's portrait in the window of the photography shop participate in the massive Second Empire economy of legal photographic portraits that were not always in very good taste and, not infrequently, exposed quite a bit of skin, such as the infamous ones of Rigolboche deplored by the Goncourts. Because the novel does not elaborate on the content of the portraits hanging in the Variétés, we are left to surmise that these photographs may well have conjured up the more scandalous images of actresses in tights and formfitting maillot. Nana's portrait recalls Pélin's lament about shop windows during the Second Empire: "Who of us has not seen the noble faces of virgins, of empresses, exhibited pell-mell next to nude courtesans?"[28] Given her sexual exploits, the reader would not be entirely remiss in assuming that Nana's photograph might well be one of the more risqué images of demimondaines showing a bit too much *décolleté* that abounded in photography shops. Indeed, hers might even be part of a supply of Nana erotica available behind the counter. Finally, the photographs of the prostitutes kept by the police are even more closely connected to photographic nudity. *Nana* is set during the Second Empire, when, as previously discussed, both prostitution and photographic nudity were regulated with similar police record keeping, and photographic nudity subsequently migrated from the pages of the BB3 to the BB1. In this context, the lists kept by the police in *Nana*, which use the photograph to perpetuate rather than prevent prostitution, almost necessarily conjure up the (entirely plausible) possibility of large official registers filled with nude or seminude photographs of women who had sold themselves for protection. The photographs in *Nana*, then, are tainted by their relationship to the economics of sex more generally and sexually explicit photographic representation more particularly. The fact that these photographs indicate Nana's changing fortunes throughout the novel—even when they are not actually photographs of her—emphasizes just how important the convergence of photographic visuality and sexual availability will be to her story.

Nana as *Nudité*

From the moment when Nana first appears on stage at the Théâtre des Variétés, moreover, the novel forges an even more substantive connection between Nana and nude photography. Even before the curtain rises for *La Blonde Vénus*, the opening pages are littered with the verb *voir* (to see), whetting the reader's appetite for a glimpse of its star: "They wanted to see Nana," Zola writes. The director Bordenave says, "You will see"; the journalist Fauchery says, "I have never seen her"; the banker Steiner, on the other hand, claims, "I've seen her somewhere."[29] From the outset, Nana is an object to behold. Everyone desires to see her and wonders if they already have. These acts of looking are amplified throughout the evening, until Nana finally makes her long-awaited appearance. Little wonder, then, that scholars have already connected this scene to other kinds of visual representation and consumption of the body, including nude paintings and erotic theater.[30] In addition to these other visual subtexts, the spectacle of Nana's unveiling at the Variétés establishes the photographic nude as the dominant representational mode governing the display of Nana's body, both in its staging and in the relationship between that body and the eyes of the men who look at it:

> A shiver stirred the room. Nana was naked. She was naked with tranquil audacity, certain of the omnipotence of her flesh. A simple gauze enveloped her; her round shoulders, her amazon bosom whose pink tips were erect and rigid as lances, her large hips that swayed with a voluptuous rocking motion, the blonde flesh of her thighs, could be divined, could be seen through the delicate foamy whiteness of the fabric. It was Venus being born from the waves, with nothing but her hair for a veil. And, when Nana lifted her arms, the golden fuzz in her armpits was visible in the glare of the footlights. There was no applause. Nobody was laughing anymore, the faces of the men, serious, were straining forward, their noses thinned, their mouths irritated and parched.[31]

Nana certainly satisfies Paris' curiosity. In the second act of the play, she takes the stage nude but for a gauze tunic. Transparent gauze notwithstanding (or indeed, all the more so because of it), Zola's description embodies a specific kind of nudity that defines Nana from this moment forward. In his preparatory notes, Zola thrice reminded himself that the purpose of this scene was not simply to introduce Nana, naked or otherwise, but "to pose Nana well as a nudity [*bien poser Nana comme nudité*]."[32] Zola there used the word nudity in a very particular way. He was not going to represent Nana "in her nudity," but "as a nudity," that is, as an object separate from Nana's substantiated self, rather than a state of that self. This usage of the word was common Second Empire shorthand for photographic obscenity, used in newspaper accounts and even by Disdéri in his polemic against the photographic nude.[33] In other words, Nana arrives not simply as a naked woman but as a nudity, a posed and explicit representation of the naked body.

To effect the transformation of Nana into a nudity, the scene at the Variétés exploits the visual language of the photograph. It records every detail of Nana's body, from "her amazon bosom" and its immodest "pink tips" to the "blond flesh" of her thighs, with the meticulous precision unique to the photographic medium. All of her womanly forms are revealed to the reader, peeking indecently through the "foamy whiteness" of her costume. Perhaps most significant among these details is the one that seems at first glance to be the least erotic: the hair under Nana's arms. Few women have pubic hair in painted nudes—it is conspicuously absent or strategically concealed—but they do in nearly all nude photographs in the nineteenth century. More than any other aspect of her description, this small detail locates Nana's body squarely in the representational realm of photography. On a theoretical level, it participates in what was, for the Goncourt brothers, the defining characteristic of the obscene photographic aesthetic, epitomized for them by the morbid and "voluptuous" foot.[34] And while Nana's fuzz seems to be an intimate detail rather than a strictly sexual one, it is a convenient substitute for the more dangerous pubic hair that Zola does not mention and that is always present in nineteenth-century photographic nudes. The exposure of Nana's downy armpits along with the rest of her body renders that body fundamentally photographic.

This kind of uncomfortably accurate description was not unique to Zola's representation of his nude heroine; it is characteristic of his prose style more generally. When Nana appears at the Variétés, however, the photographic qualities of his gaze are amplified by allusions to various compositional tropes of nude photography. Nana's enticing transparent veil, which adds to her allure precisely by veiling nothing, is one of the most common props in Second Empire nude photographs, both legal and illegal.[35] A number of authorized and unauthorized nudes from this period perfectly illustrate Zola's debt to photography. In a stereoscopic daguerreotype produced by Braquehais in the 1850s, a woman stands

[FIGURE 73]

Bruno Braquehais, ca. 1854.
Stereoscopic daguerreotype.
J. Paul Getty Museum, Los Angeles.

[FIGURE 74]
Félix Jacques Antoine Moulin,
Étude photographique, 1853.
Salt print from glass collodion negative.
Bibliothèque nationale de France.

as Nana might, with "tranquil audacity," her arms up and, thanks to the image's meticulous coloring, with her breasts showing their "pink tips." The transparent gauze enveloping her body conceals little (Figure 73). A legal photograph from the same time period by Moulin closely mimics the presentation of Nana, even in the way the model knowingly meets the viewer's gaze (Figure 74). There are countless other such images in the photographic record of the Empire (see, e.g.,

Figures 1 and 14). Although she is on stage at the Variétés rather than standing in front of a camera, there can be no doubt that Nana is styled as a photograph. Bordenave, whom Zola also describes in his notes as "posing Nana," who insists on calling the theater his brothel, and who advertises Nana on the streets of Paris, is as much Nana's photographer as her director and pimp.[36] The debut that the director orchestrates for his protégée represents the birth of a new kind of photographic Venus, forcing readers to acknowledge that their contemporary Venuses were real women, watched, looked at, observed, and desired through photographs.

In this scene, the novel even begins to sound like the Second Empire art critics who wrote about photographic nudes. An 1854 review by Charles Gaudin of a photograph by Claudet describes the image in the following terms: "Here is another masterpiece: it's a young woman whose head is covered in a long veil that descends around her body, whose delicate forms it outlines. Her graceful face alone is revealed, but the veil is so light, so transparent, that it reveals glimpses of what it is supposed to conceal."[37] Gaudin stops short of enumerating the details of the "delicate forms" that are accentuated by the gauze, where Zola specifies the contours of Nana's body that can be divined through it, but the two both identify the same mesmerizing allure of the transparent fabric that lets one see precisely what it should hide.[38] It is almost as though Zola, like Gaudin, had a photograph in front of him when he wrote the scene from which he somehow appropriated not only the style and the tropes but also the unique visual qualities resulting from the combination of the two, transferring them wholesale into the pages of his novel.

Zola's text is as attuned to the modes of perceiving the naked body as it is to modes of reproducing it. In Nana's Venus, Zola produces both a nude photograph and a reflection on the act of looking at such a photograph. The nudity at the Variétés literalizes what Abigail Solomon-Godeau has described as the "staging of desire" that occurs in erotic and obscene photographs because of their implication in "the structures of fantasy."[39] Nana reenacts just such a fantasy, with the physical stage on which Nana appears taking the place of the frame of the photograph. This kind of staging demands a spectator, for the very ontology of the erotic image (photographic or otherwise) depends on both the spectator and the desire that the spectator feels on beholding the staged body. Zola, having posed Nana (or used Bordenave to pose her) like a photograph, does not neglect this audience. He meditated his spectators' responses just as carefully in his preparatory notes as he did Nana's nudity: "To pose her well, as a nudity, in the first performance, all of the room inflamed for the cunt [cul]; in a great heat—She is the *flesh* at the center."[40] If Nana is a "nudity," then it is essential that those around respond to her as such, as an object of desire above all else, and this is precisely how the audience behaves at the Variétés:

> Little by little, Nana had taken control of the public, and now every man was enslaved. Lust flowed from her as from an animal in heat, spreading until it filled the theater. At this moment, her slightest movements fanned the flames of desire, she ruled men's flesh with a gesture of her little finger. Backs arched, quivering as though invisible violin bows had been drawn over their muscles, the napes of necks showed downy hair blown about under the warm errant breath from one knew not which woman's mouth. Fauchery saw in front of him the truant schoolboy lifted from his seat with passion. He had the curiosity to look at the Count de Vandeuvres, very pale, his lips pinched, the fat Steiner, whose apoplectic face was bursting, Labordette ogling with the astonished air of a horse dealer who admires a perfect mare, Daguenet whose ears filled with blood and twitched with pleasure. Then an instinct made him glance behind, and he was astonished by what he saw in the Muffat's box: behind the countess, white and serious, the count held himself erect, mouth agape, his face mottled with red splotches; while, close to him, in the shadows, the cloudy eyes of the Marquis de Chouard had become two cat eyes, phosphorescent and flecked with gold.[41]

From the parched mouths when Nana first takes the stage to the phosphorescent cat eyes of the Marquis de Chouard, the reader actually sees very little of Nana's body compared to how much we see of the male desire inspired by that body. An exhaustive compilation of symptoms of sexual excitement are exposed in the public space of the Théâtre des Variétés: altered breathing, diverted blood flow, goose bumps. Daguenait's ears are clearly not the only things in the room that "filled with blood and twitched with pleasure." These men have not, for the most part, ever met or seen Nana before. Yet each one of them responds as though her nudity is staged for him alone. They enact one of the primal fantasies of the erotic image: that the naked woman depicted therein, a total stranger, exists only for the eyes of the particular man looking at her, even while hundreds or thousands of other eyes are doing the same. Their eyes, glued to Nana as if to a stereograph or to the star of an early peep show, do even more than the staging of her body to insist that Nana is a sexualized visual object.

Nana's spectators surround her in a public cloud of mass desire that eradicates individual difference. The men are reduced to their conditioned sexual responses, all basically identical, and Nana herself is reduced to little more than a sexual force. She is a "beast," an embodiment of pure lust, an everywoman, or, at least, the incarnation of every woman desired by a man; her sexuality radiates out like a breath caressing them from "one knew not which woman's mouth." No longer Nana, Bordenave's long-awaited protégée, under the gaze of these men, she becomes instead the anonymous object of their undifferentiated desire. The loss of her individual identity mimics what occurs in obscene and erotic photography, where the body is reproduced for the pleasure of so many eyes that the particular person represented therein is subsumed into the general category of "sexually available woman." Her objectification also implicates the women around her. As much as she stands apart from the other actresses, who remain in their clothes on stage and whose photographic portraits can be contemplated without eliciting this kind (or perhaps degree) of reaction, Nana's exhibition must reflect back on them. Fully undressed or not, they are still on display in much the same way. In some sense, any one of them could be Nana, depending on how they are presented and who is looking at them.

After this explosive debut, Nana goes on to reenact other distinctive scenes from nude photography. When the prince and Count Muffat interrupt her, "nude down to her waist," changing in her dressing room, and then watch with visible excitement while she wanders around "in her drawers in the middle of these men," putting on makeup and changing into her gauze tunic to go on stage, it is as if they are walking in on one of the wildly popular stereographs of women dressing or undressing (see, e.g., Figures 6, 23, 28, and 29).[42] Then, just after leaving Nana's dressing room, Muffat again watches Nana naked on stage, a redundancy that reinforces the photographic qualities of her first appearance. Backstage, an increasingly agitated Muffat "put[s] his eye to a hole," like a stereoscope, and sees her body come into focus as a pale splotch against the "somber" background of the theater through a photographic trick of distorted perspective: "Nana stood out in white, enlarged, blocking the boxes from the balcony to the fly loft. He saw her from behind, her lower back taut, her arms outstretched."[43] Finally, Nana's lesbian relationship with Satin also has a counterpart in the vast array of lesbian-themed photographs produced in the mid- and late nineteenth century (see, e.g., Figures 17, 33, and 34). It, too, becomes a visual spectacle for Nana's male lovers when they watch one night in mock shock as the two women, sharing a bite of pear, "finished up the fruit in a kiss."[44] Rather than becoming more of a human being over the course of the novel, Nana becomes more and more of a "nudity," a photographically figured representation of the body avidly consumed by the men around her.

Some of these subjects were not unique to photography, appearing as situations in pornographic literature of the time as well. Most significantly, Nana's lesbian affair with Satin does have literary precedent, as does one of the most infamous scenes in the novel, in which Nana's lover, Count Muffat, watches her masturbate to her reflected image. The genesis of that scene, however, provides another example of how Zola's novel situates the representation of Nana's body in the photographic tradition. Zola's preparatory notes indicate that the idea for the scene came (as did many others) from an anecdote of his friend Henry Céard about a courtesan named Lucie Lévy. In Céard's version of the scene, Lucie's lover reclines on a low couch smoking endless cigarettes while Lucie admires herself in the mirror:

> While her lover, on a low sofa, stretched out while smoking dreamy ciga-
> rettes, she, legs in mauve stockings halfway up her thighs, boots buttoned
> to the middle of her legs, stomach nude, torso nude, chest nude, she ap-
> proached the armoire mirror and smiled at the reflection of her beauty
> that shone pink from the flames of a great fire behind her. And gently, as
> though savoring the splendor of her body, lost in the contemplation of
> the perfect lines of her flesh, with a voluptuous gesture she sent herself
> adoring salvos of kisses. Little by little, little by little her hand descended,
> and while her face took on a sensual pained expression, in the double-
> beveled mirror were her rounded fingers, and the lesbian grace of an
> obscene Venus de Medici.[45]

The masturbating woman appears in pornographic literature going back at least as far as Jean-Baptiste de Boyer d'Argens' 1740 novel *Thérèse Philosophe*, and Céard's description places Lucie Lévy squarely into that tradition. In it, Lucie's lover is present, but mentally absent. Lost in his "dreamy cigarettes," he leaves her to her own devices. Rather than focusing on Lucie's half-undressed body, Céard concentrates instead on the progression of Lucie's actions: self-admiration, narcissistic kisses, her hand descending, the expression that passes across her face. Although the scene presumes a male viewer, he fades into the background, overshadowed by Lucie's sexual behaviors and by the emphasis on masturbation as autoerotic lesbianism.

The episode is completely transformed in the pages of Zola's novel. While Zola clearly used Céard's notes, he significantly expands the scene and, most importantly, alters the perspective. He begins, like Céard, with a description of Nana playing with her reflection in the mirror, but his version luxuriates in the details:

> Nana had become absorbed in the rapture of herself. She bent her neck,
> looking closely in the mirror at a small brown mark above her right hip,
> and she touched it with the tip of her finger, she made it stand out by

bending further backward, without a doubt finding it funny and pretty. Then, amused, she studied other parts of her body, retaken by her perverted childhood curiosity. [. . .] Slowly, she opened her arms to stretch her plump Venus' torso, she twisted this way and that, examining herself front and back, stopping at the profile of her bosom and the fleeting contours of her thighs.[46]

In Zola's reimagining, the visual dominates all else; we must see every posture, each part of her body that she herself beholds. Zola may have taken the conceit from Céard, but his execution once again recalls the photographic record. Photographs of women admiring themselves in the mirror, or with mirrors strategically arranged so as to reveal their backs while they still looked at the camera, are a staple of Second Empire (and early Third Republic) photographic nudity (see, e.g., Figures 4 and 25). Women were, of course, depicted looking in mirrors in paintings as well, notably, in two paintings by Manet that are roughly contemporary with the novel (and have also been connected to the earlier episode in Nana's dressing room): *Nana* (1876) and *Before the Mirror* (1880).[47] In Zola's mirror scene, however, the staging of Nana's body and the perspective of the viewer are uncannily similar to a series of 1856 half-stereographs by Louis Camille d'Olivier. D'Olivier's photographs illustrate Zola's description from Nana's self-adoration in the mirror (Figure 75) through her turn toward self-pleasure, as, "one arm behind the nape of her neck, one hand held in the other, she threw her head back, with her elbows out, [. . .] her eyes half shut, her mouth half open, her face bathed in an amorous laugh" (Figure 76).[48] Just as when she is on stage at the Variétés, moreover, the tableau is filled with small photographic details about Nana's body, "her solid lower back, her firm warrior's bosom with its strong muscles showing below the satin texture of her skin," and her most distinctive trait, the hair that always reappears in descriptions of her body, "a rosy down [that] made her body like velour."[49] Nana vivifies d'Olivier's still images, fulfilling what is only potential in the photographs. She is like a primitive film reel, stringing together a series of erotic snapshots so that they emerge in space and time rather than simply in the flat two-dimensionality of photosensitized paper.

Once again, moreover, Zola's grasp of photography's visual regime extends to the role of the spectator. Unlike Lucie's lover, Count Muffat is fixated on Nana, and his perspective comes to dominate Zola's narrative. As he scrutinizes Nana's every movement, he oscillates between desire and repulsion. It is at this moment in the novel that Nana is famously described as the "golden beast."[50] In Muffat's eyes, she is reduced to nothing more than her animal sex lurking under "fleshy bulges cut with deep folds, which gave her sex the troubling veil of their shadow,"

[FIGURE 75]

Louis Camille d'Olivier, 1856.
Half-stereograph salt print
from glass collodion negative.
Bibliothèque nationale de France.

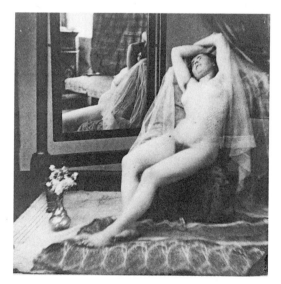

[FIGURE 76]

Louis Camille d'Olivier, 1856.
Half-stereograph salt print
from glass collodion negative.
Bibliothèque nationale de France.

and she takes on the proportions of a monster.[51] Yet he cannot look away, and under his half-spellbound, half-horrified gaze, Nana finally achieves an orgasm:

> Nana was curling up on herself. A shiver of tenderness seemed to have passed through her limbs. Her eyes misty, she was making herself smaller, as though to feel herself better. Then, she opened her hands, sliding them down along herself to her breasts, which she crushed in a nervous embrace. And throwing herself open, melting into a caress of her entire body, she rubbed her cheeks on the left and the right against her shoulders, affectionately, cajolingly. Her lustful mouth blew desire over her body. She pouted her lips, she gave herself a long kiss near her armpit, all the while laughing at the other Nana who, too, kissed herself in the mirror.[52]

Literary precedent aside, masturbation was even more closely associated with photographic representation than mirrors were. In the history of visual culture, the masturbating woman was a new motif, and one that was inextricably linked to photography. According to Abigail Solomon-Godeau, it originates with the medium, like the "beaver shot" of which it is a variation (see, e.g., Figure 19).[53] Of course, neither Nana's masturbation nor her mirror gazing was Zola's invention; they were allegedly taken from real events, not from written or photographic representations. Zola's novel, however, transposes Céard's "true story" into the visual domain in such a way as to align both mirrors and masturbation with photography. The transformation is underpinned by what Solomon-Godeau, in distinguishing the photograph from earlier forms of erotic visuality, describes as "the sexual constituted as a visual field rather than an activity as such."[54] The absentminded lover is replaced by the transfixed and omnipresent viewer-reader. The narrative action, propelled by the movement of the descending hand, is replaced by visual allusions to sexual gratification: Nana curled up, Nana crushing her breasts in an embrace, Nana melting into a postmasturbatory caress that looks like yet another suggestive photograph by d'Olivier of a woman reclining with her hand over her pubis (Figure 77). From beginning to end, Nana's pleasure is orchestrated not around the sequence of her actions but for the best display of her body, whether for her eyes, Muffat's, or the reader's. And at the very end of the scene, rather than leaving Nana basking in autoerotic satisfaction the text once again returns to the photographic conceit with which the entire scene began: the literally self-reflexive act of Nana looking at herself in the mirror (Figure 78). Wherever Nana begins, whatever she does, she always ends up as a photograph.

The reader's experience of watching Nana look at (and become a photograph of) herself is brilliantly lampooned in a contemporary cover image of *La Carica-*

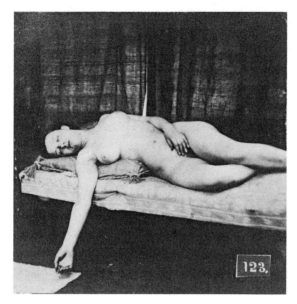

[FIGURE 77]
Louis Camille d'Olivier, 1856.
Half-stereograph salt print
from glass collodion negative.
Bibliothèque nationale de France.

[FIGURE 78]
Louis Camille d'Olivier, 1856.
Half-stereograph salt print
from glass collodion negative.
Bibliothèque nationale de France.

ture from January 1880, before the serial had been completed but when debate over the novel had already begun to rage (Figure 79). Nana is pictured in her customary state of bare-shouldered semiundress, leaning over a strange machine with a protruding tube, like a phonograph, but which also has an image of a similarly attired woman attached to the top, like a stereoscope. The image has a caption, "Chez Nana," and the machine's tag identifies it as a "Photo-Phonographe." The text below it reads,

> Do you know the Society of *photo-phonographs* for *naturalist novelists?* It is a very anonymous Society that takes care of secretly placing photo-phonographs in individuals' homes: these indiscreet instruments collect everything that is said, photograph everything that is done and report it to naturalist novelists. At a soirée hosted by M. Emile Zola, the MASTER deigned to demonstrate the functions of his phonographs of 1879 for us. The handle was turned by the hands of the famous NANA, of whom we are happy to give the first portrait. Caution! M. Zola's phonographs will talk.

The satirical photo-phonograph revives a running joke about the efforts of naturalist writers to capture reality, and the explicative text focuses not on the images but rather on the sound recordings that Zola's strange machine will capture. The text also states, however, that the photo-machine will provide the first accurate portrait of Nana, and this is of greater significance. In the caricature, Nana is presumably looking at this very photographic portrait. The photograph is not sketched out clearly, but she is obviously scantily clad and the holder into which the image is placed evokes that of a stereoscope. For contemporaries, it was evidently quite obvious that the novel's nude aesthetics were taken from photography.

Although it is humorous, the cover of *La Caricature* illustrates a very serious consequence of Nana-as-photograph. In the scene where Nana looks at herself, the juxtaposition of mirrors and masturbation simultaneously establishes the obscene aesthetic of Zola's description and reflects Nana's self-desire back to its source. Nana is both acting out photographic obscenity as Count Muffat watches and playing the part of the man who is aroused by looking at such scenes. In other words, her act of masturbation does not depict her own sexual arousal; it mirrors the desire of the men who look at her. Nana has no identity, no interiority. Unlike Lucie, who pleasures herself while her lover's attention is engaged elsewhere, Nana is merely a photographic phantasm, trapped performing the scenes of other people's desires—*never* her own. She does not even have a narrative, for that, too, is a projection of fantasy, a way to progress from one carefully posed "nudity" to another. Like Baudelaire's beheaded woman, she embodies

"Nana-Revue," *La Caricature*, 3 January 1880.

the fundamental rift between a body that is desired and one that signifies, between what is natural and what is human, as laid bare by photography. This is the source of Muffat's growing horror as he stares at Nana's body. That body—and the brute force of its sexuality—does not belong to Nana but to those who look at and stage her. Muffat's horror is the horror of recognition. It is not her sex but rather his desire that is destroying him.

☜ Sex, Class, and Nana's Photographic Body ☞

Photographic allusions aside, the mirror scene has long been the source of debate over the socioeconomic ramifications of Nana's rapacious sexuality. Zola famously wrote of the novel, "The subject of the novel is this: All of society in heat for a cunt [*cul*]."[55] Nana's sexuality is, indeed, a social issue and, more particularly, a class issue. Muffat, in part, becomes terrified of Nana's body in this scene because he has just read the famous article by the journalist Fauchery in which Nana is described as a "golden fly" produced in the Parisian slums who has come to infect Paris: "She avenged the abandoned ones of whom she was the product. With her, the filth that was left to ferment among the people rose up and contaminated the aristocracy."[56] In his reading of Fauchery's article, Peter Brooks directly connects Nana's sexuality to her lower-class origins in the text: "She is the product of the proletariat, of four or five generations of alcoholics, who represents physical and social degeneracy in the 'nervous disorder of her sex'. [. . .] One notes the equation, typical in Zola, between a strong female sexuality and the lower classes: the body as a source of class confusion, of potential revolution, as an object of fear."[57] Similarly, Charles Bernheimer, while marking a distinction between Nana as a "good girl" and Nana as sex, as nothing more than her "cunt" (with the cunt being the locus of Nana's destructiveness), also emphasizes her place in contemporary conservative discourse about the social problem of (lower-class) prostitution.[58] The novel does seems to express a fear of Nana's sexuality that is filtered through her socioeconomic position. There is certainly no question that Nana wreaks havoc on the upper classes. The end of the novel is replete with language of economic catastrophe, as she spreads financial ruin and runs through the fortunes of every male character in the novel: "This was the period of her existence when Nana illuminated Paris with redoubled splendor. She loomed on the horizon of vice, she dominated the city with the insolent display of her luxury, with her disdain for money, which made her publicly destroy entire fortunes."[59] Nana's lovers finish dead, bankrupt, or both, and as "the growing needs of her luxury enraged her appetites, she finished men off in a single bite."[60] She is a superb figure of class revenge, terrifying reviewers like Pontmartin, who were as taken aback by the novel's class implications (particularly the suggestion that middle-class institutions like the theater were the site of sexual class warfare) as they were by its nudity.

That the ruin brought down by Nana is so explicitly financial, however, suggests that the economics of sex are just as much at issue as the class status (or the monstrous force) of her own sexuality. In this sense, class or, at least, wealth comes to be of the utmost importance, but not necessarily in the way that Brooks and Bernheimer argue it is. In all her guises, as actress, prostitute, or photograph, Nana is something more than sex: she is sex for sale, sex transformed into an economic force. It is this convergence of sexual desire and economic power that is eating away at French society, not sex alone. The market dynamics of sex in the novel, moreover, are propelled not by Nana herself but by the men who desire her and have the financial means to consume her. These men are no less "beasts" than she is; as Zola would declare in May 1880, "If we are curious, if we peek through the cracks, I suspect that we will see amongst the distinguished classes, what we see amongst the people, for the human beast is the same everywhere; only its clothing changes."[61] Just as Muffat realizes with horror while watching Nana in the mirror, the point is precisely that Nana's sexuality has no class or, rather (and worse still), that the beast within the lower-class Nana is the same as that within the wealthy Muffat. In the context of the novel's sexual economics, therefore, Nana's destructive sexuality implicates less the lower class from which she hails than the upper echelon of the social structures rising above her. Again, in his preparatory notes, Zola would write, "Nana, she's the filth from below, *l'Assommoir*, standing up and corrupting the upper classes, you allow this ferment to be born, it rises up and then disorganizes you."[62] This language echoes Fauchery's newspaper article but clarifies the novel's perspective significantly. Even as the text expresses anxiety about the destructive effects of working-class sexuality, it also—perhaps even more forcefully—denounces the workings of a social system in which the upper classes are satisfied that their economic power constitutes moral superiority and leave those below to rot. *Nana* demonstrates that money, class, social status, and control of the economic system in which sexuality is deployed do not inoculate the upper classes against the ill effects of that system. Their fall into financial ruin is simply all the more spectacular when, prey to the same vices and desires as the lower classes, they cannot disentangle sex and money.[63]

Nana's photographic aesthetic is not the only evidence that Zola's novel condemns a system of sexual commerce that operates from the top of society down. Zola's critique of prostitution operates in essentially the same vein. After all, even if Nana were not represented through the photographic lens, she would still be a courtesan whose social trajectory is entirely dependent on the men who offer her fortunes to consume in a single bite. The novel's photographic aesthetic amplifies the critique of prostitution by serving as a constant and inescapable reminder that Nana is not a person but rather a thing passed from hand to hand and eye to gawking eye. It is also a reminder of the growing entanglement of the two forms of sexual exploitation that determine Nana's identity. Zola's novel both registers the historical reality of the ties between prostitution and photographic obscenity and marks out an even more fundamental theoretical connection between the two. In *Nana*, prostitution and photographic nudity are equated not because the photographic model is a prostitute (as some argued in the Second Empire) or because prostitutes use photography to sell their bodies (as was increasingly true during the Third Republic) but because they are two sides of the same coin circulating in the contemporary sexual marketplace. They both participate in a system that functions by dispossessing women of their own agency and of the bodies they are selling, whether those women are paid for sex or reproduced ad infinitum to be sold as a simulacrum of themselves.

The disruptive political implications of this critique are clarified by a brief reference to nude photography—the only explicit reference to such images in Zola's fiction—in another novel from the Rougon-Macquart cycle, *La Fortune des Rougon*. In the midst of the 1851 coup d'état, as Pierre Rougon seizes the opportunity to take control of the mayor's office, his compatriot Vuillet grasps for his own position of power. Vuillet is one of the most morally dubious characters in the novel, "a figure of damp palms, of sleazy glances," who has made his money keeping a bookstore that specializes in religious texts and devout imagery.[64] As he watches the insurgency from his window, Vuillet observes the director of the post office being arrested by revolutionaries and seizes his opportunity:

> So too, in the morning, at the same moment when Rougon was seating himself in the mayor's armchair, he had gone to tranquilly install himself in the director's office. He knew the employees; he had received them upon their arrival, telling them that he would replace their director until his return, and that they would have nothing to worry about. Then he had gone rummaging around in the morning post with a poorly disguised curiosity; he was sniffing out the letters; he seemed to be looking for one in particular. Without a doubt, his new situation answered one of his secret plans, for he went so far, in his contentment, as to give one of his employees a copy of the *Œuvres badines de Piron*. Vuillet had a well-stocked collection of obscene books, which he hid in a large drawer, under a layer of rosaries and holy images; it was he who inundated the town with shameful photographs and engravings, without that harming the sales of prayer books in the least.[65]

Vuillet is such an outrageous hypocrite that he verges on parody, hiding dirty books and photographs of naked ladies under rosaries and religious images and selling prayer books along with obscene photographs. He takes over the post office in a successful bid to protect his obscene commercial dealings from discovery. The example of Vuillet implies that, quite aside from disagreeing with its fundamental political principles, Zola conceives of the Empire as having been morally bankrupt and sexually hypocritical from its very inception, down to the most inconsequential of bureaucrats, the postal director in Plassans. Years later, *Nana* exposes this hypocrisy writ large. An empire in which positions of power are held by dealers in dirty photographs is also that in which citizens ogle the photographs sold by Vuillet and pay for sex with Nana, without any of these activities in any way endangering their social position.

From the Second Empire to the Third Republic

Ostensibly, this dark reality belongs to a different time than when Zola actually wrote *Nana*. Zola's topic is life under the Second Empire, not the Third Republic. Because Nana is rendered as a photograph, however, she becomes a Third Republic problem as much as, or even more than, an imperial one. Many aspects of the visual vocabulary of the commercial photographic nude change little from 1850 to 1900. The most popular props and poses from the Empire grace the thousands of cabinet cards for sale around the city in the 1880s, dominate the magazines of photographic nudes allegedly aimed at painters that proliferate after 1900 and even appear in the illustrated photo-novels of the fin de siècle (see, e.g., Figures 46, 59, 80, and 82). Nana's repertoire consists of many of these perennial favorites. If she was recognizable as a photographic image, she was also a disturbingly contemporary one, her nudity a harsh reminder of the continued and growing presence of the same depictions of the body in the Third Republic. Nor are the connections that Zola forges between prostitution and obscene photography merely relics of the Empire. Neither the trade in female flesh nor the trade in simulacra thereof were in any way stunted by the shift in political regimes in 1870. As the photograph became an increasingly dominant and disturbing presence on the streets of Paris during the Third Republic, its ties to prostitution were only strengthened. By cloaking the social problems of the Republic in the garb, or lack thereof, of the Empire, *Nana* revealed how little the two periods differed. And if the solution in the novel is disease and death, or purification through the cleansing destruction of war and regime change, that boded ill for the young Republic.

For all these reasons, if *Nana* is nothing more, in Ulbach's formulation, than a compendium of commentaries on illicit photographs, those commentaries constitute a scathing critique. They indict republican France for perpetuating the same political and social hypocrisy of the Empire and condemn Zola's elite contemporaries as little better than Vuillet, who seizes a government position the better to distribute his wares, or Muffat, who is destroyed by the animal lust he unsuccessfully disavows. The reaction against *Nana* confirms rather than refutes the accusation that the text levies against Zola's contemporaries, one that Zola had actually made even more explicitly elsewhere. In "La République et la littérature," Zola claimed that the republicans had sacrificed the truth in exchange for their political ascendancy. With particular prescience (the article appeared in the spring of 1879), Zola denounced idealist "Romantic" republicans for refusing to acknowledge reality and cynically deploying accusations of pornography against Naturalists to undermine their credibility: "They attempt to discredit them in throwing mud on their face, in treating them like sewer workers, pornographers, obscene novelists. [. . .] The Romantics believed one must embellish and arrange the documents of humanity for the pleasure and the profit of the nation."[66] He would later say the same of *Nana's* detractors.[67] When Zola stripped the truth bare—literally—even of the most delicate veil, critics of all political persuasions used accusations of pornography to cover it up again.

This brings us back to the many reviewers who were so disgusted by *Nana*. Even as Armand Pontmartin warned readers against it, he revealed that he did indeed recognize the truth in its pages, and its contemporary implications: "If society, if the bourgeoisie, if the theater, if the refined and lettered public, are really as the author of *Nana* paints them, the amnestied and the communards are right. [. . .] You are better off with blood than with obscenities, with fire than with filth; to suppress this deprivation, this infection, this pestilence, reforms will not be enough; one of these immense cataclysms that destroys in order to regenerate will not be too much."[68] This is exactly the book's dark message. Despite the blood and the political upheaval of the Commune, little had fundamentally changed in the transition from the Empire to the Republic. Obscenity, written and visual, was still everywhere. Prostitution was still commonplace. Yet perhaps what bothered many readers more than this harsh vision of reality was its assignment of blame. By the time the fuss over the novel had quieted down, it was clear that Nana's sin was not in taking her shirt off for Zola's camera but in implicating his readers as she did so. Nana held up a mirror in which they saw not her but themselves staring back at them. For it is precisely the educated and the elite who *are* responsible in the novel, rendering that social structure just as blighted as Pontmartin did not want it to be. It may well have been easier to for Zola's critics to decry *Nana* as a pornographic lie than to acknowledge the photographic accuracy of its unpleasant truth.

✒ CHAPTER 8 ✒

Maizeroy and the Feminist Photo-Novel

In 1897, the Paris publishing houses Offenstadt and Nilsson introduced a new product: a series of novels illustrated by photography, the first of their kind. Early the next year, an intrepid reporter from the *Mercure de France* surveyed a selection of contemporary authors on this daringly modern transformation of the book. One of those authors was Zola, who, despite deploying photographic aesthetics in service to social critique in *Nana*, resoundingly rejected the new genre. "The novel illustrated by photography," he declared, "will immediately slip into nudity."[1] Zola's response suggests not only that contemporary authors would not engage with photography for any motives other than prurience, but also that there was something in the very nature of the photographic process that lent itself to salacious nudity, and that the photo-novel would necessarily succumb to this pernicious tendency. Nor was Zola entirely wrong. While the full corpus of sixty-odd novels published between 1897 and 1908 is remarkably heterogeneous, it includes a number of sexually explicit texts adorned with nude illustrations. As a result, Zola's response has subsequently had a great influence on scholarship about the photo-novel, which generally corroborates his position and its equation of photography and obscenity.[2]

Yet while such a reading aligns with the growing anxiety at the end of the nineteenth century over the spread of photographic nudity as well as Zola's critique of nude photography in the pages of *Nana*, it also obscures the complexities of the photo-novels. The novels of the most prolific contributor to the genre, René Maizeroy, are a case study in these complexities. Though he is currently languishing in obscurity, Maizeroy, who was a disciple of Alphonse Daudet and a close friend of Guy de Maupassant (he may have been the model for *Bel-Ami*'s Duroy), was one of the most successful novelists of his time.[3] Born René Jules Jean Toussaint in Metz, Lorraine, on 2 May 1856, to a military family, Maizeroy was on the way to his own illustrious military career when the great success of his first collection of short stories, *Souvenirs d'un Saint-Cyrien,* in 1880, led him to literary endeavors.[4] Over the next three decades, Maizeroy wrote more than forty novels and a dozen short-story collections under a variety of pseudonyms, contributed to *Gil Blas, Le Figaro, La Vie moderne, Le Journal, La Presse, Fémina, Je sais tout, La Vie littéraire, La Grande Vie,* and *Les Annales politiques et littéraires,* and became literary director of *Le Matin* in 1909.[5] Maizeroy's penchant for the salacious resulted in two prosecutions for outrage aux bonnes mœurs, the first for a short story he wrote for *Gil Blas* in December 1880 (at the height of the pornography crisis), and the second for his 1885 Sapphic novel, *Les Deux Amies.*[6] His style and subject matter, however, were so varied — ranging from explicit eroticism to euphemistic libertine wit to moralizing realism — that a review of his 1888 hit *Petite Reine* asked in confusion, "To which school [of writers] does M. René Maizeroy belong? I hardly know anymore."[7]

Despite the reviewer's confusion, in the late 1880s Maizeroy settled into the style and readership that would define his career. He had developed his own strain of realism focused primarily on contemporary sexual mores. Maizeroy's style had origins in the eighteenth-century literary tradition of libertinage, in the nineteenth-century school of naturalism, and in his taste for contemporary scandal, but it became something else, what one reviewer called his own "elegant specialty," the "fin-de-siècle sensational novel of passion."[8] Maizeroy represented love and desire from a female perspective, and his unique brand of sensational novel became so popular among woman readers that from the late 1880s until his death, he was known as a "master feminist," his name synonymous with one kind of feminism of the period, a genre of writing for and about women.[9] He inspired what was described as "the nearly fanatical admiration" of his female readers, who were called the *Maizereines,* substituting *reine* (queen) for Maizeroy's *roi* (king).[10] King of this domain, Maizeroy was a cross between a literary guru and a rock star in his own time.

At the turn of the century, Maizeroy began to write extensively for the new network of photo-illustrated publications, publishing eleven photo-novels between 1898 and 1906. His photo-novels are just as concerned with sexual passion as his other works, and they make a significant contribution to his "feminist" corpus. Moreover, Maizeroy's "feminism" also played a central role in the way that his texts treat nude photography. In Maizeroy's novels, photography does fall easily into nudity, and his works contain some of the most explicit literary testimonies both to the pervasiveness of photographic nudity and to contemporary concerns about it. In his fiction, photography's distinctive exposure of the body is often associated with the worst kind of social degeneracy, and it inspires a dangerous and destabilizing sexualized gaze. Maizeroy's photo-novels, however, do not share this gaze. They deny their own photographic illustrations the privilege of representing sexual desire or even the nudity Maizeroy himself associates with the medium in his writings. Instead, any sexual content is limited entirely to the domain of the text, a text that focuses intently on female subjectivity and desire. By thus differentiating textual and visual modes of desire, Maizeroy's photo-novels present the photographic medium as appropriated by a (male) gaze that cannot comprehend (female) desire. In Maizeroy's work, only language is capable of rendering sexuality in the complex "feminist" terms so appreciated by his readers. His privileging of the feminine textual mode over the masculine photographic mode expands *Nana*'s critique of economics and sexual agency into an exploration of the intersection of gender, desire, and representation in a world saturated with photographic nudity.

◄ Nude Photography and Photographic Looking in Maizeroy ►

As discussed in Chapter 5, by the 1880s, the invention of the Kodak camera meant that the photograph could be a very personal object. In the world of Maizeroy's fiction, photography's function is inherently personal, its meaning determined by its place in the sentimental conflicts that propel his plots. These photographs are almost always portraits exchanged between lovers, and they mark the ebb and flow of sexual desire even when the images in question are not themselves explicit.[11] Portraits exchanged when love affairs start then sustain those relationships when lovers are separated.[12] Alternatively, as (male) attention wanders, photographs of new lovers betray their infidelity to their old loves.[13] And once all the many affairs have ended, the photographs that are left behind signify all the ways that love endures or fades.[14] Perhaps unsurprisingly, a number of the nudes that appear in his novels are personal photographs that function in much the same way as photographic portraits. In the photo-novel *Chérissime* (1901, republished without photographic illustrations as *Le Feu de joie* in 1909), the protagonist Solange discovers that her beloved Claude has been unfaithful by way of three incriminating photographs of her rival Simone, all inscribed to him with personal messages. In one of the portraits, Simone appears in her corset, "as though she was nude, her shoulders exposed, her breasts offered up in a little bit of gauze."[15] The short story "La Collection du Colonel," from *Au régiment* (1897), consists of a description of the quirks of Colonel Daument de Crosailles that culminates with his unique collection of photographs, made up of many nudes of his former lovers.[16] Finally, in the photo-novel *L'Amu-*

seuse, one of the heroine's clients shows her a stash of sentimental detritus (also of past loves) including letters and nude photographs.[17] These personal nudes fit neatly into the thematics of photography in Maizeroy's novels, which emphasizes the medium's important role in mediating sexual and sentimental relationships.

Personal photography, however, is not the only kind of nudity in Maizeroy's fiction. Casual allusions to commercially distributed nudes also pepper his novels. Suggestive photographs of popular actresses are displayed "in the windows of the passages, amongst these pretty girls who pull on their stockings in front of a mirror, smiling about who knows what kind of naughty dream and lacing their corsets in provocative poses."[18] These images are part of the visual phantasmagoria of the covered arcades, anchoring the *effet de réel* of Maizeroy's streetscape of nineteenth-century Paris. Similarly, commercially produced nudity often appears as a piquant detail in his sketches of military life. In the story, "La B'tite gommerce," photographs are peddled by a German Jew, Père Haarder, who travels from garrison to garrison buying and trading for various military items: "Among the lieutenants it was albums of Viennese photographs, collections of erotic nudities, that he most frequently traded for chipped sabers or tattered clothing."[19] Again, the salesman and his nudities are descriptive details meant to evoke the feeling of day-to-day life in the military, in turn suggesting just how common these kinds of objects were.

In a testament to their ubiquity, Maizeroy's fiction often scarcely seems to register the nude photographs hanging in shops or lurking in desk drawers as anything other than a fact of contemporary life. For the most part, they are presented to readers with a knowing wink and a smile. Yet Maizeroy also hints at the darker significance of nude photography by way of the kinds of looking those images inspire. The seemingly lighthearted, libertine story "Épreuves rigolos" is a perfect example of the kinds of insights masked by Maizeroy's worldly tone. In the story, a young count has an affair with a photographer's wife, occasionally meeting for trysts in her husband's studio. Yet despite the suggestive location, the count remains oblivious to the significance of her use of the nineteenth-century photographic catch phrase "*Ne bouge plus*" ("Don't move") during some of their more acrobatically amorous moments.[20] Years later, he becomes engaged to a young woman whose father has a taste for old books and "eighteenth-century erotic engravings."[21] The old man is convinced that he has seen his future son-in-law somewhere before, but cannot recall where—until he presents the count with an album of photographs. To his horror, the count discovers that

> I, myself, the count Jean de Valonnières, figured in the album; I appeared
> on every page, recognizable, striking, my feet up in the air, surprised in the

most tantalizing, the most lascivious poses. I appeared from the back, in a three-quarters shot, full-frontal and obviously compliant, a smile on my lips, pleasure in my eyes, bent, arched, swooning, victorious and pleading.

Oh, the shame! I had been the plaything of this bohemian couple, I had been used as a subject by a photographer in quest of tantalizing images and those prints had perhaps been sold by the hundreds, or the thousands, and were travelling the globe, being displayed on the tables of the best brothels.[22]

While the story's tone is flippant, the consequences of this involuntary foray into nude modeling are serious. "Épreuves rigolos" is at its heart a story about voyeurism (as I note in Chapters 2 and 5, fears about photographic voyeurism become increasingly common at the fin de siècle) and, as such, a story about the nature of looking as mediated through photography. The count is fooled because he doesn't understand who or what is looking at him, mistaking the gaze of the photographer and his camera for the gaze of a lover. His marriage prospects are then destroyed because of the people who consume the photographic representation of that mistaken gaze. Once captured on film, the count is defined by his photographic misstep. He will remain unmarriageable because he has been the object of the wrong kind of gaze. The story is funny because the count is a man, and normally these kinds of sexually determined acts of looking and their devastating consequences are reserved for women. Gender substitution aside, however, the dynamics of the erotic gaze in the story are no laughing matter. The count's misadventure suggests that once observed photographically, one is forever consigned to remain nothing more than that image of oneself.

Others of Maizeroy's stories are even more explicit about the harm of eroticized photographic looking. One of the best examples is his description of the bedroom of Colonel de Crosailles in the short story "La Collection du Colonel":

The colonel papered the walls of his room with a strange series of portraits annotated with dates and women's names. It was like a secret museum, erotic and monotone, of women's naked and dimpled bodies, photographed in the same callipygian pose wherein only their undulating buttocks and their shoulders swept by their thick hair could be seen. All of those whom he formed with his expert lessons, who passed through his alcove, who made him kneel at their feet are there, white and unsettling like vicious goddesses. And sometimes, without violating their secret, without naming them—does he even remember their names for that matter?—recognizing them once again from a forever-exposed fold of their skin, from a shadow, from a mole pricking the adorable line of a back or a round hip like a fly, the colonel recounts their stories, smiles at the memory of the most tender caresses, at the young woman from Bayonne he kidnapped during a change of garrisons as one affixes a boutonnière to one's buttonhole, at the devilish creole who imprisoned him in her hair in Mexico for three days and three nights, and at the temptress of a little countess under whose windows he always made the regiment march and play music.[23]

The colonel has papered the walls of his bedroom in nude images of former lovers, transforming it into his own secret museum. The term invokes older traditions of private and elite libertinage, not the contemporary commerce in commercial nudity, and, indeed, the colonel's photographs are deeply personal. The models are former lovers, and each one appears in the same pose. Yet while he is charitably rendered by Maizeroy, the colonel is engaged in an insidious act of looking. This is the looking that dismembers the body in Baudelaire, and with similar tropes (hair, haunches). Each woman's face has disappeared, leaving behind only those parts of her that interest the colonel: her back, her hair, her shoulders, the line of her waist and hips, her butt. These fragments surround the colonel in a kind of mnemonic kaleidoscope, their purpose only to give him the pleasure of remembering and reliving his sexual experiences with these women. The bodies that the colonel once did possess physically in sexual encounters he now can possess eternally through the photograph, enacting retrospectively photographic obscenity's promise of the sexual ownership of a body through the act of looking.

The collection also indicates another disturbing consequence of the false sense of ownership that comes with nude photographs: an obsessive urge to accumulate representations of the body as fragments rather than as constituent parts of a human being.[24] The colonel's tastes lean callipygian; another man might specialize in breasts, or knees, or eyes, with total disregard for the women to whom they belong. In his photo-novel *L'Amuseuse*, Maizeroy develops the sinister implications of this collector's compulsion. The novel tells the story of a young woman, Jeannine, as she embarks on her career as an *amuseuse* (essentially, a cross between a call girl and a courtesan). In what is the most bizarre passage in any of Maizeroy's novels, Jeannine pays a visit to the distinguished M. Marcheprime, a prospective client and purported revenant who had died in a carriage accident at Hainaut on 11 May 1745.[25] She finds herself in a gloomy *hôtel particulier* constructed according to various paranoid manias similar to those of des Esseintes in *À Rebours*. The walls are adorned with "niches where pearly nudes shimmered," the windows have all been closed to the outside world with large shutters, and inside Marcheprime has constructed a bizarre multiroom shrine to past and future lovers, with six chambers already filled and three waiting for future subjects.[26] Once they have all been filled, Marcheprime intends to hang himself with the cord woven from the locks of his great love, Marthe, who died next to him in the accident.[27]

In the inner sanctum of his grotesque temple of love, Marcheprime has Jeannine open two locked cabinets. In one cabinet are the relics of Marthe, including the cord of hair that will ultimately kill him. In the other is a kind of museum display, very much akin to the colonel's, but also with something of Dantan's crypt about it:

> One of them contained the most motley array of objects, carefully displayed on rosewood shelves, and labeled like precious museum pieces. Packets of letters and telegrams tied up in a ribbon, crumpled handkerchiefs, gloves, cheap paper fans, mismatched silk stockings, desiccated bouquets, garters, parasols, tiny patent leather shoes and feathered slippers, a cotton lawn shirt lacerated with nail scratches and bite marks, corsets, photographs of naked women pinned like dead butterflies, with long fine needles all lined up in the same position, straight through the heart.[28]

Marcheprime has assembled an impressive quantity of sentimental detritus. Unlike the colonel, he has not dissected the women in his collection and arranged them in multiple iterations of the same body parts, but somehow his "secret museum" is nonetheless far more sinister. Marcheprime has distilled the photograph's ability to capture reality into a force of classification and control, in this case of the bodies of women, lined up and pinned through the heart. The other objects around them are laden with sentimental value and imbued with personal meaning, signifying through emotion and memory. The manner of the photographs' display, however, divorces them from this realm. They are laid out like so many scientific specimens for the sadistic viewing pleasure of their owner, exposing a troubling potential for cruelty lurking in every photographic representation of the body.

✦ From Perverted Looking to Perversion and Degeneration ✦

In two of his "naturalist" novels of the 1880s, Maizeroy amplified his criticism of nude photography representing nude photographs not merely as manifestations of an objectifying sexualized gaze but as symptoms of social degeneracy. *La Dernière Croisade* (1883) narrates the destruction of France's ancient nobility by the forces of modern capitalism via the story of the Marquis de Taillemaure. Taillemaure is bankrupted by his common, profligate, and depraved young wife, Régine, and then falls into total ruin after speculating in the Crédit continental, a Catholic bank run by a converted Jew. Régine runs off with her lover, the marquis dies of a cerebral fever a week later, and his father pays the debts to save the family name. In the degenerate Paris of the novel, everyone in the upper class has a dirty secret; a particularly repulsive secret forms its second plot. Régine has one living relative, with whom she shares a taste for "naughtiness" and "erotic manuals," her cousin General Bosq.[29] Once a fine soldier, Bosq has, in his old age, become addicted to absinthe and has developed increasingly disturbing sexual proclivities: "He became, with age, more and more perverted, but with the dissolute mania of the blasé whose forces are weakening and brain is withering away like a sponge soaked in violent acids. All the proxénètes of Paris, all the shady vendors of libertine photographs, of obscene books, of aphrodisiacs, harassed him, squeezed money out of him."[30] Bosq haunts brothels and prowls the boulevards, collecting obscenity of every kind. Despite being favored by the attentions of a respectable widow, he often neglects her for prostitutes, with whom he is on a first-name basis. Whereas the erotica of *Au régiment* is all in good fun, General Bosq's taste for prostitutes and dirty pictures is yet another ominous sign of the decline of French culture.

After his inauspicious introduction, Bosq lurks in the background until about two-thirds of the way through the novel. By the time he reappears, he has sunk from prostitutes to pedophilia, entertaining "young girls picked up from all corners of Paris" in a rented house in Reuil.[31] The reader discovers him back at his club, lost in a daydream about one young girl, "fresh and pink, already perverted like a boulevard flower girl, who had arrived hatless with a schoolgirl's pinafore smudged with ink stains and a box full of writing notebooks."[32] A few days later, he is picked up at his club by a pair of policemen who discreetly inform him that he is under arrest for the rape of a minor. The police escort the general back to the scene of his iniquities, a dilapidated house with a single furnished room in which every object is an accusation against him: "The bed was still unmade and the crumpled sheets hung like rags. Children's toys lay scattered in the middle of the floor amidst erotic photographs."[33] Here, photographs are not simply a realistic detail, but are at the heart of Bosq's fall. The bed, the children's toys, and the obscene photographs together are the proof of his guilt and signifiers of his complete moral dissolution. Facing arrest, the general commits suicide.[34] The circumstances of Bosq's death encapsulate the themes of the entire novel taken to the extreme: A pedophile and avid consumer of obscenity commits suicide to conceal his crimes, and the police help to preserve his reputation by spreading the rumor that his death was not a suicide at all, but a murder. Hypocrisy and sexual deviance have invaded not only the nobility of France but the very foundations of social order, the police and the army. Everyone conspires to hide the truth about themselves and about the state of society, particularly its sexual behaviors.[35]

Nude photographs are no less a marker of degeneration in Maizeroy's *succès de scandale*, *Les Deux Amies*. The novel's heroines, Eva and Jeanne, grow up in the same building on the Champs-Élysées, attend the same convent school, and, under cover of their friendship, become lovers at a young age. Eva is thrown out of school and soon thereafter establishes a lesbian sex club in a nearby mansion with adornments including paintings of "women's bodies voluptuously sketched onto the canvas, quite modern with their sickly forms and without the chastity of the antique nude."[36] Paintings, however, are among the tamer of their vices: "The mansion ended up becoming a veritable illicit brothel. The library composed of insalubrious books, the clandestine photographs, the supple robes of transparent batiste hung on the coat hooks of the rooms, all contributed to giving it this aspect."[37] In this feminine version of Bosq's tawdry retreat, Eva and Jeanne calculatingly seduce young women, including Jeanne's cousin-in-law, whose inheritance she aspires to steal (the plot fails; Luce, as her name suggests, is too good). They, like General Bosq, are sexual predators, and they, too, are associated with illegal nude photographs.

Maizeroy is not always consistent in his attitude toward lesbianism; sometimes it is a cause, sometimes a consequence of a contemporary moral degeneration. According to his interview on the book, however, Maizeroy understood lesbianism to be a real threat to the fabric of French society. He claims to have wanted to "show the dangers to mothers of families; to make them understand that it does not suffice to surveil their daughters' male waltzing partners, that boarding-school friendships are sometimes more dangerous than the passing infatuations begun between a quadrille and a mazurka."[38] If Maizeroy is to be taken at his word (he was, after all, facing legal charges), it is neither incidental nor coincidental that Eva and Jeanne consume photographic obscenity. Such images may be the harmless pastime of young military men, but in the wrong hands, they are also a force of moral and social decay, a shared currency of the sociopath and sexually deviant. They encourage private perversions that become public problems.

In Maizeroy's fictional world, photography is the medium of sexual desire, and nude photography is ubiquitous. In some cases, nudes are tolerated, even mocked. Yet despite Maizeroy's wit, the socially disruptive effects of the nude photograph radiate through his stories, upending the accepted standards of behavior meant to dictate the terms of appropriate and socially productive sexuality. At its least troubling, in the form of personal love tokens, nude photography signifies sexual inconstancy; at its most troubling, in the form of commercially distributed obscenity, it signifies the collapse of the traditional marriage system under the pressures of sexual perversion, pedophilia, and lesbianism. These photographs have deleterious aesthetic effects as well, encouraging voyeurism, compulsive looking, and fragmentation of the body. And because photography is ultimately defined by its erotic iterations in Maizeroy's texts, such images in turn determine the broader social significance of the medium as a representational mode.

◄ Resisting the Nude in Maizeroy's Photo-Novels ►

Given the negative thematics of nude photography in Maizeroy's fiction, it seems somewhat strange that he turned to the photo-novel at all, for it did very quickly descend into nudity. Zola's brusque condemnation of the photo-novel was allegedly prompted by one of the first to be published, a sexually explicit text by a young unknown, Pierre Guédy, called *Amoureuse Trinité*.[39] In addition to a plot that turns on an incestuous ménage à trois, Guédy's photo-novel is peppered with twenty-eight naked and half-naked women. They are heavily airbrushed, but these nudes nonetheless invoke classic tropes of nude photography, such as one illustration depicting a naked woman gazing in the mirror (Figure 80). And while *Amoureuse Trinité* is perhaps the most extreme example, it certainly isn't the only one; many novels include the occasional nude or seminude woman, whether or not these images are relevant to the plot.

Yet strange though it may seem, Maizeroy evidently did not shun the photo-novel. Instead, he struck the precarious balance of embracing the genre while rejecting its problematic association with photographic nudity. Maizeroy's twelve photo-novels largely eschew nude illustrations. At their most exposed, the women adorning the pages of Maizeroy's books wear nightdresses. In evening dress, they reveal their arms or perhaps a slipping shoulder strap. If they look into the mirror, as in a photograph from *Chérissime*, they are fully clothed, as though to evoke and then deny the old erotic trope (Figure 81). Only one of Maizeroy's illustrated novels, *Au Bord du lit*, includes scantily clad women, and these are limited to two examples, one draped in gauze and the other heavily airbrushed (Figure 82). Neither is connected to erotic scenes in the text, which, contrary to the implications of its title, contains little sexual content.[40] Indeed, even beyond simply rejecting nudity, Maizeroy's photo-novels push back against their own photographic illustrations in myriad ways. Maizeroy almost always

AMOUREUSE TRINITÉ. 77

— Oui, une sœur…

Il n'accentua pas mais il eut la sensation qu'Elzen devinait que la sœur en question était trouvée, qu'il la célait en son âme pour leur commune joie.

Il murmura :

— Depuis des années ! Mon amour pour toi ne fut pas amoindri… Elle a la bouche de Paul et tout le sourire.

Elle s'attristait ; mais, désireuse de la vie répercutée à pleins coups en la poitrine, elle murmura, intéressée :

— Elle est vierge?

— Oui, vierge…, et un nom sacerdotal, Christiane.

— Christiane?

— Elle a les yeux bleus, les yeux qui t'impressionnent, les yeux qui t'énamourent. Tu as des larmes ?

Malgré elle une sensibilité l'émouvait.

— Je te croyais à moi… entièrement…

— Oh ! pardonne-moi, j'ai tout fait pour arracher

[FIGURE 80]

Page from Pierre Guédy, *Amoureuse Trinité*, 1897.
Collection of the author.

wrote and published his novels without illustrations first and then published them with photographs (the notable exception is *Chérissime*, which was only subsequently published without illustrations as *Le Feu de joie*). Within the photo-novels, the relationship between the two media is labyrinthine and avoids direct correspondence between written and illustrated scenes. Rather than working in

58   CHÉRISSIME.

Vincent-de-Paul, lui-même, le trouverait-il, s'il était encore de ce monde?

Et Madame de Faverel qui les écoutait, en nouant les brides de sa capeline devant l'une des glaces, songeait :

— Une femme comme celle-là pourrait-elle avoir un mauvais fils?

[FIGURE 81]

Page from René Maizeroy, *Chérissime*, 1901.
Collection of the author.

concert, the two media are often at odds with each other, particularly at sexually charged moments. Most importantly for this discussion, at every turn, Maizeroy's photo-novels resist the erotic imperatives of photography that he elaborates on in his fiction. They do not merely deny the photograph its affinities with nudity; they reserve the domain of the erotic for the text alone. Despite their photo-

60 AU BORD DU LIT

épanouissements de lotus, le Bouddah faisait le geste auguste de la bénédiction. Léone y glissait

furtive, inquiète, tel un fantôme dans ses longs voiles, ondulait, le visage caché, les formes perdues parmi les plis rythmiques et souples du

[FIGURE 82]

Page from René Maizeroy, *Au Bord du lit*, 1900.
Collection of the author.

graphic illustrations, Maizeroy's photo-novels assert the primacy of textual modes of the representation of sexual desire over visual ones.

At the most basic level, the resistance to photography is built into the layout of Maizeroy's photo-illustrated texts. Photo-novels generally had two kinds of illustrations, small images interspersed within the text and full-page plates. Oc-

116   POUPÉE DE JOIE

noire. Et la file s'éclaircissait comme si quelque cloche invisible eût sonné dans l'air froid la retraite, les équipages, les uns après les autres, faisaient demi-tour, s'égaillaient au grand trot vers l'Arc de triomphe.

Par instants, Hubert consultait sa montre, relisait le petit bleu de Yette et armé de patience,

Il lui dénoua d'autorité ce qui restait de sa voilette. (P. 102.)

[FIGURE 83]

Pages from René Maizeroy, *Poupée de Joie*, 1903.
Collection of the author.

casionally, images inserted into the text represent more incidental moments that correspond to the events narrated near or around them and do not require a caption. More often, however, all of the photographs, full plates or smaller images, are scattered around the text at random and require captions to connect them to the scenes that they represent. Such is the case in Mazieroy's *Poupée de joie*, for example, none of whose illustrations appears facing or embedded in the

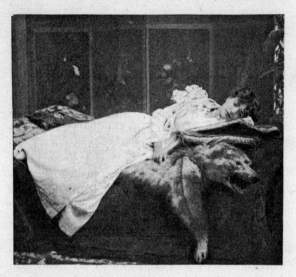

POUPÉE DE JOIE   117

dévoré d'anxiété, continuait à aller et venir. Et il
s'approchait tellement des dernières voitures que
les roues l'éclaboussaient, qu'on l'eût pris ou pour

Et confuse, elle feignit d'être fâchée, de lui en vouloir. (P. 103.)

un malheureux aux abois qui mendie, qui tente
d'apitoyer par ses prières quelque âme charitable,
ou pour un mari jaloux qui épie quelque trahison,
guette la femme qui le trompe et son complice,
tremble de manquer son coup, de ne pas atteindre

8

text to which it corresponds. In some sequences of multiple images illustrating
single scenes from the text, such as a four-photograph series of a reconciliation
between the protagonist Yette and her lover Hubert after a long quarrel, the different photographs making up the set are also separated from each other. Two of
the illustrations from the reconciliation appear facing each other fourteen pages
after the event; the other two appear together eight pages later (Figure 83). There

is no reason to break up the photographic sequence, except to emphasize its discontinuity from the text and to interrupt the narrative that it conveys to the reader, a narrative which consequently becomes entirely detached from the one in the text.[41]

This same passage from *Poupée de joie* is also a perfect example of how this disconnect extends from the layout to the content of illustrations and text, with particular significance for how those two media represent sexual desire. In the scene, Hubert and Yette are ecstatic to be reunited after a painful separation. Despite Yette's protestations that she cannot stay, Hubert "carried her to the divan, laid her down amongst the pillows, knelt at her feet, began to rub her fine, silk-sheathed ankles and legs with persuasive and suggestive caresses."[42] She resists Hubert until two paragraphs later, when she succumbs by exclaiming, "'Take me again, take all of me, take me always, I love you, I love you,'" only swiftly to reverse herself, as "confused, she then scolded Hubert [. . .] feigned being angry."[43] Yet there are no signs of these caresses or this confusion in the photographic illustration, which merely depicts Yette languishing on a divan covered in a bearskin; even stranger, Hubert has mysteriously vanished (right side, Figure 83). The text is euphemistic, but it is clear that the two lovers are not simply gazing into each other's eyes, and all of the scene's overt sexual content has been excised from the photograph. The other three images in the series do depict the scenes to which they correspond but only show Hubert removing Yette's hat on her arrival and then her preparations for departure afterward (left side, Figure 83). The photographs depict the events that frame the sexual encounter, not the encounter itself. Yette remains fully dressed, her hair, despite her protestations in the text, is neatly done, and she has little physical contact with Hubert. The story the photographs tell is not at all one of a clandestine meeting between two separated lovers; at most, it might perhaps depict an innocent flirtation. Compared to the text, which is both sensational and passionate in Maizeroy's typical fashion, the photographs are not only decorous but downright boring.[44]

An even more striking example of text and image working at cross purposes, in which the text tends toward the erotic and the illustration toward the chaste, occurs merely a few pages later. Maizeroy opens chapter 19 of the novel with an explicit description of the two lovers basking in the afterglow of sex. The illustration at the top of the page, however, depicts an entirely different scene, when Yette chastises a servant; her hat is on, she is carrying a parasol, and nothing about it suggests what Maizeroy describes in the text just below (Figure 84).

One of the joys preferred by M. de Monréal was, after their embrace, to lie by Yette's feet like an obedient dog, to contemplate her like a distant star.

Once they had quenched their thirst for pleasure again and again, they lay side by side, exhausted, without reason, their flesh aching, their ears filled by a deafening rumble of seaswells, their eyes blinded by a tumult of sparks, this self-recovery, this ineffable meditation, this effort by the soul to escape the lethargic body, to purify itself in reverie, delighted him above all else.

Paralyzed on the bed, her hair scattered, without even the energy to tie the ribbons of a negligee over her radiant nudity, Madame de Minerves seemed hypnotized, so white in the dimly lit room entirely strewn with flowers she gave the impression of some dead lover.[45]

After their multiple orgasms, Yette lies naked next to Hubert, unable even to rouse the strength to cover herself. True, Maizeroy devotes more attention to their reflections on the experience, the "flight of their souls into the realm of dreams," than to Yette's nudity, almost as though he wishes to veil Yette with his words even if she will not veil herself. Nevertheless, the content, if not graphic, is perfectly clear. The only thing more jarring than the pairing of this text with the image that precedes it is its pairing with the photograph meant to illustrate it. When the illustration of this scene does finally appear some twenty pages later, Hubert is seated fully dressed at the feet of his (always) perfectly coiffed lover (Figure 85). The two are again on the bearskin divan, and there is no sign of a bed nor even the slightest hint of exposed skin. In order to understand what is really happening in the photograph, the reader must turn to the caption and the text. The photograph is not only completely divested of its erotic associations, it is so "clean" as to cleanse the text in which it appears. Someone casually skimming through the book's illustrations would hardly think any disreputable scenes were to be found within its pages. At the same time, because one must read the text in order to truly understand the illustrations (rather than those illustrations giving away the plot at a glance), the text maintains control over the image rather than the reverse. It is as if the photographs in Maizeroy's novels are deliberately prudish and disconnected from his texts. At every turn, his photo-novels deny the photograph its affinities with nudity and sexual desire and reserve the domain of narrative control, with all of the eroticism that entails, for the text.

A scene such as this that is both sexually explicit and illustrated is a rarity in Maizeroy's photo-novels. Often, the sexier parts of the story aren't illustrated at all. Indeed, perhaps most revelatory, even when the text of the photo-novels specifically mentions photographic nudity, inviting the reproduction of such images, no such accompanying illustration appears. Marcheprime's pinned specimens are not reproduced in the illustrations for *L'Amuseuse*, nor are the seminude

La jeune femme haussa alors le ton, malmena le valet de chambre. (P. 99.)

XIX

L'une des jouissances que préférait M. de Monréal était, après l'étreinte, de se coucher aux pieds

[FIGURE 84]

Page from René Maizeroy, *Poupée de Joie*, 1903.
Collection of the author.

photographs discovered by Solange in *Chérissime*. The text pauses over these
images long enough to describe them to the reader but stops at this ekphrasis.
In the case of *Chérissime*, the novel does include an illustration of Solange examining the photographic evidence of her lover's infidelity, and this plate even appears close to the text narrating the scene (Figure 86). Clearly the episode is

L'une des jouissances de M. de Monréal était, après l'étreinte, de se coucher aux pieds
de Yette, dans une pose de chien fidèle. (P 109.)

9

[FIGURE 85]

Page from René Maizeroy, *Poupée de Joie*, 1903.
Collection of the author.

important enough to be emphasized in an illustration, but the reader never actually sees the photographs themselves. In either of these cases, reproducing the photographs would have simply amplified the "reality effect" of the novels and would not have added anything to the sexual content of the books, since the content of the images is described in the text. Yet still the corresponding photo-

dans le baguier de malachite, et d'y prendre, dans le
deuxième tiroir de gauche, une enveloppe qui contient
cinq billets de cent francs... Tu la cachèteras, et si
cela ne te dérange pas trop, tu la feras recommander
dans n'importe quel bureau...

Quel inéluctable besoin de pénétrer dans les secrets
de Claude, de savoir
ce que renfermait ce
meuble qui était tou-
jours fermé, m'a in-
citée à fouiller dans
les autres tiroirs, à
regarder ce qu'ils
célaient ?

Comment ai-je osé
agir ainsi, commet-
tre une telle indéli-
catesse ?

Est-on, à certains
moments de la vie,
le maître de soi-
même? Quelque force mystérieuse ne manie-t-elle pas
notre volonté comme de la cire?

Dans le premier tiroir de droite, sous de longs
cahiers de papier anglais marqué au chiffre de Claude,
il y avait trois grandes photographies et un paquet de
lettres.

L'une de ces photographies représentait Madame de

[FIGURE 86]

Page from René Maizeroy, *Chérissime*, 1901.
Collection of the author.

graphs are not introduced. The full significance of these omissions becomes
clearer in contrast with the photo-novel *Le Consolateur*. In that novel, a portrait
of the protagonist Maggie that has been exchanged between two of her lovers *is*
reproduced in the text (Figure 87). This photograph alludes to the sexual relationship at the heart of the story: Maggie is torn between her lover Raymond and

LE CONSOLATEUR. 177

« Je devrais
maintenant avoir
au moins une
lettre...

« Les spahis
qui font le ser-
vice du courrier
ont réussi jusqu'à
ce jour à éviter
les embuscades, à
échapper à tous
les périls qui les
menacent...

« Vous ne m'a-
vez donc pas
écrit, *une seule
fois...*

« Puis-je croire
à une pareille
indifférence, à une pareille cruauté de votre part?

« Ne faudrait-il pas que vous ayez changé d'âme,
que vous soyez devenue, par quelque sortilège, aussi
égoïste, aussi insensible que vous étiez tendre et
charitable?

« Ne faudrait-il pas, Maggie, que vous soyez
coupable envers moi, que vous m'ayez trahi et
renié?

« Ne faudrait-il pas que vous soyez acculée au fond
de quelque affreuse impasse, qu'un autre m'ait rem-
placé dans votre cœur et vous ait épousée, que je ne

12

[FIGURE 87]

Page from René Maizeroy, *Le Consolateur*, 1905.
Collection of the author.

his best friend, to whom she becomes engaged when she believes Raymond to
be dead. Its visual content, however, obscures those relationships rather than
exposes them. As a result, the photograph reproduced in the text truly appears
to be nothing more than an unmotivated realistic detail; one must absolutely
read the text in order to understand it as something more than a photographer's

portrait of a young woman. In other words, the only instance in which Maizeroy's photo-novels reproduce a sexually charged photograph mentioned in the text is one in which that photograph's content belies its sexual significance entirely. The power of representing sexual desire is given almost entirely to the written word.

⚐ Maizeroy's Feminism and the Representation of Female Desire ⚑

It bears acknowledging that whatever attitudes toward nude photography Maizeroy expressed in his fiction, the absence of explicit photographic illustrations in Maizeroy's photo-novels might well have been, in part, a practical choice. Nudes—or even illustrations representing the sexual content of his novels— would have been a gamble. They might well have appealed to a certain readership, but they also risked attracting the attention of law enforcement, which would have led to prosecution. The photographs in Maizeroy's photo-novels, on the other hand, are almost like a decoy. As a rule, they are disarmed of their erotic power and then subordinated to the text; when the text and the images each tell two different stories, the more interesting one, both sentimentally and erotically, is always the text. The subdued photographs thus shield the text, distracting attention away from its sexual explicitness and protecting it from prosecution. Yet such an explanation, while entirely plausible, also feels inadequate. Maizeroy's fiction does not merely reject photographic nudity. His work lays out a fault line dividing textual and visual expressions of desire in the yawning gap between the explicitness of his texts and the vagueness of the photographic illustrations. This division between the kinds of content permitted to each representational medium suggests another, more complex explanation, one rooted instead in the collision between the erotic imperative of photography and Maizeroy's signature style, his "feminism," which demanded an entirely contradictory approach to the representation of gender, subjectivity, and sexuality.

By the time he began publishing photo-novels, Maizeroy's reputation as a feminist had been cemented. His was not, of course, the feminism of men and women like Hubertine Auclert, Maria Deraismes, and Léon Richer, who were fighting to improve the political, economic, and social conditions of women through the right to vote, equal educational rights, and the reinstitution of divorce laws.[46] Maizeroy was a literary feminist, a writer of "novel[s] of passion" for and about women, at which he was extraordinarily successful. One of Maizeroy's greatest critics, Adolphe Brisson, who meant it as insult when he described Maizeroy as *the* paradigmatic "feminist novelist," nonetheless offers a remarkably detailed description of exactly what that meant. He wrote, "The feminist worthy of this name does not content himself with captivating his clients: he seduces them, insinuates himself into their innermost thoughts, he shows them with certain signs, difficult to determine, that they can have faith in him. He is not only an entertainer, he is the confessor and the friend of those who devour his works. [...] There is between them an affinity of temperament and a spiritual kinship."[47] In his texts, Maizeroy somehow seduced and befriended his female readers, gaining their trust by telling them stories that reflected their own experience.

In 1892, when he published *Cas Passionnels,* Maizeroy was asked for his own definition of feminism. At first glance, his response seems condescending, superficial, and not altogether different from Brisson's:

> "To love women," he said, "this is merely a question of temperament, a sort of fencing wherein the strongest and most adroit get themselves nicked by the blade, a brutish drudgery, vulgar, bestial, monotonous when it is only a matter of the eternal coupling of the sexes and no hint of dreams intermingles with the Kiss, a supreme joy when the soul alone is at stake, when we stumble across affinities of sentiment, of wild dreams, of impressions, when hearts melt together in an intimate beatitude.
>
> "Less simple is to know the women whence come all of our folly, all of our suffering, all of our ecstasy, to read their changeable complex natures, as saturated with vice as with virtue, too rebellious or too submissive, to feel with them, to speak their language without mistake. The rare ones, those who manage to do this, are the true *feminists.*"[48]

While he begins by dismissing a love of women as insufficient for "feminism," it is clearly at the basis of his entire conception of the genre. The desire to understand women proceeds directly from a sexual attraction, a notion of them as objects of desire. Furthermore, despite his lip service to their "complex natures," his characterization of "women" is one of opposing clichés, vices and virtues, rebellion and submission. His language about sex is equally reductive, with its invocation of ephemeral euphoria and bestial sensuality. And yet, what *is* remarkable about this description, and important for understanding his widespread appeal, is his language about seeking to truly comprehend women, to "read" their complexities, and to speak their language without error. His "feminism" is an act of textual interpretation, grounded in the act of reading and speaking, of understanding and communicating the female experience—both sentimental and sexual—through language.

Maizeroy's uncanny ability to give voice to women so astutely as to seem at the same time simply to allow them to speak for themselves was precisely his

appeal to female readers. As a reviewer remarked in 1889 while attempting to
explain the coining of the term "Maizereine," Maizeroy's followers were devoted
and obsessive, and they sought to understand themselves through his fiction:
"All of these qualities have already led to numerous editions of *l'Adorée*, of which
every Parisian woman has read and reread the feverish developments, the delicate analyses, the audacious, troubling conclusions. They have long assured for
the young novelist the almost fanatical admiration of an entire part of the female
audience who recognize themselves in his books and whom one of our most
spiritual chroniclers has baptized: the clan of the *Maizereines*."[49] The Maizereines
were so devoted because they recognized themselves in Maizeroy's novels, in
whose pages he permitted "a woman to speak with complete liberty."[50]

There is little doubt of what Maizeroy spoke. The novelist Lucie Delarue-
Mardrus describes the experience of reading Maizeroy's novels in her memoirs.
She was sixteen and just going through puberty: "Tumult, chaos, no word could
describe what I was at this torrential moment. Everything clashed, contradicted
itself: impure thoughts, archangelic dreams, a taste for vulgar words, a love for
high style, schoolgirl laziness, a crazy ardor to learn."[51] In the midst of her confusion, she describes the potential of sexual awakening and her anticipation of
knowledge and experience: "Under this very tulip tree, separated from the others, I read, stirred in the most impure parts of my being, the novels of René
Maizeroy. The sensuality he describes left me feverish, awaiting the life that
would let me experience them one day."[52] Maizeroy's readers found in his pages
sentimental and sexual experiences to which they could aspire, experiences that
suggested the potential for a world in which their pleasure was essential rather
than secondary.

Along with Brisson and other contemporaries who disparaged Maizeroy's
"feminine" output, some late-twentieth-century scholars, like Marc Angenot, dismiss him as catering to a niche female market by promoting "adultery and irreg-
ular situations" in quasi-pornographic "novels of adultery and salacious libertinage."[53] Angenot argues that authors like Maizeroy appealed to women only to
sell novels. Because they never explicitly espouse feminist politics, these novels
could be read as yet another example of literature produced for women at the
end of the nineteenth century that actually had as its purpose a kind of "necessary indoctrination" of women into the existing social structures and as a substitute for their sublimated desires.[54] On the other hand, Maizeroy's focus on the
sexual and emotional experiences of his many female protagonists also foreshad-
owed the works of Colette and other female novelists in the early twentieth century who explicitly took up the question of sexual desire. Indeed, in her study of
female fin-de-siècle writers, Rachel Mesch argues that their focus on female sex-

uality (specifically, the quest for orgasm) is its own kind of feminism that looks forward to the twentieth century.[55] I would argue that whatever his motives, the same is true of Maizeroy's fiction, although that is somewhat beside the point here. Whether or not Maizeroy's work can be considered feminist by our contemporary standards, his focus on female sexual expression, primarily through language, is entirely at odds with the kind of twisted and objectifying masculine desire he associates with photography. It is, therefore, also at odds with the very idea of illustrating his "feminist" novels photographically, which can be seen in the way that Maizeroy's photo-novels that present his "feminist" perspective on sex (that is, focused on female self-expression) also reject the photographic gaze. By denying photography the possibility of illustrating erotic desire, Maizeroy reaffirms the text as the medium that can capture the totality of female experience. While most of his photo-novels lend themselves to a similar analysis (including the same passages of *Poupée de joie* discussed above), I will conclude with an exemplary case of the conflict between text and image within the framework of Maizeroy's feminism, the photo-novel *Chérissime*. *Chérissime* is paradigmatic of how his feminism entails the deployment of textual representational techniques against the erotic potential of the photograph in order to prioritize (and valorize) female desire and subjectivity.

Chérissime tackles the sexual awakening of an older woman and mother, Solange, who has an affair with a younger man, Claude. In it, Maizeroy sympathetically reveals all of the embarrassment and humiliation she endures as those around her obliviously call attention to her age, refer to her as her lover's "older sister" or "a sexless friend," and consider her as nothing more than an aging mother facing the inescapable loneliness of life after forty.[56] While she finds great love and happiness with Claude for a time, she suffers the indignity of discovering Claude's dalliances with other women and watching her daughter Suzanne grow up to resent Claude's affection for her. The novel concludes with Suzanne in a convent and Solange dead of the shock of her daughter's betrayal, her lover's abandonment, and her own aging body: "When he broke through the door, Claude saw all that remained from his bygone and divine love affair, *a dead old woman next to a broken mirror.*"[57] At the end of the novel, Solange is forced to become what society has seen her to be all along, decrepit and desexualized, and the result is her death.

Yet despite its devastating conclusion, like all of Maizeroy's feminist novels, *Chérissime* is focused on its female protagonist, so that we, the readers, see not this dead older woman but rather the vibrant and living woman who loved Claude and was destroyed by his heartlessness. Her great fear, which eventually kills her, is that her contemporaries are correct to believe that she is too old to be the object of Claude's sexual desire and, by extension, that she, too, can no longer desire Claude. She is consumed by worries over her uncomfortable place in these gendered sexual roles. And the novel's plot makes clear the dangerous role of photography in these kinds of disempowering dynamics of desire. As already discussed, Solange discovers one of Claude's infidelities precisely by way of seminude photographs of another woman. The simple fact that the accompanying illustration does not reproduce these photographs but instead shows Solange looking at them already signals the novel's turn away from photographic representation in favor of a linguistic mode of expression. This visual privileging of Solange's subjectivity is reinforced in the text. Solange's perspective anchors the narrative structure of *Chérissime*. Significantly, the focus on female sexual experience emerges not simply through the novel's plot but through Maizeroy's feminist style, through his use of language to represent sexual desire. While the text offers a number of examples, the most striking involve the consummation of Solange and Claude's relationship. In representing Solange's thoughts and privileging her sensations over those of Claude, *Chérissime* uses the privileged omniscience of the narrator to lay bare a psychology of female desire, defying the twisted and objectifying gaze that Maizeroy ascribes to nude photography.

One of Maizeroy's favored narrative devices is the use of personal documents, rather than simple first-person narration, to convey unexpressed thoughts and emotions. In *Chérissime*, he deploys Solange's journal. As she prepares to leave for a trip with Claude, she writes,

> The moment approaches when I will give myself away never to take myself back, when he will possess me completely as he has wanted for so many days, and I have violent apprehensions, the ineluctable turmoil of a young girl who will be delivered to the legal rape of a husband [. . .] I fear that our love will not withstand this test and that I will not be the mistress, the lover that he dreamt of, the one that he imagined from afar, that I will seem stupid, inexperienced, ridiculous.
>
> Will he love me as I am?
>
> Will I know how to please him, seduce him, keep him?
>
> Will I be his type, as the vulgar would say?[58]

The representation of Solange's excitement and anxiety is exemplary of Maizeroy's commitment to his female protagonists (and readership). As he conveys her thoughts to the reader, he aligns the novel's trajectory with Solange's subjectivity and with her own potential future satisfaction rather than with Claude's. The woman who might have been the sexual object of the lover's photograph, or a figure in nude illustrations for a male reader, has come alive and become the subject of this monologue, as Solange expresses her worries about satisfying the demands of her lover's desire. She refuses to become a specimen, pinned through the heart, or a trophy, pasted on a bedroom wall. As the object of Claude's desire speaks, moreover, she in turn renders Claude an object, that of both her own desire and her anxiety, emphasizing the reciprocal exchange of emotion between lovers (in sharp contrast to the unidirectional contemplation of a photograph). Indeed, her subjectivity so permeates the novel that the only kind of nude photograph that feels as though it might be appropriate would be an image of Claude, a use of photography for female pleasure that was without precedent within the pages of the photo-novel and rare outside of it.

When the pair do finally consummate their relationship, the scene is rendered in third person, but once again in such a way as to focus on Solange's sensations all the while complicating sexual subject-object relations in much the same way:

> She felt *as in a dream* that hands were grasping her hands, that a burning mouth was descending upon her neck, running, pushing itself into her hair, on her neck, behind her ears, and finally reaching her lips, devouring, insatiable, victorious.
>
> Happy, *more than happy*, she abandoned herself entirely, gave herself over to the supple fingers, light, dexterous, audacious that were running the length of her bust, her hips, her legs, granting her the desired illusion of an interrupted caress, of a cajoling and experienced embrace that was transporting her submissive, crazed, towards supreme pleasure.
>
> They undid the silk laces, undressed her without indecency, without clumsiness, without violence, setting the rhythm, one might have said, of their movements on the kisses that were invading, bit by bit, her delighted, liberated, vibrant skin, that were slowly conquering it, that were quelling its instinctual rebellions.[59]

Solange is entirely given over to Claude. He acts on Solange's body, not the reverse. The narrative, however, is once again bound to her response, to what she feels and thinks. Ultimately, Claude is the mere instrument of her desire, a phantasm governed by her wishes, even if she appears to remain passive. In other renderings of the scene (Maizeroy plagiarized himself on at least two occasions), Solange becomes even more important, for Maizeroy uses the first person, presenting the scene as a "confession" written by a woman to her lover detailing "these sensations of before, during, and after of which I cannot think without exquisite trouble, without orgasming."[60] As the scene progresses in all of its versions, moreover, she takes an increasingly active role in her own seduction, undressing herself with Claude, participating in the awakening of her flesh initiated by her lover's kisses. Claude may eventually desert Solange, but in the hierarchy of desire in the text his is secondary to hers.[61] Even more striking, at the moment of Solange's ecstasy, the text appears to offer an explicit rebuttal of photography by way of its catalog of the sites of Solange's arousal. These same erotically charged body parts—breasts, hips, legs, lips—are also the ones fragmented into objects of desire in nude photography (as in the colonel's museum of buttocks). Maizeroy's novel, however, asserts their role in Solange's pleasure, not that of a viewer or a lover. Clichéd though it may be, the sex scene both confirms *Chérissime*'s "feminist" rejection of photographic illustration and clarifies the significance of that rejection for the novel's plot of photographic betrayal. Solange's emotions and her physical experience, expressed in the text, are far more important than Claude or the images produced for his enjoyment, and to show those images would be to sink into a photographic mode inimical to the telling of her story.

Reading, of course, is a fundamentally subjective experience, and another reader might understand *Chérissime* quite differently. Yet whether one is inclined to consider the exaggerated romances of Maizeroy's novels as mere escapism or as a contribution to the nascent feminist movement, they offer a unique and nuanced perspective on the social consequences of nude photography's ever-expanding cultural presence. Setting the photo-novels against the context of Maizeroy's many other allusions to nude photography elsewhere in his œuvre, it becomes clear that in *Chérissime* (as in many of his other photo-novels), text and image are more than representational techniques. They are gendered representations of desire. The text is the mode of female sexual subjectivity, while the photographs that dot the books' pages mark incursions of a sexually charged male gaze. This division places Maizeroy's photo-novels in the strange position of repudiating the terms of their own genre, of resisting the mode of representation that sets them apart—the photograph—in order to preserve their meaning. In some ways, by so gendering text and photography, Maizeroy's position is conservative and reactionary, for it reflects his contemporary reality without fully interrogating it or attempting to reclaim photographic representation for women. Yet at the same time, his work, along with that of Zola, conceives of the nude photograph in terms that are remarkably modern and entirely familiar today, whether or not we may agree with their positions. As he refuses to "fall into nudity," Maizeroy's fiction both testifies to the reach of nude photography and reveals many of the gendered fault lines that would continue to radiate out from it well into the twentieth and twenty-first centuries.

Conclusion

Over the years this book took to complete, I began to write art reviews. In the summer of 2017, I reviewed a retrospective of Irving Penn's photographs at the Metropolitan Museum of Art in New York. The exhibition included more than two hundred images, but most interesting to me were Penn's nudes from the 1950s. Having spent so much time looking at the trajectory of the photographic nude in the nineteenth century, I was struck by the way that Penn seemed to be pushing back against precisely that history, namely, the proliferation of sexualized images of the female body and the increasing association of photographic nudity with obscenity. More than that, I saw in his images something like what Baudelaire had hoped for poetry, and had categorically denied to photography, that is, the possibility to render the physical body as form, without idealizing or obscuring that body in the process. Penn's photographs overturn the gendered aesthetic hierarchy of masculine form over feminine matter, and in so doing they offer a glimpse of what one possible space of artistic nudity might look like after the nineteenth century. Excited, I posted a link to my review of Penn's show on my Facebook page, hoping I might inspire some discussion about the topic. The post immediately disappeared. It had been censored by Facebook because of the lead image: a close-up of a woman's stomach framed by a sliver of pubic hair and the edge of her breast.

Such censorship is no rarity in the age of digital media. There have been many disputes over nudity on social media platforms (pictures of women breastfeeding, for instance, have been a flashpoint). But because of Penn's engagement with the same photographic history and conventions discussed in this book, this case of censorship struck me as a particularly fitting epilogue. In the first place, it is a recent example of how important texts are for understanding how photographic nudity signifies. Facebook's algorithm did not read my review, the text that would have challenged the purportedly pornographic signification of the image. In the second place, and for this very reason, it is also an example of the way that our thinking about representations of the body in the twenty-first century is still shaped by the nineteenth. During the 1850s and 1860s, fears about the social and sexual dangers of photographic nudity were still often attended by debates about aesthetics and the province of art. As time went on, discussions of art and the nude largely disappeared in favor of the moralizing discourse of antipornography reformers at the fin de siècle who cast the photographed body—nearly always female—as a social danger that had to be contained. Facebook's algorithm, which allows the nude female body to signify only as obscenity, is the logical extension of the evolving attitudes in the nineteenth century. From several possible meanings for the female photographed body, one emerged as dominant to this day. A photograph of a nude woman is prurient and dangerous—both to that woman and to society—before it can be anything else.

There are many reasons why this narrowing of meaning is not necessarily a bad thing. Paternalistic reformers like Bérenger were not alone in perceiving the harm in nude photographic representations of the body. The novels of Maizeroy and Zola prefigured twentieth-century feminism's response to these images and the related sex industries in which they are often embedded. McCauley and Solomon-Godeau, the foremost feminist historians of the nineteenth-century photographic nude, developed the same ideas percolating in Maizeroy and Zola: that nude photographs are closely implicated with prostitution both practically and theoretically and that they are forms of representation that fundamentally deny female agency and desire. For twentieth-century antipornography feminists, just as for these nineteenth-century observers, these representations of the female body could not be art. To cast them as such obfuscates the real dangers such representations do to the women in them and the society that consumes them. In this sense, the shift toward recognizing the deleterious social consequences of nude photography is an example of the great progress that has been made in our awareness of the economic and sexual exploitation of women's bodies.

All of this is true. The facts of the nineteenth century show us very clearly the ways in which the photographic nude was embedded in economic and sexual exploitation. Even the women who may very well have chosen to represent themselves photographically, such as the Countess de Castiglione, could not escape this reality. In a fundamental way, images of naked women produced in a society that denied women sexual and political agency necessarily reinscribe the terms of women's oppression, just as Solomon-Godeau argues regarding the countess. Moreover, while debate over nude photographs did turn around questions of "art" at that time, these arguments were still marked by misogyny. For every glowing review that saw in female nudity an ideal form of beauty and grace, there was another that could see only prostitution and dangerous female sexuality, and neither accorded agency or personhood to the women involved.

And yet, I keep returning to the first photograph in this book, and to the sense of possibility glimpsed—if only briefly—in the best académies and the earliest positive reviews of the nude. I cannot help but feel that we do a great disservice to these images, not to mention to ourselves, when we assume that rhetoric about their artistry was merely a cynical cover for pornography and that these photographs represent nothing more profound than the reality of the model's exploitation. What space then is left for art? Or rather, what space is left for photographic art? There are no debates about the value of Degas' nudes, even though many of them represent prostitutes and (as I myself have argued) may well have been produced in dialogue with the conventions of explicit nude photography. We continue to marvel at Manet's *Olympia* even as we know that the shock of her arrival lay in her allusions to the dark realities of prostitution. What is it about photography that makes it so different, that by the end of the nineteenth century disqualified it, seemingly ipso facto, from the realm of art and the positive valorizations the term might carry? Why might it be important that, however briefly, the first nude photographs were perceived as having the potential to do more?

Much ink has been spilled on the ontology of the photographic image, and it is not my intention to spill more here. I will instead propose a very simple answer to both of these questions as a way of leading to my conclusion. Photography is not just any representational form. It is, at its core, the form of the *real*. No matter that almost from its inception it was manipulated to show us false versions of reality. No matter that in the digital age, seemingly documentary photographs may be entirely untethered from that which they appear to represent. Photography has not yet shaken off its ties to the real, which from its first appearance undermined its aspirations to be a medium of art. The real is the source of the endless scandals surrounding it and our enduring fascination with it. When we talk about photographs of the body, we are not merely talking about a representation of the body, we are talking about the body represented in the image. In some sense, when a photograph of the body can signify only as a marker of oppression—whether that photograph dates to the nineteenth century or to today—we are also admitting that the real body can signify only in those terms. To me, this is a profound loss. It also obscures a far more complex and nuanced way of understanding how photography changed the body's meaning.

When the first photographers claimed to capture the female body in the name of art, they did something revolutionary and dangerous. They made the actual female body into an object worthy of aesthetic contemplation. Some of their attempts were disingenuous; some are frankly repulsive. But to my eyes (and I recognize how personal this judgment is), some are among the most beautiful and moving representations of the female body to be found in Western art. That beauty is rendered without the protective gloss of marble, the formalizing lines of the pen, or the obscuring texture of paint. Photography undid the safely idealized forms of women that had for so long dominated visual representation, unveiling them as fantasy. The power of the "beaver shot" is its shocking exposure, literal and figurative. It demands that we actually look at one of the most tabooed, concealed, exploited, abused, and feared parts of the female body, and for reasons that lie outside those of titillation and possession. The first nude photographs required one of the more explicit acknowledgments of the power of the *real* female body in the history of art. The best attempts at "art" nudes accorded the real female body a legitimate metaphoric and artistic value alongside its sexual power and asked viewers to confront that body in order to understand its meaning. They represented fleshy physical women as objects of beauty and objects of desire simultaneously. They even suggested that women might be desiring subjects. They allowed the female body to signify in an unprecedented way.

I do not mean to romanticize the early history of the photographic nude, or photographic nudity as a genre. These photographs were produced in a society in which women were second-class citizens. Yet they nevertheless granted the female body a remarkable plenitude of meaning in its stark nakedness. This, for me, is the significance of the literary works in this study. They testify precisely to the immense, varied, and contested signifying power granted by photography to the body and to what we lose when we limit the scope of that meaning. Baudelaire and the Goncourt brothers wrote about the photographic nude in terms of art because there was a real debate going on about the possibility that it might represent something more than bodies for sale, whether or not they ultimately rejected that possibility. And even in rejecting photographic artistry, they were forced to acknowledge the way in which it was asking real bodies to signify in a new way. Indeed, even as these three authors posited the death of art in the arrival of nude photography, their own creative output and their theories about art were forged in reaction to the new genre. In Baudelaire's poetry, the metaphoric truth of the body is revealed in its dialogue with photographic representation. However viscerally they denounce it, the Goncourt brothers nevertheless perceived that the nude photograph would upend existing artistic conventions to the point of demanding an entirely new way of conceiving of art. In other words, protest though they did, these authors register nude photography as profoundly important to the history of art and aesthetics and grant it a complexity and depth of potential meaning that corresponded to its artistic role. Particularly in the context of the other contemporary discussions about the model's body and the art value of nude photography, Baudelaire and the Goncourt brothers point to an enlightened future when the real body's aesthetic value might be recognized in positive terms, despite their own qualms about the photographic medium (or our qualms about their attitudes toward women).

Consequently, the novels of Zola and Maizeroy simultaneously represent both advancement into greater awareness and retreat into foreclosure of the body's meaning. In contrast to Baudelaire and the Goncourt brothers, these later authors recognize the dangers of the nude photographic image in terms familiar to readers of the twenty-first century. They transform the prudery of their contemporaries into nuanced explorations of the real harm nude images could do in contemporary society, including to the women in them. *Nana* enacts the worst ways that these images represent the body's sexual objectification under capitalism and Maizeroy's novels denounce them as silencing the expression of female desire. Yet, as the broader discourse about the street and photography's place in it suggests, this awareness is at times excruciatingly paternalistic and misogynistic. It also comes at the expense of the nude photograph's right even to trespass in the realm of art and with that any pretensions to a positive or transcendent meaning for the bodies it represents. Nana's body metes out death and destruction because it can signify only in terms of harmful sexuality; Maizeroy's texts have to obscure the real female body in order to grant women the power to express their sexual desire. Once the harm of these images was recognized, it seems, there was no way to valorize their revolutionary aesthetic potential.

We no longer live in the nineteenth century, and yet we have not entirely moved past it. As Facebook's censorship suggests, we have not reconciled our increasing awareness of all the ways that nude photography can reflect and perpetuate oppression with the positive ways that it might grant meaning to the body. We have not built on the potential of early artistic discourse about nude photography. Rather than jettisoning the problematic misogyny and sociopolitical context of those discussions about art and the body, it often feels as if we have simply jettisoned those discussions altogether. Where, then, does this leave us? For one thing, with work to be done. France was surely not the only place where the photographic image overturned old concepts about the body and its representation. Nude photographs have a global history. They also have a queer history. They may well also have a role in emerging trans identities at the end of the nineteenth century. They have their own iconographical lexicon that deserves far more careful study than I could grant it here. I hope that this book inspires more work on all of these different histories and a recognition of the immense artistic and cultural importance of these representations of the body around the globe.

More than that, I hope that the work I have done on these images offers a glimpse of just how many interpretations a photograph of the body can carry, including as a work of art, and why the recognition of all these many meanings is so important. I am only too aware that for the exposed (photographed) body to stop signifying oppression and exploitation entirely would require a total transformation of our society, our laws, and our ways of thinking about the body and sexuality, so that art and beauty were not always tempered to their breaking point with these realities. I don't foresee such a revolution; indeed, the Me Too movement has revealed just how far we still are from it. But I do hope we might start with a new kind of discourse about art and pornography that is more open to the body's multivalent signification. Rather than censoring images of the body, we need to attend to the kinds of images we see and to the ways that they are made. This change is already underway in the world of art photography and across the Internet, Facebook notwithstanding, but less so in our broader image culture. The body has power; women can reclaim that power. When women — cis women, trans women, women of all socioeconomic backgrounds and ethnicities — represent their own bodies (and control the profit from those images, whatever their sexual content), those photographs do not have to signify obscenity, exploitation, or objectification. Instead, when women let fall the "veil that hid[es] their beauty," as so many have in the years since photography's invention, their photographs can represent the complexity and diversity of sexuality, artistry, desire, and transgression, and with that all of the ways that they lend meaning to human experience.

⚔ NOTES ⚔

PREFACE

1. "Chronique: Paris, 19 janvier," *Gazette des tribunaux*, 20 January 1856, 70.

2. Ibid.

3. Crary, *Techniques of the Observer*, 13.

4. Aubenas, ed. *L'Art du nu au XIXe siècle*; McCauley, *Industrial Madness*; Solomon-Godeau, "The Legs of the Countess," *Photography at the Dock*.

5. Existing studies have focused on the relationship between literature and photography more generally. See, e.g., Edwards, *Soleil noir*; Ortel, *La Littérature à l'ère de la photographie*; Montier et al., eds., *Littérature et photographie*. With the exception of a few pages in Edwards on the nude in the photo-novel, none of these works explicitly addresses the nude as a genre. The two recent books that do address nude photographs are not primarily concerned with photography as such. They are Lathers, *Bodies of Art*, and Dawkins, *The Nude in French Art and Culture*.

CHAPTER 1

1. Quinet registered the photograph in 1861. Nazarieff, however, attributes it to Félix Jacques Antoine Moulin and dates it to 1850–1852, *Early Erotic Photography*, 131–133. Based on the model and props, I think it is more likely it was taken in the late 1850s by Auguste Belloc.

2. On issues of sexual objectification, see Solomon-Godeau, "The Legs of the Countess," 65–108, and "Reconsidering Erotic Photography: Notes for a Project of Historical Salvage," in *Photography at the Dock*, 220–237; McCauley, "Braquehais and the Photographic Nude," *Industrial Madness*, 149–194. On the artistic side of the debate, see Aubenas, ed., *L'Art du nu*.

3. "Décret organique sur la presse du 17 février 1852," 321. On the censorship law and photography generally, see English, "Anxiety and Official Censorship," 107, and Goldstein, "France," *Political Censorship of the Visual Arts*, 79–80.

4. "Loi du 17 mai 1819," 465, 467. On this law and nude photography, see also Demange, "Nu et nudité devant la loi," *L'Art du nu*, 38, and Solomon-Godeau, "The Other Side of Venus," *The Sex of Things*, 134. While photographs might have been subject to censorship under the 1835 September Laws until 1848, I have found no records of photographic nudes—or indeed any photographs—approved or rejected by the censors during that period. See A.N. F*18 VI 48 (accessible via *Image of France*) and *Régistres des estampes déposées*, 1839–1848. In the 1840s, most photographic images were daguerreotypes, which circulated in small numbers and may

not have been targeted for censorship. Goldstein's discussion of the September Laws excludes photography, "France," *Political Censorship of the Visual Arts*, 61–80.

5. "Chronique: Paris, 24 juillet," *Gazette des tribunaux*, 25 July 1851, 724. See also "Jurisprudence de la presse," 167. I will use either the French original or the English terms "affront to public decency" and "indecency" to refer to legal charges under the 1819 law.

6. Font-Réaulx, *Painting and Photography*, 221.

7. During the Empire, prosecutions under either statute were tried by a judge in the *tribunaux correctionnels*. Donovan, *Juries and the Transformation of Criminal Justice in France*, 93.

8. On the intent of the law, see Bérenger, *Manuel pratique*, 13–16.

9. "Décret organique sur la presse du 17 février 1852," 321.

10. "Code des photographes," *Moniteur de la photographie*, 15 June 1862, 56.

11. See, e.g., "Faits divers," *La Presse*, 26 May 1859; "Tribunal correctionnel de Paris," *Gazette des tribunaux*, 26 October 1860, 1028–1029; "Chronique: Paris, 18 September," *Gazette des tribunaux*, 19 September 1861, 916; "Art. 1251," 371–375; "Art. 1400," 54–55.

12. On the 1863 case, see "Code des photographes," *Moniteur de la photographie*, 1 October 1863, 111–112. On the 1864 case, see "Jurisprudence générale—1864," 21–22. An 1868 appeal confirmed that the censorship law determined sentencing because of its harsher penalties. "Paris, 28 février 1868: Peine, cumul, contravention, lois spéciales," 340. The defense that unregistered images were not necessarily obscenity had been attempted before 1863 unsuccessfully, "Chronique: Paris, 16 Octobre," *Gazette des tribunaux*, 17 October 1861, 1013.

13. "Jurisprudence générale—1864," 21.

14. On the first nude daguerreotypes, see Aubenas, "Le Nu académique existe-t-il en daguerréotype?" *L'Art du nu*, 24–29; Buerger, *French Daguerreotypes*, 129–132; Solomon-Godeau, "The Legs of the Countess," 95; Starl, "A New World of Pictures," *A New History of Photography*, 52–53.

15. Aubenas, "Modèles de peintre, modèles de photographe," *L'Art du nu*, 61–62; Frizot, "Automated Drawing: The Truthfulness of the Calotype," *A New History of Photography*, 73.

16. Untitled, *Le Corsaire*, 25 February 1847. Quoted by Aubénas, "Modèles de peintre, modèles de photographie," 42.

17. Aubenas, "Le Nu académique existe-t-il en daguerréotype?" 25–27.

18. Lerebours, *Traité de photographie*, 86.

19. See, e.g., Nazarieff, *Early Erotic Photography* and *The Stereoscopic Nude 1850–1930*, as well as Koetzle, *Uwe Schweid Collection*.

20. On collodion negatives and albumen prints, see Frizot, "The Transparent Medium," *A New History of Photography*, 91–95; on the carte-de-visite, see Sagne, "All kinds of portraits," *A New History of Photography*, 109–110; on the stereograph, see Richard, "Life in Three Dimensions," *A New History of Photography*, 175–183.

21. Aubenas, "Modèles de peintre, modèles de photographe," 42–65; Aubenas, "Eugène Delacroix et la Photographie," *L'Art du nu*, 92–95; Aubenas, "Les albums de nus d'Eugène Delcroix," *Delacroix et la photographie*, 23–51; Font-Réaulx, "Courbet et la photographie," *L'Art du nu*, 84–91; Font-Réaulx, *Painting and Photography*, 227–235.

22. Lerebours, *Traité*, 86.

23. See also Aubenas, "Reflets et miroirs," *L'Art du nu*," 130–131; Pinet, "Chevelure," *L'Art du nu*, 120–123; Pinet, "Le Masque, l'anonymat du mystère," *L'Art du nu*, 124–129; and Rexer, "Stockings and Mirrors," *Degas: A Strange New Beauty*, 137–141. The fixation with the visual effects of gauze is my own observation.

24. Lerebours, *Traité*, 86.

25. Clark, *The Painting of Modern Life*, 136.

26. Ibid, 123–127.

27. She was Laure Braquehais, wife of Bruno. See Lacan, "Revue photographique," *Le Moniteur de la photographie*, 15 January 1863, 161, and McCauley, *Industrial Madness*, 185. Apparently, a female student of Auguste Belloc proposed opening an atelier for woman photographers to produce académies, but it does not seem to have materialized. "Des dames photographes," *Revue photographique*, 5 November 1856, 196. On this atelier, see also Buerger, *French Daguerreotypes*, 130.

28. Aubenas, "Modèles de peintre, modèles de photographe," 42–65, and Font-Réaulx, "Courbet et la photographie," 84–91.

29. Images authorized for sale at the École des beaux-arts, see A.N. F*18 VIbis 1: 1 January 1865–1 June 1869, 389, 392. Authorization for export only, or on condition that they not be displayed, see, e.g., Lamy, below.

30 For example, ad for Charles Gaudin, *La Lumière*, 9 September 1854.

31. In 1855 and 1857, "nudities" were explicitly excluded. "Première exposition dans les salons de la Société," *Bulletin de la Société française de photographie*, March 1855, 40. "Exposition annuelle de la Société française de photographie," *Bulletin de la Société française de photographie*, October 1856, 295. In 1859, they were not explicitly excluded. "Exposition de la Société française de photographie," *Bulletin de la Société française de photographie*, January 1859, 27. See also McCauley, *Industrial Madness*, 156, and Solomon-Godeau, *Photography at the Dock*, 233.

32. "Réunion photographique," *La Lumière*, 25 March, 1854, 45–46; "Réunion photographique," *La Lumière*, 21 February 1855, 29–30.

33. "Défense de la photographie: De la photographie comme art," *Revue photographique*, 5 March 1857, 262–263; "Rapport sur l'Exposition ouverte par la Société en 1857," *Bulletin de la Société française de photographie*, August 1857, 260–263; A. Belloc, "L'Avenir de la photographie," *Revue photographique*, 5 August 1858, 109–110; "Exposition photographique," *Revue photographique*, 5 May 1859, 116–117; "Des rapports de la photographie avec les beaux-arts; par M. Claudet" *Revue Photographique*, 5 November 1860, 285–297; "L'Art et la photographie," *Revue photographique* 5 June 1860, 162–164. See also Mayer and Pierson, *La Photographie*, 129 ff.

34. Lacan, "De la photographie et de ses diverses applications aux beaux-arts et aux sciences (Extrait du *Moniteur* du 12 janvier 1855)," *La Lumière*, 27 January 1855, 16.

35. Wey, "De l'influence de l'héliographie sur les beaux-arts (suite)," *La Lumière*, 16 February 1851, 6. For a different reading of Wey, see McCauley, *Industrial Madness*, 154.

36. Gaudin, "Réunion d'artistes photographes," *La Lumière* 25 March 1854, 45. See also Buerger, *French Daguerreotypes*, 130–132, on Gouin.

37. Gaudin, "Réunion photographique," *La Lumière*, 24 February 1855, 30.

38. On the Braquehais and Gouin families, see McCauley, *Industrial Madness*, 151, and Buerger, *French Daguerreotypes*, 126–133.

39. Lacan, "Revue photographique: Études d'après nature: M. Braquehais," *La Lumière*, 16 September 1854, 147. See also McCauley, *Industrial Madness*, 152.

40. BB3, 1, 3, 5–6, 7, 10–11, 13, 17, 20–22, 29–30, 69 79–81, 82–84, 89, 95, 103, 110–115, 120, 136 154–155, 161, 177, 185 186 191–193, 259, 278.

41. Stanhopes, BB3, 8, 150, 151, 160, 172, 175–176, 178, 179, 190, 192, 202, 204, 207, 221, 251, 252, 260, and 265. See also McCauley, *Industrial Madness*, 160, and Demange, "Nu et nudité devant la loi," 40.

42. An 1860 raid yielded 1,458 photographs; another in 1865 produced nearly 800 images and 300 negatives. BB3, 85, 252.

43. BB3, 104. See also "Tribunal correctionnel de Paris," *Gazette des tribunaux*, 26 October 1860, 1028.

44. The government commissioner cited 64 prosecutions involving 172 individuals between July 1863 and June 1865. "Séance du 22 juin, 1865," 132.

45. Both the content of photographs pasted into the BB3 and their overlap with photographs in the Enfer collection suggest that photographs used for identification in the BB3 were seized in raids. Only a handful of suspects appear fully dressed (usually photographers).

46. Solomon-Godeau, "The Legs of the Countess," 74–75.

47. Solomon-Godeau, *Photography at the Dock*, 233–235, and "The Other Side of Venus," 134. Significantly, Solomon-Godeau attributes this scopic regime to all nudes, not just sexually explicit ones. While it certainly isn't absent from academic nudity, I only consider it a defining quality of erotic photographic nudity.

48. Solomon-Godeau, "The Legs of the Countess," 97, "The Other Side of Venus," 134, and *Photography at the Dock*, 233. David Ogawa on the other hand argues that the "beaver shot" anonymizes the model in response to police activity, "Arresting Nudes in Second Empire Paris," 346–347. Solomon-Godeau's claims about photography and the invention of the beaver shot refer specifically to the realm of erotic imagery. It bears noting that medical drawings of genitals— particularly anomalous genitalia—from this perspective considerably predated the advent of photography. For an early nineteenth-century example, see, e.g., Jacquemin, "Description de l'organisation vicieuse." I am grateful to Anne Linton for drawing my attention to this fact and providing this source. See Linton, "Prescribed Fictions" and "Hermaphrodite Outlaws." On Belloc and medical imagery specifically, see also Aubenas and Comar, *Obscénités*, 27-28.

49. On lesbian images, Solomon-Godeau, *Photography at the Dock*, 235.

50. Aubenas, "Les photographies de l'enfer," *L'Enfer de la bibliothèque*, 259.

51. I count thirty-one photographers in the BB3 who also registered legal images of any kind: Augé, Belloc, Bertrand, Billon, Bilordeaux, Brisson, Bucquet, Cordier, Delbarre, Durand, Fronti, Gentil, Jouvin, Ken, Lacroix, Lamiche, Lamy, Léautté, Leymarie, Lorinet, Plaut, Petit, Quinet, Speisser, Segoffin, Thiébault, Thomassin, Torbéchet, Tongue, and Weyler. Additionally, although their names do not appear in the BB3, Malacrida and Moulin were the first to be tried for outrage aux bonnes mœurs in 1851 (see note 5), and Nazarieff has attributed illegal nudes to Gouin and Braquehais. Nazarieff, *Erotic Photography*, 38–57, 88–107. Marconi was arrested in 1873 for unauthorized nudity, Drujon, *Catalogue des ouvrages, écrits et dessins*, xxxi. McCauley's count is different, *Industrial Madness*, 158, 391.

52. BB3, 71, 137, 259.

53. BB3, 240–242, 250.

54. BB3, 106, 202. "Cours et Tribunaux," *La Presse*, 15 February 1862.

55. BB3, 6, 10, 40, 49–50 55, 56, 85, 92, 141, 145, 160, 179, 194, 198, 202–203, 221, 248, 255, 260, 265, 271.

56. "Chronique: Paris, 8 septembre," *Gazette des tribunaux*, 9 September 1857, 895, refers to this change in policy. Models were apparently already being sentenced in June of that year. See "Chronique," *La Lumière*, 20 June 1857, 99.

57. BB3, 43, 46, 55, 65, 70–72, 78, 89, 126, 129, 143, 181, 182–184, 193, 196, 235, 236, 283.

58. "Photographies obscènes," *Revue photographique*, 5 August 1860, 220; "Chronique: Paris, 8 septembre," *Gazette des tribunaux*, 9 September 1857, 895.

59. The professional model, BB3, 52. For crossover models, see, e.g., photographs by Lamy discussed below.

60. Sexual majority (i.e., the age of sexual consent), legal majority, and the marriage age were all different. On the age of sexual consent, see Daniel, *De la protection des jeunes filles mineures*, 26–27.

61. "Photographies obscènes," *Revue photographique*, 5 August 1860, 220. Child pornography only began to be discussed in the later part of the century.

62. BB3, 24, 51–53, 72–74, 76–77, 86–88, 93, 96–99, 100, 101, 118–120, 123, 125–126, 128, 130, 132–133, 140, 143–144, 149, 186, 195, 200–201, 237–238, 242–243, 250, 255, 258, 267, 283. See also "Cours et Tribunaux," *La Presse*, 11 October 1860, for a representative survey of professions.

63. BB3, 54, 55, 76, 87–88, 93, 147, 253, 284.

64. McCauley, 183–184. For McCauley and Solomon-Godeau, prostitution defines the photographic model. Solomon-Godeau, "The Legs of the Countess," 94–95, 99–103.

65. "Chronique: Paris, 24 juillet," *Gazette des tribunaux*, 25 July 1851, 724. See also Desportes, "Revue mensuelle," 142; Pélin, *Les Laideurs du beau Paris*, 13–18; "Photographies Érotiques," *Le Tintamarre* 13 May 1860, 4, which is cited at length in A. Méphis, "Chronique," *La Lumière* 19 May 1860, 79; "Séance du 22 juin, 1865," 128; and "Untitled," *Le Triboulet*. See also McCauley, *Industrial Madness*, 155.

66. Pélin, *Les Laideurs du beau Paris*, 14.

67. BB3, 1, 6, 39, 41, 63, 66, 152, 217, 219, 301, 302.

68. Commissions, BB3, 70, 96, 131. McCauley notes a commission (likely a lithograph), *Industrial Madness*, 157. From entries that refer to neither a storefront nor peddling, I deduce that photographers used their studios, BB3, 49 and 119.

69. BB3, 1, 63, 160, 179, 198, 202, 221, 260, 265.

70. BB3, 30.

71. BB3, 4, 6, 10, 23, 34, 40, 55, 60, 65, 71, 82, 83, 85, 117, 193, 194, 285.

72. Vendors designated as "peddlars" or those with no storefront, BB3, 7, 32, 33, 175, 176, 197, 216–217, 219–220, 225–226, 229, 229–233, 243, 247, 251, 259–260, 299. See also "Chronique et faits divers," *Le Temps*, 28 June 1862.

73. BB3, 295.

74. BB3, 171, 249, 273, 285.

75. Larousse, "Crémerie," *Grand Dictionnaire universel du XIXe siècle*, V: 486. In 1866, a man was arrested for showing obscene photographs to female customers of a creamery. "No. 997," 784–786, and "Art. 1400," 54–55.

76. BB3, 6, 9, 14, 17, 18, 30, 46, 58–59, 68, 71, 79, 106, 122, 127, 130, 139, 144, 147, 150–151, 159, 163, 166, 174, 178, 190, 199, 204, 207, 210, 212, 214, 234, 239, 241, 270 (*2nd), 273. Various servants were also arrested while making deliveries for their employers, BB3, 39, 162, 202. The BB3 also indicts a wine merchant's assistant who stored his friend's wares (199), a hairdresser (47), and two cooks as accomplices (6, 167), without specifying their roles.

77. BB3, 7, 39, 302, 175, 176, 282. See also Andral, "Outrage à la morale," *Courrier de la librairie*, 179.

78. BB3, 191. BB3, 249. BB3, 218. BB3, 257. BB3, 286–287.

79. BB3, 249, 163–164, 165, 276, 286.

80. "Cours et Tribunaux," *La Presse*, 15 April 1862.

81. Larousse, "Collégien," *Grand Dictionnaire universel du XIXe siècle*, IV: 608. Pélin also mentions "lycéens" consuming nude photographs, *Les Laideurs du beau Paris*, 15.

82. Goncourt, *Journal:* II: 24–25, 161–162, 304. On Dantan's collection, see also "Courrier de Paris," *Le Figaro*, 12 April 1860.

83. "Échos de Paris," *Le Figaro*, 27 March 1864.

84. On the provinces, see McCauley, *Industrial Madness*, 164; BB3, 216–217; Lavedan, "Les Événements du mois," *Le Correspondant*, 704; "Jurisprudence Générale—1864," 21–22; "Correspondance de Bayonne," *La Petite Revue*, 23 January 1864, 175–176. On Mexico, see "Art. 1251," 371–375; "Cass.—crim. 11 août 1864," *Journal du Palais*, 574; and McCauley, *Industrial Madness*, 161. On Peru and Japan, see Maxime Ducamp, *Paris, ses organes, ses fonctions et sa vie*, II: 30. On export to Spain, "Tribunaux," *La Lumière* 14 August 1858, 131 (reprinted as "La Photographie au Palais," *Revue photographique*, 5 September 1858, 137), and "Tribunal correctionnel de Paris," *Gazette des tribunaux*, 26 October 1860. On Russia, "Untitled," *Le Triboulet*. On imports from Switzerland, BB3, 207.

85. "Séance du 22 juin, 1865," 128, 132.

86. Pélin, *Les laideurs du beau Paris*, 14.

87. "Photographies érotiques," *Le Tintamarre*, 13 May 1860, 4.

88. "Code des photographes," *Moniteur de la photographie*, 1 October 1863, 112.

89. Lecour, *La Prostitution à Paris et à Londres*, 250.

90. On these photographs, see Solomon-Godeau, "The Legs of the Countess," 91–93.

91. "Chronique," *La Lumière*, 19 May 1860, 79.

92. Solomon-Godeau, "The Legs of the Countess," 74–75, 87–94.

93. Pélin, *Les Laideurs du Beau Paris*, 15. On the mix in shop displays, see also McCauley, 158.

94. See again Pinet, "Chevelure," 120–123; Pinet, "Le Masque, l'anonymat du mystère," 124–129; Aubenas, "Reflets et miroirs," 130–131; and Rexer, "Stockings and Mirrors," 137–141.

95. On the erotic appeal of stereoscopic three-dimensionality, see Solomon-Godeau, "Legs of the Countess," 95, and Crary, *Techniques of the Observer*, 127.

96. Homberger, "The model's unwashed feet," *Artistic Relations*, 140; Weingarden, "Manet's Realism and the Erotic Gaze," *Efficacité/Efficacy*, 292; Solomon-Godeau, "The Legs of the Countess," 98.

97. McCauley, *Industrial Madness*, 170–173.

98. "Untitled," *La Lumière*, 26 June 1856, 100.

99. Gouin, Malacrida, Moulin, Belloc, Cordier-Billon, Bertrand, Torbéchet, Lamy, Bisson, Marconi, Léautté, Tongue, Weyler, and Braquehais made illegal nudes and submitted legal nudes.

100. Figure 26 corresponds to entries for Lamy, A.N. F*18 VI 67: November 1860–July 1861, 94. Figures 27 and 28 correspond to A.N. F*18 VI 67: November 1860–July 1861, 314. They were granted authorization by special order and also appear in a register of special authorizations and authorization denials, A.N. F*18 VI 133, 162.

101. Figure 29 is from the Enfer of the Bibliothèque nationale. For other illegal images from the series, see BB3, 118, and Koetzle, *Uwe 1000 Nudes*, 356–359.

102. BB3, 104. Copies of his output are preserved today in the Bibliothèque nationale's *Enfer*.

103. BB3, 31.

104. These include large-format nudes submitted by Marconi, as well as stereographs submitted under the name Billon, attributed by Nazarieff to Belloc, *Early Erotic Photography*, 18–35. See also entries submitted under his own name, A.N. F*18 VI 67: November 1860–July 1861, 196, 199, 264, 299. It is not clear whether Figure 30 was submitted for authorization by Belloc, although it is in the collections of the Bibliothèque nationale.

105. Molard, "Bibliographie: *Les Quatre branches de la photographie*; par M. Belloc," *Bulletin de la Société française de photographie*, September 1855, 274–276; "Bibliographie photographique: *Compendium des quatre branches de la photographie* Par A. Belloc, Professeur de la photographie," *Revue photographique*, 5 July 1858.

106. "Défense de la photographie: De la photographie comme art," *Revue photographique*, 5 March 1857, 262. For other praise of Belloc, see Untitled, *La Presse*, 24 October 1844; Durieu, "Rapport sur l'Exposition de la Société francaise de la Photographie," *Revue photographique*, 5 May 1856, 110; Paul Périer, "Exposition universelle," *Bulletin de la Société française de photographie*, September 1855, 266.

107. For more on Belloc, see Aubenas and Comar, *Obscénités*, and Ogawa, "Arresting Nudes," 342–347.

108. On Courbet's photographs, Font-Réaulx, "Courbet et la photographie," 86. On "beaver shot" photographs and *The Origin of the World*, Aubenas, "Postface," in Schopp, *L'Origine du monde*, 138–139; Font-Réaulx, *Painting and Photography*, 230–231; Frizot, "Body of Evidence: The Ethnophotography of Difference," *A New History of Photography*, 271; McCauley, *Industrial Madness*, 178. Solomon-Godeau on the other hand cites the painting as an exception to her own claim that photography "invents" the beaver shot, "The Legs of the Countess," 97.

109. BB3, 293.

110. Font-Réaulx, "Courbet et la photographie," 85.

111. Needham, "Manet, 'Olympia,' and Pornographic Photography," *Woman as Sex Object*, 81–89. Weingarden expands on Needham's analysis in "Manet's Realism and the Erotic Gaze," 287–298.

112. Solomon-Godeau, "The Legs of the Countess," 99.

113. Moigno, "Biographie: M. Moulin," *Revue photographique*, 5 December 1855, 27; "Tribunaux," *La Lumière*, 14 August 1858, 131 (reprinted as "La Photographie au Palais," *Revue photographique*, 5 September 1858, 137).

114. "Cours et Tribunaux," *La Presse*, 9 September 1857.

115. This is the position (with variations) taken by Lathers, *Bodies of Art*, 234; McCauley, *Industrial Madness*, 154; Ogawa "Arresting Nudes," 338; and Solomon-Godeau, *Photography at the Dock*, 220–237.

116. D'Apremont, "Nouveaux Horizons photographiques," *La Lumière*, 25 September 1858, 154.

117. Ibid.

118. Ibid.

119. "Photographies érotiques," *Le Tintamarre*, 13 May 1860, 4.

120. "Ce que peut faire un photographe," *Le Figaro*, 3 November 1861.

121. Ibid. The prosecutor in the case of Eugene Darnay also condemns him for his crime against both the honor of the models and the "admirable art" of photography. See "La Photographie au Palais," *Revue photographique*, 5 September 1858, 137. Also reported as "Tribunaux," *La Lumière*, 14 August 1858, 131.

CHAPTER 2

1. See McCauley, *Industrial* Madness, 183–184; Solomon-Godeau, "The Legs of the Countess," 94–95, 99–103; Robert "Le photographe, le modèle et le commerce des corps," *Splendeurs et misères: Images de la prostitution 1850–1910*, 68–79.

2. Lathers, *Bodies of Art*, 19; Clark makes a similar claim about Manet's *Olympia*, arguing that her class is encoded onto her body, "Olympia's Choice," *The Painting of Modern Life*, 118–119, 146.

3. On the sexual status of the painter's model and her connection to prostitution, see Lathers, *Bodies of Art*, 13, 54–55.

4. Proudhon also targets paintings and engravings, *Du principe de l'art et de sa destination sociale*, 259.

5. Clark, 103. See also Bernheimer, *Figures of Ill Repute*, and Clayson, *Painted Love*.

6. BB3, 191, 218, 249, 257, 286–287.

7. BB3, 31.

8. Untitled, *Le Corsaire*, 25 February 1847. Cited by Aubénas, "Modèles de peintre, modèles de photographie," *L'Art du Nu*, 42.

9. Pélin, *Les Laideurs du beau Paris*, 16.

10. Claude, *Mémoires de Monsieur Claude*, II: 80. That they are possibly fabricated, see Harsin, *Policing Prostitution*, 160.

11. "Ce que peut faire un photographe," *Le Figaro*, 3 November 1861.

12. "Code des photographes," *Moniteur de la photographie*, 1 October 1863, 112.

13. Untitled, *Le Triboulet*, 28 March 1857.

14. Harsin, *Policing Prostitution*, 94–95.

15. For another approach to pose in the guilt of the model, see David Ogawa, "Arresting Nudes," 338.

16. "Photographies érotiques," *Le Tintamarre*, 4. Also, A. Méphis, "Chronique," *La Lumière*, 19 May 1860.

17. Pélin, *Les Laideurs du beau Paris*, 15.

18. "Chronique: Paris, 8 septembre," *Gazette des tribunaux*, 9 September 1857, 895. Another article in the *Gazette des tribunaux* similarly (but less strikingly) described the photographs as "visible proof" of their guilt, "Chronique: Paris, 16 Octobre," *Gazette des tribunaux*, 17 October 1861, 1013.

19. On the legal status of prostitution, see Harsin, *Policing Prostitution*, 80–81, 94–95, 331.

20. See also Ogawa on the gender imbalance of those arrested for modeling, "Arresting Nudes," 339–340.

21. BB3, 24. Despite her story, Parant paid 100 francs and served a six-month prison sentence. See also "Chronique: Paris, 13 juin," *Gazette des tribunaux*, 14 June 1857, 583.

22. "Cours et Tribunaux: Tribunal correctionnel de la Seine," *La Presse*, 26 October 1860. Similar language was used in "Chronique: Paris, 19 janvier," *Gazette des tribunaux*, 20 January 1856, 70.

23. "Ce que peut faire un photographe," *Le Figaro*, 3 November 1861.

24. On photographic models and the professions of prostitutes, see McCauley, *Industrial Madness*, 183–184. She cites Parent-Duchâtelet, whose work is summarized by Corbin, *Les Filles de noce*, 46–51, and Harsin, *Policing Prostitution*, 115, 123, 206–209.

25. Lecour, *La Prostitution à Paris et à Londres*, 250.

26. The concern over the sexual status of photographic models is clearly related to the broader anxiety about the problematic distinction between prostitute and "honest" woman, which were equally fraught categories. See Corbin, *Les Filles de noce*, 82–83; Harsin, *Policing Prostitution*, 116, 279. On the problematic distinction in relation to nude photography in particular, see McCauley, *Industrial Madness*, 166–167, and Abigail Solomon-Godeau, "The Legs of the Countess," 94–95, 101–105. For an overview of discourse about prostitution in the nineteenth century, see Corbin, *Les Filles de noce*, 13–53.

27. "Ce que peut faire un photographe," *Le Figaro*, 3 November 1861.

28. On the eleven-year-old model, "Photographies obscènes," *Revue photographique*, 5 August 1860, 220.

29. In one case, a man reported that a photographer had taken seminude pictures of his daughter. BB3, 137. In another, a seventeen-year-old told police she had posed nude at the behest of her lover, BB3, 131–132.

30. "Cours et Tribunaux: Tribunal correctionnel de la Seine," *La Presse*, 16 September 1857.

31. Ibid.

32. "Tribunaux," *La Lumière*, 14 August 1858, 131. Reprinted as "La Photographie au Palais," *Revue photographique*, 5 September 1858, 137.

33. "Chronique: Paris, 8 septembre," *Gazette des tribunaux*, 9 September 1857, 895.

34. On the charge of "debauching of a minor," see Rogron, *Code pénal expliqué*, 495–496. For photographers charged with "excitation to debauchery," see "Tribunaux," *La Lumière*, 14 August 1858, 131 (reprinted as "La Photographie au Palais," *Revue photographique*, 5 September 1858, 137), and "Cours et Tribunaux: Cour de cassation," *La Presse*, 18 January 1861. In the 1858 case, the models were charged as accomplices; in 1861, the BB3 indicates they were not, BB3, 128.

35. "Photographies obscènes," *Revue photographique*, 5 August 1860, 219.

36. Tardieu, *Étude médico-légale*, 12.

37. Ibid., 12.

38. Ibid., 12.

39. Ibid., 13.

40. Solomon-Godeau, "The Legs of the Countess," 69.

41. "Cours et Tribunaux: Cour de cassation," *La Presse*, 18 January 1861. The model, Julie Vériot (or Verriot), also appears in the BB3, 130.

42. "Chronique," *La Lumière*, 3 September 1859, 143.

43. Ibid.

44. Ibid.

45. Ibid.

46. Ibid.

47. Ibid.

48. For Matlock, these fears about looking and exposure turn on issues of realist representation (including but not limited to photography). "Censoring the Realist Gaze," *Spectacles of Realism*, 37.

49. For some of these humorous references, see Untitled, *Le Triboulet*, 28 March 1857, and "La Semaine parisienne," *Le Figaro*, 7 March 1870.

50. On Pesme's prosecution, "Art. 778," 80, and Demange, "Nu et nudité: le nu devant la loi," *L'Art du nu*, 39. On the mania for Léotard and his photographs, see "Tribunal de commerce de la Seine," *Gazette des tribunaux*, 29 September 1860, 936, and Goncourt, *Journal*, I: 775.

51. Cogniard and Clairville, *Oh! La, la! Qu'c'est bête tout ça*, 18.

52. Claude, *Mémoires de Monsieur Claude*, II: 81.

53. Ibid., 92.

54. Ibid., 93.

55. Ibid., 94.

56. Disdéri, *L'Art de la photographie*, 302.

57. Ibid.

58. Ibid., 303.

59. Ibid.

60. Ibid., 304.

61. Ibid., 304–305.

62. "Tribunaux," *La Lumière*, 14 August 1858, 131 (reprinted as "La Photographie au Palais," *Revue photographique*, 5 September 1858, 137).

63. Moigno, "Biographie: M. Moulin, *Revue photographique*, 5 December 1855, 26.

64. Lacan, "Exposition universelle: Photographie," *La Lumière*, 13 October 1855, 161–162; Périer, "Exposition universelle," *Bulletin de la Société française de photographie*, September 1855, 273. Lacan, "Exposition photographique," *La Lumière*, 11 June 1859, 93; "Exposition photographique," *Revue photographique*, 5 May 1859, 116.

65. Gaudin, "Imprimerie photographique," *La Lumière*, 22 January 1853, 13. Lacan, "De la photographie et de ses diverses applications aux beaux-arts et aux sciences (Extrait du *Moniteur* du 12 janvier 1855)," *La Lumière*, 27 January 1855, 16.

66. Lacan, "La Photographie de genre: M. Moulin," *La Lumière*, 20 August 1853, 135. For further praise of Moulin, see Lacan, "Revue photographique: Mm Disdéri, Moulin," *La Lumière*, 17 June 1854, 95, and "Untitled," *Le Propagateur*, 4 December 1853, cited in Nazarieff, *Early Erotic Photography*, 111–112.

67. "Chronique: Paris, 24 juillet," *Gazette des tribunaux*, 25 July 1851. Nazarieff has attributed an explicit stereoscopic daguerreotype to him, *The Stereoscopic Nude, 1850–1930*, 47.

68. Moigno, "Biographie: M. Moulin," *Revue photographique*, 5 December 1855, 27.

69. Périer, "Exposition universelle," *Bulletin de la Société française de photographie*, September 1855, 273. The final phrase, "on ne saurait voir," likely alludes to Molière, *Tartuffe*, III, 2, 860–862.

70. "Ce que peut faire un photographe," *Le Figaro*, 3 November 1861.

71. Lacan, "Revue photographique: Études d'après nature: M. Braquehais," *La Lumière*, 16 September 1854, 147.

72. Ibid.

73. Gaudin, "Réunion d'artistes photographes," *La Lumière*, 25 March 1854, 45.

74. "Untitled," *Le Propagateur*, 4 December 1853. Cited in Nazarieff, *Early Erotic Photography*, 111–112. Nazarieff indicates that it refers to Figure 38.

75. "Bloc-Notes Parisien: Le droit à la photographie," *Le Gaulois*, 21 August 1889, 1; "Nouvelles et echoes," *Le Gil Blas*, 29 August 1887, 1. As a fictional type, see Jules Demolliens, "Chez le photographe," *La Caricature*, 8 October 1881, 322; "Le Reporteur indiscret," *La Vie de Paris*, 1901,

reproduced in Edwards, *Soleil noir*, 260. On the origins of the word "voyeurism" in connection to the brothel and photography, see also Robert, "Le photographe, le modèle et le commerce des corps," in *Splendeurs et misères*, 77–78, and McCauley, "Sneak Previews," in *Snapshot*, 56.

76. See, e.g., Fransois, "Le Photographe amateur."

77. Delcourt, *Le Vice à Paris*, 30–31. The same fear appears in fictional form in an 1879 story about a photographer pasting the faces of "women of Parisian society" onto nude bodies until an angry husband intervenes. L'Épine, "Les Coupeurs de Têtes," *La Vie à grand orchestre*, 222.

78. Bergon and Le Bègue, *Le Nu et le drapé*, 12.

79. "Chronique: Paris, 8 septembre," *Gazette des tribunaux*, 9 September 1857.

CHAPTER 3

This chapter is derived in part from "Baudelaire's Bodies, or Redressing the Wrongs of Nude Photography, *Word and Image*, 35, no. 2 (2019): 126–140. ©Taylor & Francis. Available online at http://www.tandfonline.com/10.1080/02666286.2018.1549428.

Epigraph: Baudelaire, *Œuvres complètes*, I: 1206 (henceforth OC).

1. See "Chronique: Paris, 8 septembre," *Gazette des tribunaux*, 9 September 1857; "Tribunal correctionnel de la Seine," *La Presse*, 16 September 1857.

2. Weiss, "La Littérature brutale," 178.

3. De Laincel, "Impressions de lecture: *Les Fleurs du Mal*," 441.

4. Schlossman, "Baudelaire: Liberté, Libertinage and Modernity," 75. Ladenson, *Dirt for Art's Sake*, 54.

5. Baudelaire, OC, I: 677.

6. Ladenson, on lesbians, the dandy, and the unnatural, *Dirt for Art's Sake*, 74; quotation, Sanyal, *The Violence of Modernity*, 95. For similar observations on women, the natural, and art, see Burton, *Baudelaire in 1859*, 96 ff., especially 98, 133–134, 143–144; Wing, *The Limits of Narrative*, 22; and Rosemary Lloyd, *Baudelaire's World*, 93. On similar thematics in relation to the prostitute more specifically, see Bernheimer, *Figures of Ill Repute*, 74, and Sanyal, *The Violence of Modernity*, 102 ff. These arguments are all consistent with that of Schor, who situates Baudelaire in the tradition of "the sexual stereotypes of Western philosophy, which has, since its origins, mapped gender onto the form-matter paradigm, forging a durable link between maleness and form (eidos), femaleness and formless matter." Schor, *Reading in Detail*, 16.

7. In connecting Baudelaire's poems and obscene photography Weingarden similarly argues his poems are obscene, "Manet's Realism and the Erotic Gaze," *Efficacité/Efficacy*, 296–299.

8. Unlike Sanyal, Wing, or Burton, who emphasize the problematic contradiction between natural woman and woman as signifier, I argue that all of Baudelaire's art necessarily exists between the real and the ideal as the two are always in dialogue. See Sanyal, *The Violence of Modernity*, 104; Burton, *Baudelaire in 1859*, 98; Wing, *The Limits of Narrative*, 22.

9. On "l'art pour l'art" and realism, see Lloyd, *Baudelaire's World*, 65–67, 121; Claude Pichois, *Album Baudelaire*, 130–135; Avice and Pichois, *Passion Baudelaire*, 70, 94; Hiddleston, "Art and Its Representation," in *The Cambridge Companion to Baudelaire*, 136; Starkie, *Baudelaire*, 227; and Terdiman, "Baudelaire's 'Le Cygne': Memory, History and the Sign," *Present Past*, 134.

10. Baudelaire, OC, II: 685.

11. Baudelaire, OC, II: 493.

12. Baudelaire, OC, II: 59.

13. Baudelaire, OC, II: 598.

14. Baudelaire, OC, II: 596.

15. Baudelaire, OC, I: 11. The idea of "correspondances" is also discussed in the *Exposition universelle de 1855*, OC, II: 577. On correspondences, see Judd Hubert, "Symbolism, Correspondence and Memory," 46–47, and Starkie, *Baudelaire*, 227–237; on the real and the imagination, see Hiddleston, "Art and Its Representation," 136–137; Lloyd, *Baudelaire's World*, 80–82; Burton, *Baudelaire in 1859*, 170–182; and Nicolae Babuts, *Baudelaire: At the Limits and Beyond*, 20–21, 43–45, 117–121. A classic symbolist reading of this poem emphasizes the way in which the natural world is a hieroglyph for the symbolic one. I have emphasized the importance of the real (and the senses) as part of this conception.

16. Baudelaire, OC, II: 456.

17. Ibid., 457.

18. Ibid.

19. Ibid., 456.

20. On Tassaert, see Farwell, "Courbet's 'Baigneuses' and the Rhetorical Feminine Image," in *Woman as Sex Object*, 69–70.

21. Baudelaire, OC, II: 443.

22. Ibid., 445.

23. Ibid., 618.

24. Ibid.

25. Baudelaire, letter to Nadar, 14 May 1859, *Correspondance*, I: 574. In 1863, he would also request prints from Étienne Carjat. Letter to Étienne Carjat, 6 October 1863, *Correspondance*, II: 322.

26. Baudelaire, OC, II: 618–619.

27. On photography as inimical to a symbolist Baudelairian poetics, see Starkie, *Baudelaire*, 293. For Walter Benjamin, Baudelaire's reaction stems from his awareness of the destructive effect of the photograph to the aura of the work of art, *Charles Baudelaire*, 145–154. Blood focuses on the combination of the mechanical and metaphorical in Baudelaire's reaction to photography, *Baudelaire and the Aesthetics of Bad Faith*, 150–172. Raser reads Baudelaire's rejection of photography through the Lacanian "mirror stage" of development, *Baudelaire and Photography*, 63–70. For a completely different approach to Baudelaire and photography, see Marder, who reads the poem "À une passante" as a negative photographic image, *Dead Time*, 77–87.

28. Baudelaire, OC, II: 617.

29. Ibid., 621. See Avice and Pichois on Baudelaire, photography, his relationship to Nadar, and his theorizing of the imagination in 1859, *Passion Baudelaire*, 116–123.

30. On photography in the context of copying, salon painters, and the imagination in the *Salon de 1859*, see Raser, *Baudelaire and Photography*, 17–27.

31. In the *Salon de 1846*, Baudelaire described Lottier's paintings as "of a marvelously cruel truth. One might say they were made with a color daguerreotype." Baudelaire, OC, II: 484.

32. Baudelaire, OC, II: 617. This passage has been frequently cited, including (but not exclusively) by Solomon-Godeau, *Photography at the Dock*, 222, and Raser, *Baudelaire and Photography*, 25–26.

33. Baudelaire, letter to Nadar, 14 May 1859, *Correspondance* I: 574.

34. Blood describes Baudelaire's response to photography as "reactionary," noting that he "seems to [. . .] collapse aesthetic issues into questions of public morality," *The Aesthetics of Bad Faith*, 152–153.

35. Baudelaire, OC, II: 443.

36. Ibid., 619.

37. Ibid.

38. Baudelaire here sounds like Disdéri (see Chapter 2), except that where Disdéri attributes this unavoidable descent into obscenity to the flaws of the models, Baudelaire attributes it to photography.

39. Baudelaire, OC, II: 619–620.

40. Pichois, *Album Baudelaire*, 135. Ladenson, *Dirt for Art's Sake*, 53.

41. This intentional rejection of photography is a premise of Raser's study of Baudelaire, *Baudelaire and Photography*, 3–7, 61–62, 68.

42. Baudelaire, OC, II: 713.

43. Ibid., 715.

44. Ibid.

45. Ibid., 717.

46. Sanyal, *The Violence of Modernity*, 96.

47. Baudelaire, OC, II: 714.

48. Stephens argues that Baudelaire perceives something of his own poetry in Guys' method and art, "Esquisse d'incomplétude," 528. Pichois notes that Baudelaire produced sketches that are strikingly similar to those of Guys, *Album Baudelaire*, 180–182. Lloyd also remarks that the article is largely about Baudelaire himself, *Baudelaire's World*, 106.

49. Baudelaire, OC, I: 31.

50. Ibid., 31–32.

51. Ibid.

52. Baudelaire, OC, II: 455. See also "L'Art mnémonique," in *Le peintre de la vie moderne*, OC, II: 697–700. On memory, see Babuts, *Baudelaire: At the Limits and Beyond*, 21–22, 121 ff.; Hiddleston, *Baudelaire and the Art of Memory*; Hubert, "Symbolism, Correspondence and Memory," 46–55; Lloyd, *Baudelaire's World*, 17–18; Stephens, "Esquisse d'incomplétude," 532–533; and Terdiman, *Present Past*, 107–150.

53. Baudelaire, OC, I: 31.

54. Ibid., 112.

55. Ibid.

56. On the erotics of stockings, see Solomon-Godeau, "The Legs of the Countess," 74–75. Notably, Solomon-Godeau cites Baudelaire in making her argument. The garter is my own addition to her discussion.

57. Baudelaire, OC, I: 112.

58. Ibid., 113.

59. Ibid.

60. Ibid., 58.

61. Ibid.

62. Ibid.

63. Ibid., 84.

64. Ibid., 111.

65. Ibid., 85.

66. Ibid., 39.

67. Babuts, *Baudelaire: At the Limits and Beyond*, 19–23, Hubert, "Symbolism, Correspondence and Memory," 49.

68. Burton, *Baudelare in 1859*, 98.

69. Sanyal, *The Violence of Modernity*, 104.

70. Aristotle, *The Rhetoric and the Poetics of Aristotle*, 255. Roman Jakobson, "The Metaphoric and Metonymic Poles," 81.

71. Baudelaire, OC, I: 158.

72. Ibid.

73. Ibid.

74. Baudelaire, letter to Auguste Poulet-Malassis, 6 July 1860, *Correspondance*, II: 60.

75. Pinet, "La Chevelure," *L'Art du nu*, 120.

76. Baudelaire, OC, I: 26.

77. Ibid.

78. Ibid.

79. Ibid., 27.

80. Ibid.

81. For Burton, the poem acknowledges the physical aspect of woman only to transcend it, rather than to unite the real and the ideal, *Baudelaire in 1859*, 89–104.

82. Baudelaire, OC, II: 496.

CHAPTER 4

1. Goncourt, *Journal*, I: 852.

2. Goncourt, *Journal*, II: 476.

3. For readings of Manette as a painter's model, see Lathers, "Models, Monkeys and Naturalism: The Goncourt Brothers' *Manette Salomon*," in *Bodies of Art*, 142–168; Bell, "The Jew as Model," 825–847; and Dolan, "Musée Goncourt: *Manette Salomon* and the Nude," 172–185.

4. Ricatte, *La Création romanesque*, 337.

5. Goncourt, *Journal*, II: 90.

6. Ibid., 166.

7. Goncourt, *Journal*, I: 847–848.

8. Ibid., 286.

9. Ibid., 847.

10. Ibid., 1084.

11. Goncourt, *Journal*, I: 360.

12. Goncourt, *Journal*, II: 355.

13. Ibid., 376.

14. Goncourt, *Journal*, I: 633.

15. Ibid., 744. They were infuriated that the government sanctioned the taste for Rigolboche while pursuing writers like themselves. "It rains trivial books, *rigolbochades*, tolerated, authorized, encouraged by the gouvernment, who is careful not to prosecute them. [The government] reserves criminal court for people like Flaubert and us." Ibid., 774. On Rigolboche, see also Solomon-Godeau, "The Legs of the Countess," 91.

16. The Goncourts are referring to Count Nieuwerkerke, lover to Princess Mathilde Bonaparte. Goncourt, *Journal*, I: 1230.

17. Goncourt, *Journal*, II: 304.

18. Ibid., 161–162.

19. Goncourt, *Journal*, I: 633.

20. Ibid., 640.

21. Ibid., 864.

22. Goncourt, *Journal*, II: 24–25.

23. Bernheimer, *Figures of Ill Repute*, 2.

24. Ibid.

25. Ricatte describes the book as containing three novels in one: the story of an artistic couple (Coriolis and Manette), a novel of the Bohemian painter, and a chronicle of contemporary artistic life. *La Création romanesque*, 309.

26. Dolan, "Musée Goncourt," 173–174.

27. On the Goncourts' sex lives, see Ricatte, *La Création romanesque*, 309–315. On love and sex in relation to *Manette Salomon* and their own lives, see Champeau, "Les Goncourt et la passion de l'artiste," *Les Frères Goncourt: Art et écriture*, 58–60. On the text's anti-Semitism in relation to its artistic themes, see Ricatte, *La Création romanesque*, 318–320; Bell, "The Jew as Model"; and Lathers, "Models, Monkeys and Naturalism."

28. Goncourt, *Manette Salomon*, 158, 147. Text from the Charpentier et Fasquelle edition, Paris, 1896.

29. Ibid., 147, 148.

30. Ibid., 331.

31. Ibid., 322.

32. Ibid.

33. On *Le Peintre de la vie moderne* and Chassagnol, see Bell, "The Jew as Model," 832–836, and Dolan, "Musée Goncourt," 181.

34. Baudelaire, *Salon de 1846*, OC, II: 493.

35. Ibid.

36. Baudelaire, *Le Peintre de la vie moderne*, OC, II: 685.

37. Ibid., 885.

38. Goncourt, *Journal*, II: 275.

39. Baudelaire and Chassagnol argue the *habit noir* is only an impediment to inferior artists, *Manette Salomon*, 322, 325, and Baudelaire, *Salon de 1846*, OC, II: 494–495. In addition to the praise of Balzac, Chassagnol borrows Baudelaire's language about high and low subjects and the poetry of the modern streets. Goncourt, *Manette Salomon*, 323–324; Baudelaire, *Salon de 1846*, OC, II: 495–500.

40. Bell argues that the Goncourt brothers attempt to redeem the ideal by grounding it in the real, but they are plagued by an ambivalence about these categories that is manifested in Manette's stereotypical Jewish materialism. I agree entirely, but I believe that their ambivalence is conditioned specifically by Baudelaire's use of the real and the ideal to define the modern artist, and the ambiguous role he grants to the artist in navigating these categories in a photographic world. Bell, "The Jew as Model," 825–847. For another take on idealism and material reality in in the novel's discussion of light as "impalpable reality," see Christin, "Matière et idéal dans *Manette Salomon*," 938.

41. Baudelaire, *Le Peintre de la vie moderne*, OC, II: 685–686.

42. *Manette Salomon*, 322, 323. Baudelaire, "Laquelle est la vraie?" OC, I: 342. First published in June 1863 in *Le Boulevard*. Baudelaire, OC, I: 1344.

43. Baudelaire, *Salon de 1846*, OC, II: 456.

44. *Manette Salomon*, 182–183

45. Ibid., 184. The description continues onto p. 185.

46. Ibid., 187.

47. Ibid.

48. Ibid., 170.

49. Ibid., 183.

50. Ibid., 196.

51. Ibid., 187.

52. Ibid., 331.

53. Ibid., 137.

54. Ibid., 162.

55. Ibid., 208–209.

56. Edmond de Goncourt, *Manette Salomon: Pièce en neuf tableaux*, 72–74.

57. *Manette Salomon*, 140.

58. Ibid., 196.

59. Ibid., 209.

60. Ibid., 327.

61. Ibid., 412–413.

62. Ibid., 414.

63. Ibid., 331.

64. Ibid., 332.

65. Ibid., 358.

66. Ibid., 456. Critics agree on the importance of the ending but not on its meaning. For various readings, see Armstrong, *Manet Manette*, 60–61; Lathers, "Models, Monkeys and Naturalism," 160; Bell, "The Jew as Model," 846–847.

67. *Manette Salomon*, 456.

CHAPTER 5

1. Wey, *Chronique du siège de Paris*, 175; "Chronique du jour," *La Presse*, 26 October 1871; "Échos de Paris," *Le Figaro*, 29 August 1872.

2. Reprinted as "Paris au jour le jour," *Le Figaro*, 15 March 1871.

3. "Loi relative à la presse du 11 May 1868," 397–400; "Décret qui abolit le cautionnement des journaux du 10 octobre 1870," 114; "Loi relative aux poursuites à exercer en matière de délits commis par la voie de la presse, du 15 avril 1871," 101–102; "Loi qui rétablit le cautionnement pour tous les journaux et écrits périodiques du 6 juillet 1871," 2–4; "Loi sur la répression des délits qui peuvent être commis par la voie de la presse ou par tout autre moyen de publication, et sur la levée de l'état de siège, du 29 décembre 1875," 1048–1050. These laws are summarized by Albert Eyquem in *De la répression des outrages à la morale publique*, 128–129. An October 1870 decree established jury trials for images facing indecency charges but was incorrectly promulgated and therefore had no standing. "Art. 9259," 87–88. An 1873 appeals case confirmed

that the censorship decree of 1852 remained in effect for photographs. "Angers, 26 mai 1873," 859–860.

4. In 1881, the language about "morale publique" was excised from the law. "Loi sur la liberté de la presse du 29 Juillet 1881," 130. Henceforth I will continue to use either the English terms "affront to public decency" and "indecency" as before or the new terminology in French to refer to such prosecutions.

5. On jury trials for images, see "Loi sur la liberté de la presse du 29 Juillet 1881," 133. For a detailed analysis of the law of 1881, see Albert Faivre and Edmond Benoit-Lévy, *Code manuel de la presse*, 117–124, 294–295.

6. Moulin abandoned photography in 1862; Belloc died in 1867. Nazarieff, *Early Erotic Photography*, 21, 39, 113. Braquehais went bankrupt and then died in 1875. McCauley, *Industrial Madness*, 191.

7. For producers of legal nudes from the Empire, e.g., Marconi, A.N. F*18 VIbis 3, p. 96, and Quinet, A.N. F*18 VIbis 4, pp. 294, 296. For producers of illegal nudity, e.g., Thiébault and Lamiche (BB3, 4, 31). They submitted photographs for authorization in the early 1870s. A.N. F*18 VIbis 3, pp. 85, 96.

8. These likely correspond to images registered by Welling, A.N. F*18 Vibis 4, p. 309.

9. For example, the same series of nudes by Welling, note 8. On the Dépôt légal in the early Third Republic, see also Dawkins, *The Nude in French Art and Culture*, 11–16.

10. Gaillardin, "Chronique," *La Presse*, 31 May 1873; Menus propos," *La Presse*, 23 August 1880.

11. In 1873 Marconi was arrested for selling nudes without authorization. However, he had long registered nudes and did so in that same year. It seems likely there was some confusion about the law after 1871. Drujon, *Catalogue des ouvrages*, xxxi.

12. "Tribunaux," *Le Temps*, 7 May 1892.

13. "L'Affaire des photographies," *La Presse*, 23 January 1892; "Menus faits," *La Justice*, 22 January 1892.

14. Entries dating to 1884 by Léar, A.N. F18* Vibis 6, p. 92.

15. Mannoni, "Kirchner, Albert (a.k.a. Léar)," *Encyclopedia of Early Cinema*, 360.

16. Gautrand, "Photography on the Spur of the Moment," *A New History of Photography*, 233–241.

17. Print runs, e.g., A.N. F*18 Vibis 6, pp. 38, 52, 90.

18. For others of these periodicals not discussed here, see Lathers, *Bodies of Art*, 225, and Pinet, "De L'étude d'après nature au nu esthétique," *L'Art du nu*, 30–37, especially 32–33.

19. Comte, "Inventaire de la pornographie," *Premier congrès national contre la pornographie*, 30.

20. Compared to other such publications, *Le Stéréo-nu* includes a significant number of male nudes, possibly related to the growing cult of the male body builder discussed by Garb in "Modelling the Male Body: Physical Culture, Photography and the Classical Ideal," *Bodies of Modernity*, 55–79.

21. Lathers similarly describes *Mes Modèles* as presenting its models as "sexually available," *Bodies of Art*, 229. However, she gives some credence to their claims to act as aides to artists, *Bodies of Art*, 234.

22. Pinet, "De L'étude d'après nature au nu esthétique," 36.

23. "Notre But," *Le Nu académique*, 1 July 1905.

24. For a general overview of fin-de-siècle photo-illustrated publications, see Edwards, *Soleil noir*, 230–264.

25. "Faits divers," *La Presse*, 4 July 1883.

26. Quotes, "Tribunaux," *Le Temps*, 24 November 1883. Also reported in "Faits divers," *La Justice*, 30 June 1883; "Faits divers," *La Presse*, 3 July 1883; "Tribunal correctionnel de Paris," *Gazette des tribunaux*, 30 November 1883, 1150.

27. "Tribunaux," *Le Temps*, 24 November 1883; "Tribunal correctionnel de Paris," *Gazette des tribunaux*, 30 November 1883, 1150. Dawkins also mentions Lafontaine, *The Nude in French Art and Culture*, 31.

28. *Guide complèt des Plaisirs mondains*, 196–197.

29. The site archivesderos.com, run by a dealer in Paris, is one of the best resources for later nineteenth-century images. Unfortunately, many of his 22,000 images are neither attributable nor dateable and thus this collection can only suggest general trends.

30. Fiaux, *Les Maisons de tolérance*, 167.

31. Rexer, "Stockings and Mirrors," *Degas: A Strange New Beauty*, 137–141.

32. BB6, 11. "Faits divers," *La Justice*, 29 September 1891; "La Journée à Paris," *La Presse*, 1 October 1891; "Faits divers," *Le Temps*, 14 November 1883; "Faits divers," *La Presse*, 16 November 1883; "Tribunaux," *Le Temps*, 31 January 1884; "Nouvelles diverses," *Le Figaro*, 30 August 1896; "Faits divers," *Le Temps*, 30 August 1896; "Faits divers," *La Presse*, 31 August 1896.

33. "Informations," *Le Figaro*, 22 June 1875; Bigeon, *La Photographie et le droit*, 212–213.

34. "Informations," *Le Figaro*, 22 June 1875; Tribunaux," *Le Temps*, 7 May 1892. See also Dawkins, *The Nude in French Art and Culture*, 31.

35. "Faits divers," *La Justice*, 29 September 1891; "La Journée à Paris," *La Presse*, 1 October 1891; Fiaux, *Les maisons de tolérance*, 168.

36. "Chronique du jour," *La Presse*, 26 October 1871; "Faits divers," *Le Temps*, 1 April 1882; "Faits divers," *La Presse*, 5 April 1882; "Gazette des tribunaux," *Le Figaro*, 31 January 1883; "Tribunaux," *Le Temps*, 1 February 1883; "Faits divers," *Le Temps*, 18 June 1883; "Nouvelles diverses," *Le Gaulois*, 29 July 1883; "Faits divers," *La Presse*, 3 July 1883; "Faits divers," *La Presse*, 4 July 1883; "Gazette des tribunaux," *Le Figaro*, 8 July 1883; "Chronique des tribunaux," *Le Gaulois*, 8 July 1883; "Tribunaux," *Le Temps*, 9 July 1883; "Tribunaux," *Le Temps*, 24 November 1883; "Nouvelles diverses," *Le Figaro*, 23 September 1885; "Faits divers," *La Justice*, 21 June 1888; "Question du jour: La Chasse aux livres," *La Presse*, 1 April 1890; "Nouvelles diverses," *Journal des débats politiques et littéraires*, 14 June 1891; "Échos," *La Presse*, 15 June 1891; "La Journée a Paris," *La Presse*, 1 October 1891; "Nouvelles diverses," *Le Figaro*, 8 January 1892; "Faits divers," *La Presse*, 4 August 1897; "Gazette des tribunaux," *Le Figaro*, 2 December 1897; "Tribunaux," *Le Temps*, 3 and 10 December 1897; "Nouvelles diverses," *Journal des débats politiques et littéraires*, 4 August 1898; "Gazette des tribunaux," *Le Figaro*, 23 October 1900; "Nouvelles diverses," *Le Figaro*, 30 November 1900. See also Bérenger et al., "La Question de la pornographie," 217.

37. "Paris Au Jour le Jour," *Le Figaro*, 15 March 1871. Gaillardin, "Chronique," *La Presse*, 31 May 1873; "Menus propos," *La Presse*, 23 August 1880; "Nouvelles diverses," *Le Figaro*, 23 September 1885; "Le R P Ollivier et l'interpellation sur la moralité," *Le Gaulois*, 11 April 1897; Colin, "Annexe no. 648," 39 (repeats the text of Guillier, "Annexe no. 159," 414).

38. "Faits diverses," *La Justice*, 21 June 1888; "Échos," *La Presse*, 20 April 1891.

39. "Nouvelles diverses," *Le Figaro*, 27 August 1901; "Monsieur Bérenger," *Le Figaro*, 22 July 1902; "Nouvelles diverses," *Le Figaro*, 24 June 1903; Comte, "Inventaire de la pornographie," 40.

40. BB6, 35; "Journal du Palais," *La Justice*, 6 May 1892; "Faits divers," *Le Temps*, 24 October 1884.

41. "Gazette des tribunaux," *Le Figaro*, 31 January 1883. Also reported in "Tribunaux," *Le Temps*, 1 February 1883." See also Meunier, *Les clameurs du pavé*, 107–109.

42. "Les coulisses de la politique," *Gil Blas*, 12 May 1882, 2. On wine shops, see also "Journée parisienne," *La Presse*, 25 May 1881, and "Faits divers," *La Justice*, 29 September 1891 (rereported in "La Journée à Paris," *La Presse*, 1 October 1891).

43. "Gazette du jour," *La Presse*, 31 December 1873; "Informations," *Le Figaro*, 6 February 1874; "Informations," *Le Figaro*, 22 June 1875; "Informations," *Le Figaro*, 15 September 1875; "Tribunaux," *La Presse*, 19 December 1880; "Nouvelles diverses," *Le Gaulois*, 19 May 1881; "Faits divers," *La Presse*, 20 May 1881; "Faits divers," *Le Temps*, 20 May 1881; "Journée parisienne," *La Presse*, 25 May 1881; "Tribunaux," *Le Temps*, 19 January 1882; "Nouvelles diverses," *Le Figaro*, 10 April 1882; "Faits divers," *Le Temps*, 11 April 1882; "Tribunaux," *Le Temps*, 23 April 1882; "Tribunaux," *Le Temps*, 7 July 1882; "Faits divers," *La Presse*, 7 April 1883; "Faits divers," *La Presse*, 3 August 1884; "Bulletin judiciaire," *Journal des débats politiques et littéraires*, 10 June 1887; "La Journée à Paris," *La Presse*, 18 October 1891; "Faits divers," *Le Temps*, 26 July 1892; "Photographies obscènes," *L'Intransigent*, 27 July 1892; "Frère et soeur," *La Presse*, 3 September 1895; "Le Palais," *La Presse*, 27 July 1897; "Tribunaux," *La Presse*, 14 October 1900; "Tribunaux," *Le Temps*, 15 and 24 October 1900; "Gazette des tribunaux" *Le Figaro*, 23 October 1900. See also Bérenger et al., "La Question de la pornographie," 217.

44. BB6, 49; "Poursuites et condamnations judiciaires," 324, 325, 327; "Revue judiciaire et administrative," 18; "Nouvelles diverses," *Le Gaulois*, 19 May 1881; "Faits divers," *La Presse*, 20 May 1881; "Faits divers," *Le Temps*, 20 May 1881; "Tribunaux," *La Presse*, 14 August 1890; "Bulletin judiciaire," *Journal des débats politiques et littéraires*, 13 August 1890; "Dernières dépêches des correspondants particuliers du Temps," *Le Temps*, 28 May 1891; "Nouvelles diverses," *Le Figaro*, 8 January 1892; BB6, 2, 35, 129,164, 204.

45. BB6, 216. The portrait is by Achille Zo.

46. "Bulletin judiciaire," *Journal des débats politiques et littéraires*, 10 June 1887; "Faits divers," *La Presse*, 31 March 1883; "Faits divers," *La Presse*, 7 April 1883; "Nouvelles diverses," *Le Gaulois*, 27 March 1883; "Faits divers," *Le Temps*, 26 July 1892; "Photographies obscènes," *L'Intransigent*, 27 July 1892.

47. Possession remained legal through the end of the century. Faivre and Benoit-Lévy, *Code Manuel de la Presse*, 124.

48. Scholl, *L'Orgie parisienne*, 203.

49. "Informations," *Le Figaro*, 6 February 1874; Taxil, *La Corruption fin-de-siècle*, 293; L'Épine, "Les Coupeurs de Têtes," *La Vie à grand orchestre*, 222. The photograph of Sarah Bernhardt was sold in 1997 and is currently held in an unknown collection, *L'art du nu*, 41.

50. "Gazette du jour," *L'Intransigent*, 2 August 1882; Trascaze, "Tabac," *Dictionnaire général*, 1802.

51. Pinet, "De L'étude d'après nature au nu esthétique," 32.

52. Comte, "Inventaire de la pornographie," 37.

53. Fabreguettes, *Des atteintes ét attentats aux mœurs en droit civil et pénal*, 29. This is part of a discussion of the undesirable publications and photographic images in shops and on public thoroughfares, 29–30.

54. Celliez and Le Senne, *Loi de 1881 sur la presse*, 432. See also debates of the 1882 law. "Chambre des députés: Séance du 2 mai 1882," 476; "Chambre des députés: Séance du 26 juin 1882," 1031.

55. "Le Colportage," *Le Figaro*, 23 July 1881.

56. "Faits divers," *La Justice*, 30 June 1883

57. "Nouvelles Diverses," *Journal des débats politiques et littéraires*, 13 October 1895, 2.

58. "Faits Divers," *L'Intransigent*, 25 August 1900.

59. "Tribunaux," *Le Temps*, 7 May 1892. "Bulletin judiciare," *Journal des débats politiques et littéraires*, 6 May 1892. "Journal du Palais," *La Justice*, 6 May 1892; "Revue judiciaire," 165.

60. Bérenger, "La Question de la pornographie," 217.

61. "Correspondance anglaise du Figaro," *Le Figaro*, 19 July 1875; "Faits divers," *Le Temps*, 11 April 1882; "Bulletin du jour," *Le Temps*, 12 May 1888; "Étranger," *Journal des débats politiques et littéraires*, 29 July 1888; "Bulletin de l'étranger," *Le Temps*, 29 July 1888; "L'Affaire Parnell et l'incident Pigott," *Le Temps*, 28 February 1889; "Bulletin de l'étranger," *Le Temps*, 24 April 1891; "Étranger," *Journal des débats politiques et littéraires*, 22 October 1891; "Étranger," *Journal des débats politiques et littéraires*, 26 October 1891; "Au pays des bonnes mœurs," *Le Matin*, 10 January 1892; "Bulletin de l'étranger," *Le Temps*, 13 June 1892; "Paris: Une Saisie" *Le Petit Parisien*, 31 January 1895; "Paris: Photographies et livres saisis," *Le Petit Parisien*, 26 February 1895; "Images pornographiques," *La Presse* 18 January 1896; "Nouvelles diverses," *Journal des débats politiques et littéraires*, 4 August 1898; "Une nouvelle affaire d'espionage," *L'Intransigent*, 7 February 1899; "Faits divers," *L'Intransigent*, 25 August 1900. See also "Faits et informations: Suisse," 1098–1099.

62. "Lettres de Palestine," *Le Temps*, 28 September 1898; Courtois, *Le Tonkin français contemporain*, 8; Armand Corre, *L'Ethnographie criminelle*, 391, 394; Cahun, "Untitled," *Journal des débats politiques et littéraires*, 18 August 1878.

63. "Journal du Palais," *La Justice*, 6 May 1892; "L'Affaire des photographies," *La Presse*, 23 January 1892; "Menus faits," *La Justice*, 22 January 1892.

64. Étranger," *Journal des débats politiques et littéraires*, 22 October 1891; "Images pornographiques," *La Presse*, 18 January 1896.

65. Comte, "Inventaire de la Pornographie," 41.

66. "Art. 1251," 371–375; "Cass.—crim. 11 août 1864," 574; "Jurisprudence: France," 496–497.

67. "Faits et informations: Suisse," 1098.

68. "Le congrès de Lausanne contre la littérature immorale," *Journal des débats politiques et littéraires*, 17 September 1893.

69. "Loi du 16 mars 1898, modifint la loi du 2 août 1882 sur la répression des outrages aux bonnes moeurs," 94, note 3. See also "Sénat: Séance du 11 juin 1897," 970–971; D'Estournelles, "Annexe no. 2839," 156; "Cour de cassation, 15 mai 1884," 586; "Jurisprudence: France," 496–497; "Article 628," 116–119.

70. "Le Congrès de Lausanne contre la littérature immorale," *Journal des débats politiques et littéraires*, 17 September 1893. "Images pornographiques," *La Presse*, 18 January 1896. Bérenger, "Annexe no. 81," 127. "Sénat: Séance du 8 avril 1897," 786–788. Bérenger, *Manuel pratique pour*

la lutte contre la pornographie, 19. For examples, see ads from *Gil Blas*, 9 December 1890, 10 May 1891, and 10 January 1892, p. 4.

71. "Nouvelles du jour," *Le Temps*, 4 January 1899; "Outrages aux bonnes mœurs," *Journal des débats politiques et littéraires*, 5 January 1899.

72. Bérenger, "Annexe no. 81," 124–127. See also Bérenger, "Annexe no. 50," 255–256; Bérenger, "Annexe No. 142," 434.

73. Paris: Une Saisie," *Le Petit Parisien*, 31 January 1895; "Paris: Photographies et livres saisis," *Le Petit Parisien*, 26 February 1895; "Gazette du jour," *L'Intransigent*, 28 February 1895.

74. "Loi modifiant la loi du 2 août sur la répression des outrages aux bonnes moeurs, du 16 mars 1898," 105. On publicity and the 1898 law, see Eyquem, 82–83; 183. On the 1895 affair, "Loi du 16 mars 1898, modifint la loi du 2 août 1882 sur la répression des outrages aux bonnes mœurs," 95, note 1; "Sénat: Séance du 27 mai 1895," 556; "Sénat: Séance du 28 mai 1895," 559; "Sénat: Séance du 8 avril 1897," 788.

75. "Loi relative à la répression des outrages aux bonnes mœurs, du 7 avril 1908," 2012.

76. "Paris au jour le jour," *Le Figaro*, 15 March 1871.

77. On sensationalism and the "faits divers," see Schwartz, *Spectacular Realities*, 36–40.

78. "Gazette des tribunaux," *Le Figaro*, 5 December 1873; "Faits divers," *La Presse*, 12 August 1874; "Gazette des tribunaux," *Le Figaro*, 12 September 1875; "Informations," *Le Figaro*, 15 September 1875; "Tribunaux," *Le Temps*, 19 January 1882; "Nouvelles diverses," *Le Figaro*, 10 April 1882; "Faits divers," *Le Temps*, 14 November 1883; "Faits divers," *La Presse*, 16 November 1883; Aurélien Scholl, "Chronique parisienne: Rastacouères," *Le Figaro*, 19 April 1887; "La Journée a Paris," *La Presse*, 20 October 1890; "Nouvelles diverses," *Journal des débats politiques et littéraires*, 12 February 1892; "Frère et sœur," *La Presse*, 3 September 1895; "Nouvelles diverses," *Le Figaro*, 30 August 1896; "Faits divers," *Le Temps*, 30 August 1896; "Faits divers," *La Presse*, 31 August 1896; "Faits divers," *Gil Blas* 30 June 1897.

79. Bérenger, "Annexe No. 81," p. 123.

80. Freund, *Photography and Society*, 86–87, and Gautrand, "Photography on the Spur of the Moment," *A New History of Photography*, 238.

81. Parts of Pierre Louÿs' collection are in Louÿs, *Le Cul de la femme*, and Goujon, *Dossier secret*.

82. This album is held at the reserve of the Bibliothèque de l'Arsenal.

83. "Un Scandale," *La Presse*, 24 October 1894; "Echos et nouvelles: Les Méfaits de la photographie," *Gil Blas*, 6 March 1898.

84. Fransois, "Le Photographe amateur."

85. Freund, *Photography and Society*, 83–89.

86. See Font-Réaulx, "La Photographie assemblée en rêves: Gustave Moreau," *L'Art du nu*, 108–111; Perego, "Intimate Moments and Secret Gardens: The Artist as Amateur Photographer," *A New History of Photography*, 335–345; Pinet, "De l'étude d'après nature au nu esthétique," 31–32; Pinet, "Alexandre Falguière (1831–1900)," *L'Art du nu*, 96–99. On Degas' nudes and figure studies, see Malcolm Daniel, "The Atmosphere of Lamps or Moonlight," *Edgar Degas, Photographer*, 38–46, plates 35–36.

87. Gravier, "La Nouvelle École de la photographie et l'épreuve originale," *Bulletin du Photo-club de Paris*, 1 September 1899, 308. On the Pictorialists, see Hammond, "Naturalist Vi-

sion and Symbolist Vision: The Pictorialist Impulse," *A New History of Photography*, 293–309 and Rexer, *Photography's Antiquarian Avant-Garde*, 13–14.

88. Delaye, "Études critiques sur le premier salon d'art photographique," *Bulletin du Photo-club de Paris*, 1 February 1894, 35.

89. "Bibliographie: *Le Nu et le drapé en plein air*," *Bulletin du Photo-club de Paris*, 1 January 1899, 32.

90. Bergon and Le Bègue, *Le Nu et le drapé en plein air*, 10.

91. Ibid., 9, 10.

92. Ibid., 45.

93. For example, Daelen, *La Moralité du nu: Le Nu d'après nature: La Femme*.

94. Reyner, "Le Nu en photographie," *Bulletin du Photo-club de Paris*, 1 July 1899, 219–220; D'Assche, "Le Sujet de genre," *Bulletin du Photo-club de Paris*, 1 March 1898, 81–82.

95. Bergon and Le Bègue, *Le Nu et le drapé*, 12.

96. "Troisième exposition d'art photographique du Photo-club de Paris," *Bulletin du Photo-club de Paris*, 1 June 1896, 198; Charles Gravier, "La Nouvelle École de la photographie et l'épreuve originale," *Bulletin du Photo-club de Paris*, 1 September 1899, 308; Albert Reyner, "Le Nu en photographie," *Bulletin du Photo-club de Paris*, 1 July 1899, 219–220; "Salon de photographie: 4ᵉ année 1897," *L'Écho photographique*, May 1897, 52.

97. "Exposition d'art photographique du Photo-Club de Paris," *L'Écho photographique*, June 1896, 65; "Troisième Exposition d'art photographique du Photo-club de Paris," *Bulletin du Photo-club de Paris*, 1 June 1896, 207.

98. "Salon photographique de Londres," *Bulletin du Photo-club de Paris*, 1 October 1896, 375.

99. On morality leagues, see Stora-Lamarre, "Le Temps des ligues," *L'Enfer de la IIIᵉ République*, 79–104, and Kerley, "Mobilizing Against Immorality," *Uncovering Paris*, 101–123.

CHAPTER 6

1. "Gaietés de la semaine: la carte du ciel," *Gil Blas*, 20 April 1891. Originally printed as "Les Gaietés de la semaine," *Gil Blas*, 19 April 1887.

2. "Gaietés de la semaine: la carte du ciel," *Gil Blas*, 20 April 1891.

3. Schwartz, *Spectacular Realities*, 28.

4. There are many passing references to shop displays and to commercial distribution in the street cited in Chapter 5. I have focused on the more compelling discussions here.

5. Gaillardin, "Chronique," *La Presse*, 31 May 1873.

6. Ibid.

7. "Menus propos," *La Presse*, 23 August 1880.

8. "Nouvelles diverses," *Le Figaro*, 23 September 1885.

9. "Faits divers," *La Justice*, 21 June 1888; "Échos," *La Presse*, 20 April 1891.

10. Colin, "Annexe no. 648," 39. Repeats the text of Guillier, "Annexe no. 159," 414.

11. "Faits divers," *La Presse*, 20 May 1881. "Nouvelles diverses," *Le Gaulois*, 19 May 1881.

12. "Faits divers," *Le Temps*, 21 September 1889.

13. Scholl, *L'Orgie parisienne*, 203.

14. "Faits divers," *La Presse*, 3 August 1884; "Le Palais," *La Presse*, 27 July 1897; "Nouvelles diverses: Une Bagarre Place Pigalle," *Le Figaro*, 1 July 1897.

15. Mirbeau, "Nocturne parisien," *Le Figaro*, 31 August 1882. Reprinted in *Les Grimaces*, 94–103.

16. Another contemporary describes child beggars who sell obscene photographs. D'Haussonville, *L'Énfance à Paris*, 188–189.

17. Haine, *The World of the Paris Café*, 156.

18. "Faits divers," *Le Temps*, 21 September 1889.

19. A similar catalog of iniquities (including nude photographs) appears in Enne, "La Rentrée au quartier latin," 319–320.

20. Macé, *La Police parisienne*, 330–331.

21. Ibid., 275.

22. Ibid., 276, 277.

23. Ibid., 277.

24. Ibid., 281.

25. Ibid., 330–332.

26. D'Autrec, *L'Outrage aux moeurs*, 13. Flax, *Les Hommes du jour*. See also Lela Kerley, *Uncovering Paris*, 40–49.

27. On the 1898 laws as the "loi Bérenger," see "Menus propos: La Nouvelle Loi Bérenger," *La Presse*, 4 November 1897. Dean also discusses Bérenger's legislative leadership, *The Frail Social Body*, 34.

28. Lamarre, "Bérenger, René, 1830–1915," *Les Immortels du Sénat*, 222–225. Stora-Lamarre, *L'Enfer de la IIIᵉ République*, 90, 95. On the founding at the time, see, e.g., "La Licence des rues," *Le Figaro*, 4 February 1892; "Contre la licence des rues," *Le Petit journal*, 9 March 1892.

29. Stora-Lamarre, *L'Enfer de la IIIᵉ République*, 90.

30. Bérenger, "Annexe no. 50," 249.

31. Bérenger, "Annexe no. 81," 123. For a full list of targeted objects and behaviors, see "Annexe no. 81," 123–127, and "Annexe no. 50," 249–257.

32. "Sénat: Séance du 27 mai 1895," 552.

33. Ibid.

34. Gaillard, "La Licence des vitrines," 8.

35. Bérenger, "Annexe no. 81," 126. Despite using quotation marks, Bérenger's language is not entirely the same as that in Bérenger et al., "Une ligue de l'honnêteté publique," 72–74, especially 72–73. For more discussion of obscene photography, see also Bérenger, "Annexe no. 50," 255–256.

36. "Sénat: Séance du 20 mars 1893," 337.

37. Ibid. I believe "private balls" refers to the infamous 1893 public "Bal des Quat'z-Arts." See Kerley, *Uncovering Paris*, 21–62.

38. "Sénat: Séance du 20 mars 1893," 338.

39. Ibid.

40. Ibid.

41. The same attitude is shared by other reformers. See, e.g., Macé, *La Police parisienne*, 278, and Comte, "Inventaire de la pornographie," 30.

42. Bérenger, "Annexe no. 142," 434–435. He also spoke during deliberations on the 1898 law. "Sénat: Séance du 11 juin 1897," 970–975; "Sénat: Séance du 18 juin 1897," 1017–1018. Then

again in 1908 he produced a Senate report on potential changes to the law. Bérenger, "Annexe no. 87," 61–62.

43. Citation: "Sénat: Séance du 8 avril 1897," 786. Response: "Sénat: Séance du 9 avril 1897," 800–805. Similarly, in 1905 Louis Comte, secretary general of the Ligue française pour le relèvement de la moralité publique, noted that it wasn't all that easy to publicly obtain "truly obscene photographs," Comte, "Inventaire de la pornographie," 40.

44. Some of these critics are discussed by Dean, *The Frail Social Body*, 37–39. See also Kerley, *Uncovering Paris*, 49–52, for the feud between Bérenger and the *Courrier Français*. For a voice in support of Bérenger, see "Les Idées de M. Bérenger," *Le Figaro*, 18 June 1897.

45. Corbin, *Les Filles de noce*, 296–303. See also Harsin on the increase in clandestine prostitution at the fin de siècle, *Policing Prostitution*, 247–248.

46. Macé, *La Police parisienne*, 330–332.

47. "Sénat: Séance du 27 mai 1895," 552.

48. "Nouvelles diverses," *Le Figaro*, 10 April 1882.

49. "Faits divers," *La Presse*, 12 August 1874; Fiaux, *Les Maisons de tolérance*, 45; Taxil, *La Corruption fin-de-siècle*, 127.

50. "Gazette du Jour," *La Presse*, 11 July 1874; Carlier, *Études de pathologie sociale*, 25–26; D'Urville, *Les Ordures de Paris*, 219; Virmaître, *Trottoirs et lupanars*, 91. On the photographic bait and switch, see Delcourt, *Le Vice à Paris*, 29. The use of photographs to facilitate prostitution was fictionalized by Maizeroy in "L'Agence Stephenson, Liffey et Co.," *Lalie Spring*, 186–187.

51. Reuss, *La Prostitution au point de vue de l'hygiène*, 152.

52. Delcourt, *Le Vice à Paris*, 27–31.

53. Taxil, *La Corruption fin-de-siècle*, 292–293. See also Comte, "Inventaire de la pornographie," on the use of photographs by prostitutes as "excitants" for their clients, 51.

54. Fiaux, *Les Maisons de tolérance*, 108, 167, 169.

55. "Article 628," 116–119.

56. Fiaux, *Les Maisons de tolérance*, 168.

57. Ibid.

58. Ibid., 167–168. For cases linking photographic obscenity and underage prostitution, see "Faits divers," *La Presse*, 12 August 1874; "Faits divers," *La Presse*, 4 July 1883; "Carnet judiciaire," *Gil Blas*, 7 May 1892, 3; "Au Palais: Affaire des mœurs," *La Presse*, 1 July 1897. Some models in *Le Stéréo-nu* and *Le Nu académique* are visibly prepubescent; on *Le Nu académique* and young models, see Comte, "Inventaire de la pornographie," 30. Although many models in the Second Empire were under twenty-one, the use of models younger than the age of sexual consent was rarely mentioned, and I have found no extant photographic examples of child pornography from the period. I have, however, found examples from the Third Republic, when images using underage models furthermore came under increasing scrutiny.

59. Gaillardin, "Chronique," *La Presse*, 31 May 1873.

60. Ibid.

61. Comte, "Inventaire de la pornographie," 30.

62. "Faits divers" *Le Temps*, 18 June 1883; "Chronique des tribunaux," *Le Gaulois*, 8 July 1883; "Gazette des tribunaux," *Le Figaro*, 8 July 1883; "Tribunal correctionnel de Paris," *Gazette des tribunaux*, 8 July 1883, 654; "Tribunaux," *Le Temps*, 9 July 1883; "Chronique: On ne rend pas

la monnaie," *La Presse*, 10 July 1883. Madame Desmett was the likely subject of a piece in *La Presse* as well, "Faits divers," *La Presse*, 4 July 1883. She is also mentioned by Dawkins, *The Nude in French Art and Culture*, 32.

63. "Gazette des tribunaux," *Le Figaro*, 8 July 1883. The wording of the letter is slightly different as reprinted in "Tribunal correctionnel de Paris," *Gazette des tribunaux*, 8 July 1883, 654.

64. "Gazette des tribunaux," *Le Figaro*, 8 July 1883, 654.

65. "Chronique: On ne rend pas la monnaie," *La Presse*, 10 July 1883.

66. Ibid.

67. Whether she sold obscene photographs isn't clear. "Nouvelles diverses," *Le Figaro*, 8 January 1892.

68. Leca, *Pour s'amuser*, 155.

69. Ibid., 155–156.

70. On the pornography epidemic and the redefinition of the word pornography at the end of the nineteenth century, see Rexer, "*L'Année pornographique.*"

71. Wolff, "Courrier de Paris," *Le Figaro*, 14 August 1880.

72. Macé, *La Police parisienne*, 277.

73. Bataille, "Gazette des tribunaux, police correctionelle: Un pornographe," *Le Figaro*, 21 October 1880.

74. "Tribunaux: Alphonse et Nana," *La Presse*, 19 December 1880.

75. "Échos de Paris," *Le Gaulois*, 3 August 1880. For additional articles linking sales of pornographic literature and obscene photography, see also "Chronique: La Vertu," *Le Temps*, 5 August 1880, and "Le Divin Marquis," *Le Figaro*, 27 April 1885.

76. "Arrestation de deux pornographes," *Le Gaulois*, 19 May, 1881; "Arrestation de deux pornographes," *La Presse*, 20 May 1881.

77. "Gazette des tribunaux," *Le Figaro*, 8 July 1883.

78. Rexer, "*L'Année pornographique.*" On arguments for and against the new law, see, e.g., "Annexe no. 450," 123–124. For more on the press laws of 1881 and 1882, see also Dawkins, *The Nude in French Art and Culture*, 26–30.

79. Grandlieu, "Le Colportage," *Le Figaro*, 23 July 1881.

80. See Bérenger, "Annexe no. 142," 434; "Annexe no. 81," 126; "Annexe no. 87," 61; and "Sénat: Séance du 8 avril 1897," *Journal officiel*, 9 April 1897, 786–788. Again, the full history of the word's transformation is in Rexer, "*L'Année pornographique.*"

81. Searches run on Gallica, 11 April 2017. This single citation is Lafenestre, "Salon de 1873," 491.

82. Sarcey, "Chronique," *Le XIXe siècle*, 8 May 1892, 1.

83. "La Jeunesse," *Le Figaro*, 17 February 1883.

CHAPTER 7

This chapter is derived in part from "Nana in the Nude: Zola and Early Nude Photography," *Dix-Neuf*, 22, nos. 1–2 (2018): 73–97. ©Taylor & Francis. Available online at http://www.tandfonline.com /10.1080/14787318.2018.1487172.

1. Pontmartin, "*Nana* Partout," *Nouveaux Samedis*, 362–365. First printed as Pontmartin, "*Nana* Partout: L'Assommoir à Athènes," *La Gazette de France*, 26 October/1 November 1879.

2. Pontmartin, *Nouveaux Samedis*, 364. For more on the publicity push, see Henri Mitterand, *Zola*, II: 498–501; Alexis, *Notes d'un Ami*, 117; and Auriant, *La Véritable Histoire de Nana*, 87–91. On the publication data, see Alexis, *Notes d'un Ami*, 119.

3. Gille, "La Littérature," *Le Figaro*, 2 January 1880. For a detailed account of the critical reaction against *Nana*, see Mitterand, *Zola*, II: 510–513. Many reviews are excerpted and summarized in Auriant, *La Véritable Histoire de Nana*, 88–108, 119–123.

4. "A Travers la presse," *Le Gaulois*, 24 December 1879.

5. Ulbach, "Comptes rendus analytiques des publications nouvelles: Question du jour: *Nana* par M. Émile Zola," *Le Livre* (1880), I: 200.

6. Wolff, "Courrier de Paris," *Le Figaro*, 21 November 1879.

7. Chapron, "Chronique de Paris: Ça et là," *l'Événement*, 26 February 1880.

8. Pontmartin, *Nouveaux Samedis*, 373. "Proxénètes" were female go-betweens in the prostitution industry; "proxénétisme" is something like female pimping.

9. Many nineteenth-century reviews accused realist authors of untruth. See Weinberg, *French Realism*, 193. The accusation appears in the following reviews of *Nana*: Wolff, "Courrier de Paris," *Le Figaro*, 21 November 1879; "Courrier de Paris," *La Gazette de France*, 7 November 1879; and "Un Apôtre," *Le Siècle*, Nov 12, 1879. The most detailed attacks on the novel's veracity came from Léon Chapron and Aurélien Scholl in a series of articles in *L'Événement* in 1879–1880. Drawing on a personal experience, small inconsistencies in the novel's time line (Nana's age), and a letter from a reader, they undertook to prove just how impossibly false the novel was. Scholl, "Littérature expérimentale," *L'Événement*, 24 October 1879; "Courrier de Paris," *L'Événement*, 31 October 1879; and "Propos de ville et de théâtre," *L'Événement*, 14 March 1880. Chapron, "Chronique de Paris: L'Expérimentalisme," *L'Événement*, 20 October 1879; "Chronique de Paris: M. Zola," *L'Événement*, 3 November 1879; and "Chronique de Paris: Ça et là," *L'Événement*, 26 February 1880. See also Mitterand, *Zola*, II: 511, and Auriant, *La Véritable Histoire de Nana*, 98–101, for excerpts of other reviews accusing Zola of untruths. Zola responded vehemently to these accusations in "Nana," *Le Voltaire*, 28 October 1879. See also Paul Alexis' defense of Zola's research, *Notes d'un Ami*, 113–119, and Alexis, "*Nana* et l'œuvre d'Émile Zola," *Le Figaro: Supplément littéraire du dimanche*, 12 March 1881. Auriant also discusses Zola's research at great length, *La Véritable Histoire de Nana*, 7–85.

10. Pontmartin, *Nouveaux Samedis*, 370.

11. Émile Zola, "La Littérature obscène," in *Émile Zola, Œuvres complètes*, IX: 485. Originally published in *Le Voltaire*, 31 August 1880.

12. Ibid., 487.

13. For a full discussion of the place of Zola's novel in the discussions of pornography and the word's changing meaning at the fin de siècle, see Rexer, "*L'Année pornographique.*"

14. Ulbach, "Question du jour: *Nana* par M. Émile Zola," *Le Livre* (1880) I: 200. The same review in the *Gil Blas* contains a similar formulation that does not reference photography: "Ce n'est pas un mauvais livre, c'est un mauvais geste." Ulbach, "À Propos de Nana," *Gil Blas*, 24 February 1880.

15. Ulbach, "Question du jour: *Nana* par M. Émile Zola," *Le Livre* (1880) I: 200.

16. Ulbach had previously likened *Thérèse Raquin* to Courbet's *Origin of the World*. Brooks, "Nana at last Unveil'd? Problems of the Modern Nude," *Body Work*, 144.

17. Other reviews that link Zola to photography include "Un Apôtre," *Le Siècle*, 5 Novem-

ber 1879; Pontmartin, "*Nana* Partout," *La Gazette de France*, 26 October 1879; Aurélien Scholl, "La Littérature experimentale," *L'Événement*, 24 October 1879. Mitterand makes the case that Pontmartin's reference to photography is a veiled accusation of sexual voyeurism, Mitterand, *Zola*, II: 505.

18. Two of the most notorious examples were *L'Événement parisien* and *Alphonse et Nana*. Both are discussed in Rexer, "*L'Année pornographique*."

19. For a description and analysis of contemporary pornographic literature, see Stora-Lamarre, *L'Enfer de la IIIe République*, 14–48. See also Gay, *Education of the Senses*, 358–379.

20. On Zola and photography generally, see the special issue of *Les Cahiers naturalists* (1992), as well as Lambeth, "Zola Photographer," *Émile Zola and the Arts*, 55–60. For examples of Zola's own photographic output, see Émile-Zola and Massin, *Zola: Photographer*. Schincariol also reads *Nana* through photography, arguing generally for photographic techniques in the text without reference to contemporary photographic iconography. *Le Dispositif photographique chez Maupassant, Zola et Céard*, 73–101.

21. Zola, *Nana*, in *Les Rougon-Macquart: Histoire naturelle et sociale d'une famille sous le Second Empire*, II: 1333. Henceforth *Nana*.

22. Ibid., 1110.

23. Ibid., 1299.

24. Ibid., 1315.

25. Ibid., 1346.

26. Ibid., 1097, 1098, 1122.

27. Ibid., 1301–1302.

28. Pélin, *Les Laideurs du beau Paris*, 15.

29. Zola, *Nana*, 1100, 1109.

30. On painting, see Brooks, *Body Work*, 123–161. On theater, see Kerley, *Uncovering Paris*, 73–78.

31. Zola, *Nana*, 1118.

32. Zola, *La Fabrique des Rougon-Macquart*, III: 174, 176, 436.

33. See e.g., Disdéri, *L'Art de la photographie*, 302 and newspaper articles *Le Triboulet*, 28 March 1857, and "Ce que peut faire un photographe," *Le Figaro*, 3 November 1861.

34. Goncourt, *Journal*, I: 640.

35. On the visual representation and the cultural importance of the face-covering veil in nineteenth-century France rather than veiling of the body, see Kessler, *Sheer Presence*.

36. Zola, *La Fabrique des Rougon-Macquart*, III: 176.

37. Gaudin, "Réunion d'artistes photographes," *La Lumière*, 25 March 1854, 45.

38. Zola, *Nana*, 118.

39. Solomon-Godeau, *Photography at the Dock*, 232. In making this point, Solomon-Godeau refers to the work of three feminist theorists, Beverly Brown, Elizabeth Cowie, and Annette Kuhn. *Photography at the Dock*, note 1, p. 303.

40. Zola, *La Fabrique des Rougon-Macquart*, III: 436.

41. Zola, *Nana*, 1119–1120.

42. Ibid., 1207, 1209.

43. Ibid., 1220–1221.

44. Ibid., 1367.

45. The notes of Henri Céard are printed in Zola, *Carnets d'enquêtes*, 321–322.

46. Zola, *Nana*, 1270.

47. See, for example, Clayson, *Painted Love*, 67–79; Lethbridge, "Zola's Manets," in *Critical Perspectives on Manet*, 104; Brooks, *Body Work*, 145.

48. Zola, *Nana*, 1271.

49. Ibid.

50. Ibid.

51. Ibid. Schincariol also notes the reader's implication as a spectator in a scene that includes photographic details. Without reference to any actual photographs, he argues that Nana's body is represented in the scene three-dimensionally, like a stereograph, exaggerating the monstrousness of her body. *Le Dispositif photographique*, 93–101.

52. Zola, *Nana*, 1271.

53. Solomon-Godeau, *Photography at the Dock*, 233.

54. Ibid.

55. Zola, *La Fabrique des Rougon-Macquart*, III: 430.

56. Zola, *Nana*, 1270.

57. Brooks, *Body Work*, 140.

58. Bernheimer, "Decomposing Venus: The Corpse of Naturalism," *Figures of Ill Repute*, 200–233. For Bernheimer, this division enables Zola to place both Nana as a "bonne fille" and Nana as sex/death, *cul*, and rotting corpse into a conservative narrative of "natural generation, corruption, and regeneration." *Figures of Ill Repute*, 213. The mirror scene is for Bernheimer, on the other hand, one of Freudian castration and fear, *Figures of Ill Repute*, 223–224.

59. Zola, *Nana*, 1432.

60. Ibid., 1454.

61. Zola, "De la moralité," in *Émile Zola, Œuvres complètes*, IX: 451.

62. Zola, *La Fabrique des Rougon-Macquart*, III: 166.

63. Bernheimer admits that "Nana is right to protest that she is being blamed for the failure of the upper classes to perform their duties within the organism." However, he sees these duties as repression and sublimation of the lower classes and locates the "illness" represented by Nana firmly in the slums: "The conservative patriarchal ideology that Zola, in this context, can be said to underwrite defines the working class's functions within the social organism as libidinal sexuality, primitive instinct, and excremental release. A healthy society keeps these base functions in their proper place." *Figures of Ill Repute*, 217.

64. Zola, *La Fortune des Rougon*, in *Les Rougon-Macquart*, I: 79.

65. Ibid., 235.

66. Zola, "La République et la littérature," in *Émile Zola, Œuvres complètes*, IX: 497.

67. Zola, "De la Moralité dans la littérature," in *Émile Zola, Œuvres complètes*, X: 821. What Zola says in 1881 on this topic within the context of his essay "De la Moralité dans la littérature" is largely a reprint and expansion of what Zola said in self-defense in "Nana," *Le Voltaire*, 28 October 1879.

68. Pontmartin, *Nouveaux Samedis*, 377.

CHAPTER 8

1. Ibels, "Enquête sur le roman illustré par la photographie," 115.

2. See Edwards, "Roman 1900 et photographie," 135–136, and Grivel, "Le Roman mis à nu par la photographie même," 145–147. Edwards's piece was then integrated into "Le Roman-photo illustré," *Soleil noir*, 230–243. For a discussion of photo-novels that does not mention nudity, see also Amelunxen, "Quand la photographie se fit lectrice," 89–91.

3. Thibaudet, "La Question *Bel-ami*," 746–752.

4. "Echos," *La Presse*, 9 November 1918; "Sur le mort d'un Messin: René Maizeroy, officier et romancier," *La Presse*, 16 November 1918; "René Maizeroy," in Maizeroy, *L'Amour perdu*, n.p.; Colby et al., eds., "René Maizeroy," *New International Encyclopedia*, XII: 723.

5. "René Maizeroy," *L'Amour perdu*, n.p.; Colby et al., eds., "René Maizeroy," *New International Encyclopedia*, XII: 723; Dawson, "Giraudoux: De Harvard au Quai d'Orsay," 722; "Les Deux Femmes de mademoiselle," *Le Livre* (1881): 41; "*L'Amour qui saigne*," *Le Livre* (1883): 15; Guy de Maupassant, "*Le Mal d'aimer*," *Le Gaulois*, 9 March 1882. Baron Toussaint is identified as "Coq Hardy," "Frascata," and "René Maizeroy" by Joliet, *Les Pseudonymes du jour*, 51.

6. Maizeroy, "Le Chef-d'œuvre du maître," *Gil Blas*, 5 December 1880. On the prosecution for the short story, see, "Chronique," *Le Droit populaire*, 25 December 1880; "Nouvelles judiciaires," *La Presse*, 15 December 1880. Maizeroy was not convicted, but the printer of *Gil Blas* was sentenced to three months in prison and one thousand francs in fines. On *Les Deux Amies*, see "Ouvrages poursuivies," *Le Livre* (1885): 224; "Fausse morale," *Le Matin*, 24 April 1885; "Outrages aux bonnes mœurs. –'Deux Amies,' roman de M. Maizeroy," *Le Livre* (1885): 446; "Gazette des tribunaux," *La Presse*, 29 April 1885. The novel's publisher, Havard, was acquitted and Maizeroy received a one-thousand-franc fine.

7. Gille, "Réalistes et naturalistes: René Maizeroy," in *La Bataille littéraire, 4ième série*, 145–146.

8. "*P'tit mi*," *Le Matin*, 14 June 1889. For another similar description of his style, see also "*Le Boulet*," *Le Livre* (1886): 287–288.

9. "A Travers Paris," *Le Figaro*, 2 May 1896. On Maizeroy as a feminist, see also "Critique littéraire du mois: *Petite Reine*," *Le Livre* (1888): 340; and Bois, "Revue des livres: Livres féministes," *Les Annales politiques et littéraires*, 4 August 1907, 101–102. Of note, there were also male fans of Maizeroy, e.g., Mathieu, "Feuilles de présence: *La Remplaçante*," *La Presse*, 20 December 1906.

10. "*P'tit Mi*," *Le Matin*, 14 June 1889. Émile Bergerat references the Maizereines in *La Lyre comique*, 166.

11. I discuss the sexual economy of portrait photography in Maizeroy's work at length in a forthcoming article in *Yale French Studies*.

12. On the exchange of photographs between lovers, see Maizeroy, *Trop jolie*, 207, republished as Maizeroy, *Le Consolateur*, 177; Maizeroy, "L'Envie de la baronne," *Amours de garnison*, 234; Maizeroy, "Le Saint-Joseph sans nez," *Les Deux Femmes de mademoiselle*, 42; Maizeroy, *Journal d'une rupture*, 6.

13. Maizeroy, *Petite Reine*, 81; Maizeroy, *Chérissime*, 198.

14. See, e.g., Maizeroy, "Avant le combat," *Les Deux Femmes de mademoiselle*, 80; Maizeroy, "Dent pour dent," *Bébé Million*, 188; *Papa la vertu*, 154.

15. Maizeroy, *Chérissime*, 198.

16. Maizeroy, "La Collection du Colonel," *Au régiment*, 48.

17. Maizeroy, *L'Amuseuse*, 192.

18. Maizeroy, "Don Juan (dernier acte)," *Bébé Million*, 295–296.

19. Maizeroy, "La B'tite gommerce," *Au régiment*, 89.

20. Maizeroy, "Épreuves rigolos," *Cas passionnels*, 281.

21. Ibid., 283.

22. Ibid., 286–287.

23. Maizeroy, "La Collection du Colonel," *Au régiment*, 49–50.

24. On photography's "erotics of the fragment," see Solomon-Godeau, *Photography at the Dock*, 236.

25. Maizeroy, *L'Amuseuse*, 185.

26. Ibid., 177, 185.

27. Ibid., 195–196.

28. Ibid., 192.

29. Maizeroy, *La Dernière Croisade*, 104.

30. Ibid., 103.

31. Ibid., 207.

32. Ibid., 208.

33. Ibid., 215.

34. Ibid., 217.

35. Maizeroy was known for his thinly veiled *romans à clef*, and some alleged that Bosq was inspired by the suicide of one General Ney—a witness in a military espionage case—in 1881. See "*La Dernière Croisade*," *Le Livre* (1883): 444. On Ney, see "La Mort du Général Ney," *Le Figaro*, 25 February 1881; "Gazette des tribunaux," *Le Figaro*, 6 May 1881. However, in an alternate version of the story from his collection *Celles qu'on aime* of the same year, Bosq is not a general but a duke, and other aspects of the plot are also different. "La Dégringolade," *Celles qu'on aime*, 65–79.

36. Maizeroy, *Les Deux Amies*, 39–40.

37. Ibid., 42.

38. "'*Les Deux Amies*': Un Entretien avec M. Maizeroy autour du livre poursuivi," *Le Matin*, 27 February 1885.

39. Edwards, "Roman 1900 et la photographie," 135.

40. I have been unable to consult two of his photo-novels, *Lorette* and *Le Premier pas*, because of their rarity.

41. For Edwards, the separation of text and image is a way to avoid redundancy, to create anticipation, or to remind the reader of certain passages, and it "confers at times an equivocal double meaning on the photographs." "Roman 1900 et photographie," 138.

42. Maizeroy, *Poupée de joie*, 102.

43. Ibid., 103.

44. "P'tit mi," *Le Matin*, 14 Juin 1889.

45. Maizeroy, *Poupée de joie*, 109–110.

46. Moses, "Republican Feminism," in *French Feminism in the Nineteenth Century*, 196–236; Scott, "The Rights of 'the Social': Hubertine Auclert and the Politics of the Third Republic,"

in *Only Paradoxes to Offer*, 90–124. See also Offen, *Debating the Woman Question in the French Third Republic*, for a comprehensive overview of the history of political feminism in the period. Notably, Offen's etymology of the word "feminism" does not discuss its literary meaning. Offen, *Debating the Woman Question*, 157–160.

47. Brisson, "René Maizeroy," *Pointes sèches: Physionomies littéraires*, 69. For more of Brisson's invective against Maizeroy, see also Brisson, "Livres et revues: *L'Ange*, par M. René Maizeroy," *Les Annales politiques et littéraires*, 1 December 1895, 348. Brisson was joined by some other reviewers in heaping scorn on Maizeroy. A review in *Le Matin*, for instance, describes all of Maizeroy's later work after *Souvenirs d'un Saint-Cyrien* as "effeminate and vicious," "*Le Boulet*," *Le Matin*, 20 May 1886.

48. Ginisty, "Romans, contes, nouvelles," *L'Année littéraire*, 1892, 176.

49. "P'tit mi," *Le Matin*, 14 June 1889.

50. Gale, "La Vie qui passe: Le Carnet des heures," *La Presse*, 12 March 1901.

51. Delarue-Mardrus, *Mes Mémoires*, 71.

52. Ibid., 75.

53. Angenot, "Des romans pour les femmes," 337. Similarly, Edwards reads the photonovels as cynically exploiting contemporary social issues for commercial gain in "Roman 1900 et photographie," 135.

54. Angenot, "Des romans pour les femmes," 346. Angenot elsewhere classifies Maizeroy within the genre of the "depraved-voluptuous-and-well-written," *Le Cru et le faisandé*, 111.

55. Mesch, "The Right to Pleasure: Sex and the Sentimental Novel," in *The Hysteric's Revenge*, 175, 189.

56. Maizeroy, *Chérissime*, 77, 74.

57. Ibid., 266.

58. Ibid., 90.

59. Ibid., 105–106.

60. Maizeroy, *Les Jeux de l'amour*, 70. The passage cited above from *Chérissime* appears on p. 72. Also in Maizeroy, *Sur l'amour: La Possession*, 139–141.

61. The reviewer Paul Mathieu astutely characterized Maizeroy's male characters as "feeble beings, irresolute, cowardly, and as timid as children," entirely servants of their mistresses. Mathieu, "Feuilles de présence: *La Remplaçante*," *La Presse*, 20 December 1906.

⊰ BIBLIOGRAPHY ⊱

ARCHIVAL SOURCES

Abbreviations

The registers from the Archives de la Préfecture de police have been referred to using their call
  numbers alone: BB1, BB3, and BB6.

All call numbers from the Archives nationales in Paris are referred to by the abbreviation A.N.

ARCHIVES CONSULTED

Archives de la Préfecture de police, Paris
  Registers BB1, BB3, and BB6.
Archives nationales de France
  A.N. F*18 VI 48; A.N. F*18 VI 50–A.N. F*18 VI 72; A.N. F*18 VI 133; A.N. F*18 VIbis 1–
  A.N. F*18 VIbis 11.
Image of France, 1795–1880, via ARTFL. https://artflproject.uchicago.edu/content/image-france.
Photographic collections of the Département des estampes et de la photographie, Bibliothèque
  nationale de France.
Private photographic collection of Les Larmes d'Éros, Paris.
Régistres des estampes déposées, 1839–1848. Département des estampes et de la photographie,
  Bibliothèque nationale de France.

PERIODICALS (MULTIPLE YEARS/ISSUES CONSULTED)

Les Annales politiques et littéraires, 1892–1908
La Caricature, 1880–1882
Le Charivari, 1857–1865, 1880–1882
L'Événement, 1879–1880
Le Figaro, 1854–1908
Le Gaulois, 1868–1908
La Gazette de France, 1879
Gazette des tribunaux, 1851, 1856, 1857, 1860, 1861
Gil Blas, 1879–1880
L'Intransigent, 1882–1900.

Le Journal des débats politiques et littéraires, 1840–1908

La Justice, 1880–1908

Le Livre: Bibliographie moderne, 1880–1889

Le Matin, 1882–1908

Le Petit Parisien, 1876–1908

La Presse, 1840–1908

Le Siècle, 1879

Le Tintamarre, 1860, 1881

Le Voltaire, 1879–1880

MAGAZINES AND COMPILATIONS OF PHOTOGRAPHIC NUDES

Mes Modèles, 1905

Le Nu académique, 1905–1906

Le Stéréo-nu, 1905

PORNOGRAPHIC NEWSPAPERS

Alphonse et Nana: Journal satirique illustré, 1880

L'Événement parisien, 1880

PHOTOGRAPHY PERIODICALS

Bulletin de la Société française de photographie, 1855–1884

Bulletin du Photo-club de Paris, 1891–1899

L'Écho photographique, 1896–1906

La Lumière, 1851, 1853–1857

Le Moniteur de la photographie, 1861–1873

Revue photographique, 1855–1865

GOVERNMENT REPORTS

Bérenger, René. "Annexe no. 81: Proposition de loi sur la prostitution et les outrages aux bonnes mœurs (27 avril 1894)." *Annales du Sénat: Documents parlementaires. Session ordinaire et session extraordinaire de 1894, du 9 janvier au 27 décembre 1894.* Vols. 29–30, 123–127. Paris: Imprimerie des Journaux officiels, 1895.

———. "Annexe no. 50: Rapport fait au nom de la commission chargée d'examiner la proposition de loi de M. Bérenger sur la prostitution et les outrages aux bonnes mœurs, par M. Bérenger, sénateur (26 mars 1895)." *Annales du Sénat: Documents parlementaires. Session ordinaire et session extraordinaire de 1895, du 8 janvier au 28 décembre 1895.* Vols. 31–32, 249–258. Paris: Imprimerie des Journaux officiels, 1895.

———. "Annexe no. 142: Rapport fait au nom de la commission chargée d'examiner le projet de loi ayant pour objet de modifier la loi du 2 aout 1882 sur la répression des outrages aux bonnes mœurs (2 juin 1897)." *Annales du Sénat: Documents parlementaires. Session Ordinaire de 1897, du 12 janvier au 20 juillet 1897.* Vol. 35, 434–435. Paris: Imprimerie des Journaux officiels, 1898.

———. "Annexe no. 87: Rapport fait au nom de la commission chargée d'examiner le projet de loi, adopté par le Sénat, adopté avec modifications par la Chambre des députés, ayant pour objet la répression des outrages aux bonnes moeurs (27 mars 1908)." *Annales du Sénat: Documents parlementaires. Session ordinaire de 1908, du 14 janvier au 13 juillet 1908.* Vol. 48, 61–62. Paris: Imprimerie du Journal officiel, 1908.

Challemel-Lacour, Paul. "Annexe no. 1456: Proposition de loi, adoptée par le Sénat sur la prostitution et les outrages aux bonnes moeurs, transmise à la Chambre des députés, au nom du Sénat, par M. le Président du Sénat (6 juillet 1895)." *Annales de la Chambre des députés: Documents parlementaires. Session ordinaire de 1895, du 28 mai au 13 juillet 1895.* Vol. 47, 132–133. Paris: Imprimerie des Journaux officiels, 1896.

Colin, Maurice. "Annexe no. 648: Rapport fait (au cours de la précédente législature), au nom de la commission de la réforme judiciaire et de la législation civile et criminelle, sur le projet de loi, adopté par le Sénat, ayant pour objet la répression des outrages aux bonnes moeurs (14 janvier 1907)." *Annales de la Chambre des députés: Documents parlementaires. Session ordinaire de 1907, première partie, du 8 janvier au 11 juillet 1907.* Vol. 73, 39–41. Paris: Imprimerie du Journal officiel, 1908.

Darlan, Jean. "Annexe no. 130: Projet de loi ayant pour objet de modifier la loi du 2 août 1882 sur la répression des outrages aux bonnes moeurs, présenté au nom de M. Félix Faure, Président de la République française, par M. J. Darlan, garde des sceaux (18 mai 1897)." *Annales du Sénat: Documents parlementaires. Session ordinaire de 1897, du 12 janvier au 20 juillet 1897.* Vol. 35, 417. Paris: Imprimerie des Journaux officiels, 1898.

———."Annexe no. 2555: Projet de loi, adopté par le Sénat, ayant pour objet de modifier la loi du 2 août 1882 sur la répression des outrages aux bonnes moeurs, présenté au nom de M. Félix Faure, Président de la République française, par M. J. Darlan, garde des sceaux (25 juin 1897)." *Annales de la Chambre des députés: Documents parlementaires. Session ordinaire de 1897, du 3 avril au 20 juillet 1897.* Vol. 52, 1446. Paris: Imprimerie des Journaux officiels, 1898.

Devaux, Louis-Édouard-Joseph. "Annexe no. 450: Rapport fait au nom de la commission chargée d'examiner le projet de loi, adopté par la Chambre des députés, ayant pour objet la répression des outrages aux bonnes moeurs (25 juillet 1882)." *Annales du Sénat et de la Chambre des députés: Documents parlementaires. Session ordinaire de 1882, du 27 juin au 9 août 1882, première partie, Sénat.* N.S. Vol. 6, 123–124. Paris: Imprimerie du Journal officiel, 1882.

Dreyfus, Ferdinand. "Annexe no. 927: Rapport fait au nom de la commission chargée d'examiner le projet de loi ayant pour objet la répression des outrage aux bonnes moeurs et la modification de l'article 330 du code pénal (8 juin 1882)." *Annales du Sénat et de la Chambre des députés: Documents parlementaires. Session ordinaire de 1882, du 27 mars au 24 juin 1882, deuxième partie, Députés.* N.S. Vol. 5, 577–578. Paris: Imprimerie du Journal officiel, 1882.

D'Estournelles, Paul-Henry-Benjamin. "Annexe no. 2839: Rapport fait au nom de la commission chargée d'examiner le projet de loi, adopté par le Sénat, et ayant pour objet de modifier la loi du 2 août 1882 sur la répression des outrages aux bonnes moeurs (25 novembre 1897)." *Annales de la Chambre des députés: Documents parlementaires. Session extraordinaire de 1897, du 19 octobre au 23 décembre 1897.* Vol. 53, 155–157. Paris: Imprimerie des Journaux officiels, 1898.

Guillier, Pierre Ernest. "Annexe no. 159: Rapport fait au nom de la commission chargée d'examiner le projet de loi ayant pour objet la répression des outrages aux bonnes moeurs (29 mai 1903)." *Annales du Sénat: Documents parlementaires. Session ordinaire et session extraordinaire de 1903, du 13 janvier au 30 décembre 1903.* Vol. 42, 414–416. Paris: Imprimerie du Journal officiel, 1904.

———."Annexe no. 82: Rapport supplémentaire fait au nom de la commission chargée d'examiner le projet de loi ayant pour objet la répression des outrages aux bonnes mœurs (17 mars 1904)." *Annales du Sénat: Documents parlementaires. Session ordinaire et session extraordinaire de 1904, du 12 janvier au 28 décembre 1904.* Vol. 43, 170–171. Paris: Imprimerie du Journal officiel, 1905.

Lefèvre, Alexandre. "Annexe no. 103: Rapport sommaire fait au nom de la 4ᵉ commission d'initiative parlementaire chargée d'examiner la proposition de loi de M. Bérenger, sur la prostitution et les outrages aux bonnes mœurs (28 mai 1894)." *Annales du Sénat: Documents parlementaires. Session ordinaire et session extraordinaire de 1894, du 9 janvier au 27 décembre 1894.* Vols. 29–30, 143–144. Paris: Imprimerie des Journaux officiels, 1895.

Vallé, Ernest. "Annexe no. 8: Projet de loi ayant pour objet la répression des outrages aux bonnes mœurs, présenté au nom de M. Émile Loubet, Président de la République française, par M. Vallé, garde des sceaux, ministre de la justice (16 janvier 1903)." *Annales du Sénat: Documents parlementaires. Session ordinaire et session extraordinaire de 1903, du 13 janvier au 30 décembre 1903.* Vol. 42, 27. Paris: Imprimerie du Journal officiel, 1904.

GOVERNMENT PROCEEDINGS

"Séance du 22 juin, 1865." *Annales du Sénat et du Corps législatif. Du 19 au 16 Juin 1865.* Vol. 8, 128–133. Paris: L'Administration du Moniteur universel, 1865.

"Séance du 14 avril 1871." *Annales de l'Assemblée nationale: Compte-rendu in extenso des séances. Du 12 Mars au 12 Mai 1871.* Annexes, Vol. 2, 489–502. Paris: Imprimerie du Journal officiel.

"Séance du 15 avril 1871." *Annales de l'Assemblée nationale: Compte-rendu in extenso des séances. Du 12 Mars au 12 Mai 1871.* Annexes, Vol. 2, 516–525. Paris: Imprimerie du Journal officiel.

"Chambre des députés: Séance du 2 mai 1882." *Journal officiel*, 3 May 1882, 475–476.

"Chambre des députés: Séance du 24 juin 1882." *Journal officiel*, 25 June 1882, 1019–1022.

"Chambre des députés: Séance du 26 juin 1882." *Journal officiel*, 27 June 1882, 1030–1037.

"Sénat: Séance du 20 mars 1893." *Journal officiel*, 21 March 1893, 337–340.

"Sénat: Séance du 27 mai 1895." *Journal officiel*, 28 May 1895, 552–556.

"Sénat: Séance du 28 mai 1895." *Journal officiel*, 29 May 1895, 559–565.

"Sénat: Séance du 30 mai 1895." *Journal officiel*, 31 May 1895, 567–571.

"Sénat: Séance du 14 juin 1895." *Journal officiel*, 15 June 1895, 613–617.

"Sénat: Séance du 27 juin 1895." *Journal officiel*, 28 June 1895, 689–691.

"Sénat: Séance du 8 avril 1897." *Journal officiel*, 9 April 1897, 786–791.

"Sénat: Séance du 9 avril 1897." *Journal officiel*, 10 April 1897, 800–805.

"Sénat: Séance du 11 juin 1897." *Journal officiel*, 12 June 1897, 970–975.

"Sénat: Séance du 18 juin 1897." *Journal officiel* 19 June 1897, 1017–1018.

"Sénat: Séance du 25 février 1904." *Journal officiel* 26 February 1904, 218–221.

LAWS

"Loi du 17 mai 1819 relative à la répression des crimes et délits commis par la voie de la presse." *Bulletin des lois du Royaume français.* Ser. 7, vol. 8, 465–471. Paris: Imprimerie royale, 1819.

"Décret organique sur la presse du 17 février 1852." *Bulletin des lois de la République française.* Ser. 10, vol. 9, 317–324. Paris: Imprimerie nationale, 1852.

"Loi relative à la presse du 11 May 1868." *Bulletin des lois de la République française*, Ser. 11, vol. 31, 397–400. Paris: Imprimerie nationale des lois, 1868.

"Décret qui abolit le cautionnement des journaux du 10 octobre 1870." *Bulletin des lois de la République française*. Ser. 12, vol. 1, 114. Paris: Imprimerie nationale des lois, 1871.

"Loi relative aux poursuites à exercer en matière de délits commis par la voie de la presse, du 15 avril 1871." *Bulletin des lois de la République française*. Ser. 12, vol. 2, 101–102. Paris: Imprimerie Nationale des Lois, 1872.

"Loi qui rétablit le cautionnement pour tous les journaux et écrits périodiques du 6 juillet 1871." *Bulletin des lois de la République française*. Ser. 12, vol. 3, 2–4. Paris: Imprimerie nationale des lois, 1872.

"Loi sur la répression des délits qui peuvent être commis par la voie de la presse ou par tout autre moyen de publication, et sur la levée de l'état de siège, du 29 décembre 1875." *Bulletin des lois de la République française*. Ser. 12, vol. 11, 1048–1050. Paris: Imprimerie nationale des lois, 1876.

"Loi sur la liberté de la presse du 29 Juillet 1881." *Bulletin des lois de la République française*. Ser. 12, vol. 23, 125–137. Paris: Imprimerie nationale, 1882.

"Loi ayant pour objet la Répression des Outrages aux bonnes mœurs du 2 août 1882." *Bulletin des lois de la République française*. Ser. 12, vol. 25, 145. Paris: Imprimerie nationale, 1883.

"Loi modifiant la loi du 2 août sur la répression des outrages aux bonnes moeurs, du 16 mars 1898." *Bulletin des lois de la République française*. Ser. 12, vol. 56, 105–106. Paris: Imprimerie nationale, 1898.

"Loi relative à la répression des outrages aux bonnes moeurs, du 7 avril 1908." *Bulletin des Lois de la République* Française. Ser. 12, vol. 76, 2012. Paris: Imprimerie nationale des lois, 1908.

ANNOTATED LAWS

Faivre, Albert and Edmond Benoit-Lévy. *Code manuel de la presse*. Paris: A. Cotillon, 1882.

Celliez, Henry and Charles Le Senne. *Loi de 1881 sur la presse, accompagnée des travaux de rédaction*. Paris: Librairie A. Maresque Ainé, 1882.

"Loi du 16 mars 1898, modifiant la loi du 2 août 1882 sur la répression des outrages aux bonnes moeurs." *Annuaire de législation française*. Vol. 18, 89–97. Paris: Libraire Cotillon, 1899.

LEGAL JOURNALS/CASE LAW

"Art. 778." *Annales de la propriété industrielle, artistique, et littéraire* 8 (1862): 80.

"Jurisprudence générale: Décisions du conseil d'état et documents divers: Troisième partie. — 1864." *Jurisprudence générale: Recueil périodique et critique de jurisprudence, de législation, et de doctrine en matière civile, commerciale, criminelle, administrative, et de droit public* (1864): 21–22.

"Art. 1251." *Annales de la propriété industrielle, artistique, et littéraire* 11 (1865): 371–375.

"Cass. — crim. 11 août 1864." *Journal du Palais* (1865): 574.

"No. 997." *Bulletin de la Cour impériale de Paris* (1866): 784–786.

"Art. 1400." *Annales de la propriété industrielle, artistique, et littéraire* 13 (1867): 54–55.

"Paris, 28 février 1868: Peine, cumul, contravention, lois spéciales." *Journal du Palais* (1868): 340.

"Poursuites et condamnations judiciaires." *Journal des commissaires de police* (1871–1872): 323–327.

"Art. 9259." *Journal du droit criminel, ou jurisprudence criminelle de la France* (1872): 87–88.

"Angers, 26 mai 1873." *Journal du Palais* (1874): 859–860.

"Revue judiciaire et administrative." *Journal des commissaires de police* (1874): 18.

"Cour de cassation, 15 mai 1884." *La France judiciaire: Revue bi-mensuelle de jurisprudence et législation. Volume 8, Partie 2, Jurisprudence et législation* (1884): 586.

"Jurisprudence: France." *Journal du droit international privé et de la jurisprudence comparée* 17 (1890): 496–497.

"Faits et informations: Suisse." *Journal du droit international privé et de la jurisprudence comparée* 19 (1892): 1098–1099.

"Revue judiciaire." *Journal des commissaires de police* (1892): 165.

"Article 628." *Journal des Parquets* 10 (1895): 116–119.

OTHER PRIMARY SOURCES

Alexis, Paul. Émile *Zola: Notes d'un Ami*. Paris: G. Charpentier, 1882.

Andral, Paul. "Outrage à la morale." *Courrier de la librairie: Journal de la propriété littéraire et artistique*, 22 March 1856, 179.

Aubry, Roger, dir. *L'Épreuve photographique*. 1st. Ser. Paris: Librairie Plom, 1904.

Autrec, Lionel d'. *L'Outrage aux moeurs*. Paris: Éditions de l'Epi, 1923.

Baudelaire, Charles. *Correspondance*. 2 Vols. Paris: Bibliothèque de la Pléiade, 1973.

———. *Œuvres complètes*. 2 Vols. Paris: Bibliothèque de la Pléiade, 1975–1976.

Bérenger, René. *Manuel pratique pour la lutte contre la pornographie*. Paris: P. Rouillot, 1907–1910.

Bérenger, René, Frédéric Passy, and Jules Simon. "Une ligue de l'honnêteté publique." *La Reforme sociale: Bulletin de la Société d'économie sociale*, Ser. 3, Vol. 3. Paris: Secrétariat de la Société d'économie sociale, 1892, 72–74.

Bérenger, René, Arthur Desjardins, Charles Franquet de Franqueville, and Frédéric Passy. "La Question de la pornographie." *Séances et travaux de l'académie des sicences morales et politiques*, Vol. 37. Paris: Alphonse Picard, 1892, 207–223.

Bergerat, Émile. *La Lyre comique*. Paris: A. Lemerre, 1889.

Bergon, Paul, and René Le Bègue. *Art photographique: Le Nu et le drapé en plein air*. Paris: Charles Mendel Editeur, 1898.

Bigeon, Alphonse-Armant. *La Photographie et le droit*. Paris: C. Mendel, 1894.

Brisson, Adolphe. *Pointes sèches: Physionomies littéraires*. Paris: Armand Colin, 1898.

Carlier, F. *Études de pathologie sociale: les deux prostitutions*. Paris: E. Dentue, 1887.

Claude, Antoine. *Mémoires de Monsieur Claude, Chef de police de sûreté sous le Second Empire*. 10 Vols. Paris: Jules Rouff, 1881.

Cogniard, Théodore and Clairville, *Oh! La, la! Qu' c'est bête tout ça! Revue de l'année 1860*. Paris: Michel-Levy, 1861.

"Contre la licence des rues." *Le Petit Journal*, 9 March 1892.

Corre, Armand. *L'Ethnographie criminelle d'après les observations et les statistiques judiciaires recueillies dans les colonies françaises*. Paris: C. Reinwald, 1894.

"Correspondance de Bayonne." *La Petite Revue*, 23 January 1864, 175–176.

Le Corsaire, 25 February 1847.

Courtois, Edmond. *Le Tonkin français contemporain: Études, obsvertaions, impressions et souvenirs*. Paris: Henri-Charles Lavauzelle, 1891.

Daelen, Edouard. *La Moralité du nu*. Paris: Librairie d'Art Technique, 1905.

Delarue-Mardrus, Lucie. *Mes Mémoires*. Paris: Gallimard, 1938.

Daniel, Émile. *De la protection des jeunes filles mineures*. Bourges: H. Sire, 1885.

Delcourt, Pierre. *Le Vice à Paris*. Paris: A. Piaget, 1888.

Desportes, Jules. "Revue mensuelle: 1ᵉʳ Septembre 1851." *Annales de l'imprimerie*, 1 September 1851, 142–144.

Disdéri, André-Adolphe-Eugène. *Essai sur l'art de la photographie*. Paris: Chez l'auteur, 1862.

"Chronique." *Le Droit populaire*, 25 December 1880.

Drujon, Fernan. *Catalogue des ouvrages, écrits et dessins de toute nature, poursuivis, supprimés ou condamnés depuis le 21 Octobre 1814 jusqu'au 31 Juillet 1877*. Paris: Edouard Rouveyre, 1879.

Ducamp, Maxime. *Paris, ses organes, ses fonctions et sa vie dans la second moitié du XIXe siècle*. Vol. 2. Paris: Hachette, 1872.

D'Urville, Flévy. *Les Ordures de Paris*. Paris: Librairie Sartorius, 1874.

Encyclopédie amoureuse. Paris: Édition photographique, 1901.

Enne, Francis. "La Rentrée au quartier latin." *La Jeune France*, 4 (1881–1882): 319–320.

L'Épine, Ernest. *La Vie à grand orchestre: Charivari parisien. Par Quatrelles*. Paris: J. Hetzel, 1879.

Eyquem, Albert, *De la répression des outrages à la morale publique et aux bonnes mœurs, ou de la pornographie*. Paris: Marchal et Billard, 1905.

Fabreguettes, M. P. *Des atteintes et attentats aux mœurs en droit civil et pénal, et des outrages aux bonnes mœurs, prévus et punis par les lois du 29 juillet 1881 et 2 août 1882*. Paris: Librairie Maresque, 1894.

Fiaux, Louis. *Les Maisons de tolérance, leur fermeture*. Paris: G. Carré, 1892.

Flax. *Les Hommes du jour no. 20: René Bérenger*, 1908.

Fransois, Henry. "Le Photographe amateur." *La Nouvelle Vie de Paris*, no. 10, 1903.

Gaillard, Louis. "La Licence des vitrines." *Le Journal la photographie pour tous*, 30 August 1897, 6–10.

Gille, Philippe. *La Bataille littéraire. 2ième série (1792–1882)*. Paris: Victor Havard, 1890.

———. *La Bataille littéraire, 4ième série (1887–1888)*. Paris: Victor Havard, 1891.

Ginisty, Paul. *L'Année littéraire 1892*. Paris: Bibliothèque Charpentier, 1893.

Goncourt, Edmond. *Manette Salomon: Pièce en neuf tableaux*. Paris: Charpentier et Fasquelle, 1896.

Goncourt, Edmond, and Jules de. *Journal: Mémoires de la vie littéraire*. Edited by R. Ricatte. 2 vols. Paris: Flammarion, 1959.

———. *Manette Salomon*. Paris: L'Harmattan, 1993. Reprint of Charpentier et Fasquelle edition, Paris, 1896.

Guédy, Pierre. *Amoureuse Trinité*. Paris: Nilsson, 1897.

———. *L'Heure bleue*. Paris: P. Lamm, n.d.

Guide complèt des plaisirs mondains et des plaisirs secrets à Paris. Paris: A. Hall, 1905.

Haussonville, Vicomte d'. *L'Enfance à Paris*. Paris: Calmann Levy, 1879.

Ibels, André. "Enquête sur le roman illustré par la photographie." *Mercure de France*, 25, no. 97 (January 1898): 97–115.

Jacquemin. "Description de l'organisation vicieuse de l'appareil génital d'une prétendue Hermaphrodite." *Journal général de médecine, de chirurgie et de pharmacie ou recueil périodique de la Société de Médecine de Paris*, 53 (1815): 372–375.

Joliet, Charles. *Les Pseudonymes du jour*. Paris: E. Dentu, 1884.

"Jurisprudence de la presse." *Annales de l'imprimerie*, 1 September 1851, 166–168.

Lafenestre, Georges. "Salon de 1873." *Gazette des beaux-arts*, 1 June 1873, 473–500.

Laincel, Louis de. "Impressions de lecture: *Les Fleurs du mal*." *La France littéraire, artistique, scientifique*, 6 April 1861, 440–442.

Larousse, Pierre. *Grand Dictionnaire universel du XIXe siècle: français, géographique, mythologique, bibliographique*. Vols. 4 and 5. Paris: Administration du grand Dictionnaire universel, 1869.

Lavedan, Léon. "Les Événements du mois." *Le Correspondant: Recueil périodique: Religion, philosophie*, 61 (1864): 704.

Leca, Victor. *Pour s'amuser: Guide du viveur à Paris.* Paris: P. Fort, 1904.

Lecour, Charles-Jérôme. *La Prostitution à Paris et à Londres, 1789–1870.* Paris: P. Asselin, 1870.

Lerebours, Noël-Marie Paymal. *Traité de photographie: Derniers perfectionnements apportés au daguerréotype.* Paris: Béthune et Plon, 1843.

Lorrain, Jean. *La Dame turque.* Paris: P. Lamm, 1898.

Louÿs, Pierre. *Le Cul de la femme.* Paris: Astarté, 2009.

Macé, Gustave. *La Police parisienne: Un joli monde.* Paris: Charpentier, 1887.

Maizeroy, René. *Amours de garnison.* Paris: Librairie Illustrée, 1886.

———. *L'Amour perdu*, Paris: La Renaissance du Livre, 1912.

———. *L'Amuseuse.* Paris: Nilsson, 1900.

———. *Au bord du lit.* Paris: Nilsson, 1900.

———. *Au régiment.* Paris: Paul Ollendorff, 1897.

———. *Bébé million.* Paris: Paul Ollendorff, 1886.

———. *Cas passionnels.* Paris: Paul Ollendorff, 1892.

———. *Celles qu'on aime.* Paris: Paul Ollendorff, 1883.

———. *Chérissime.* Paris: Nilsson, 1901.

———. *Le Consolateur.* Paris: Nilsson, 1905.

———. *La Dernière Croisade.* Paris: Victor Havard, 1883.

———. *Les Deux Amies.* Paris: Victor Havard, 1885.

———. *Les Deux Femmes de mademoiselle.* Paris: Victor Havard, 1880.

———. *Le Feu de joie.* Paris: Alphonse Lemerre, 1909.

———. *Les Jeux de l'amour.* Paris: Nilsson, 1902.

———. *Journal d'une rupture.* Paris: Ollendorf, 1895.

———. *Lalie Spring.* Paris: Marpon et Flammarion, 1887.

———. *Papa la vertu.* Paris: Victor Havard, 1890.

———. *Petite Reine.* Paris: Paul Ollendorf, 1897.

———. *Poupée de joie.* Paris: Nilsson, 1903.

———. *Souvenirs d'un Saint-Cyrien.* Paris: V. Havard, 1880.

———. *Sur l'amour: La Possession.* Paris: Nilsson, 1900.

———. *Trop jolie.* Paris: Paul Ollendorf, 1902.

Maupassant, Guy de. *Œuvres complètes de Guy de Maupassant.* 29 vols. Paris: L. Conard, 1908–1910.

Mayer, Ernest, and Louis Pierson. *La Photographie considérée comme art et comme industrie.* Paris: Hachette, 1862.

Meunier, Lucien-Victor. *Les clameurs du pavé.* Paris: L. Baillière, 1884.

Mirbeau, Octave. *Les Grimaces et quelques autres chroniques.* Paris: Flammarion, 1927.

Le Nu d'après nature: La Femme. Paris: Librairie d'Art Technique, 1904.

Pélin, Gabriel. *Les Laideurs du beau Paris: Histoire morale, critique et philosophique des industries, des habitants et des monuments de la capitale.* Paris: Lécrivain et Toubon, 1861.

Photo-club de Paris. *Troisième Exposition d'art photographique.* Paris: Photo-club de Paris, 1896.

Pontmartin, Armand de. *Nouveaux Samedis.* Ser. 19. Paris: Michel-Lévy frères, 1880.

Premier congrès national contre la pornographie, Bordeaux, 14–15 Mars 1905: Rapports, discussions, vœux et conférences. Bordeaux: Imprimerie Commerciale et Industrielle, 1905.

Le Propagateur, 4 December 1853.

Proudhon, Pierre-Joseph. *Du principe de l'art et de sa destination sociale.* Paris: Garnier Frères, 1865.

Reuss, L. *La Prostitution au point de vue de l'hygiene et de l'administration en France et à l'étranger.* Paris: Librairie J.-B. Baillière, 1889.

Rogron, J. *Code pénal expliqué par ses motifs, par des exemples et par jurisprudence.* Paris: Videcoq, 1840.

Sarcey, Francisque. "Chronique." *Le XIXe siècle*, 8 May 1892.

Scholl, Aurélien. *L'Orgie parisienne.* Paris: E. Dentu, 1883.

Tardieu, Ambrose. *Étude médico-légale sur les attentats aux mœurs.* Paris: J.-B. Baillière et Fils, 1862.

Taxil, Léo. *La Corruption fin-de-siècle.* Paris: G. Carré, 1894.

Trescaze, Aimé. *Nouvelle Édition du Dictionnaire général, ou Manuel alphabétique des contributions indirectes, des octrois et des manufactures de l'État, suivi des tableaux des délits et contraventions et de modèles d'actes.* Poitiers: Oudin, 1884.

Le Triboulet, 28 March 1857.

Virmaître, Charles. *Trottoirs et lupanars.* Paris: H. Perrot, 1893.

Weiss, J. J. "La Littérature brutale." *Revue contemporaine*, 2, no. 1 (1858): 144–185.

Wey, Francis. *Chronique du siège de Paris, 1870–1871.* Paris: Librairie Hachette, 1871.

Zola, Émile. "Nana." *Le Voltaire*, 28 October 1879.

———. *Carnets d'enquêtes: Une ethnographie inédite de la France par Émile Zola.* Edited by Henri Mitterand. Paris: Series Terre Humaine, Librairie Plon, 1986.

———. *Correspondance.* Edited by B. H. Bakker. 11 vols. Montreal: Les Presses de l'Université de Montréal, 1978–1995.

———. *Emile Zola, Œuvres complètes.* 21 vols. Paris: Nouveau Monde Éditions, 2002–2010.

———. *La Fabrique des Rougon-Macquart: Édition des dossiers préparatoires.* Edited by Colette Becker and Véronique Lavielle. 6 vols. Paris: Honoré Champion, 2003–2013.

———. *Les Rougon-Macquart: Histoire naturelle et sociale d'une famille sous le Second Empire.* Edited by Henri Mitterand. 5 vols. Paris: Bibliothèque de la Pléiade, 1960–1967.

SECONDARY SOURCES

Abel, Richard, ed. *Encyclopedia of Early Cinema.* London: Routledge, 2005.

von Amelunxen, Hubertus. "Quand la photographie se fit lectrice: Le Livre illustré par la photographie au XIXème siècle." *Romantisme*, 15, no. 47 (1985): 85–96.

Angenot, Marc. "Des romans pour les femmes: Un secteur du discours social en 1889." *Études littéraires* 16, no. 3 (1983): 317–350.

———. *Le Cru et le faisandé: Sexe, discours social et littérature à la Belle Époque.* Brussels: Éditions Labor, 1986.

Apraxine, Pierre, and Xavier Demange. *"La Divine Comtesse": Photographs of the Countess de Castiglione*. New Haven: Yale University Press, 2000.

Aristotle. *The Rhetoric and the Poetics of Aristotle*. New York: Modern Library, 1984.

Armstrong, Carol. *Manet Manette*. New Haven: Yale University Press, 2002.

Aubenas, Sylvie, ed. *L'Art du nu au XIXe siècle: Le Peintre et son modèle*. Paris: Hazan/ Bibliothèque nationale, 1997.

Aubenas, Sylvie, and Philippe Comar. *Obscénités*. Paris: Michel Albin/ Bibliothèque nationale de France, 2001.

Auriant. *La Véritable Histoire de Nana*. Paris: Mercure de France, 1942.

Avice, Jean-Paul, and Claude Pichois. *Passion Baudelaire: L'Ivresse des images*. Paris: Textuel, 2003.

Babuts, Nicolae. *Baudelaire: At the Limits and Beyond*. Newark: University of Delaware Press, 1997.

Bakker, Nienke, Isolde Pludermacher, Marie Robert, and Richard Thomson. *Splendeurs et misères: Images de la prostitution 1850–1910*. Paris: Musée d'Orsay/ Flammarion, 2015.

Bell, Dorian. "The Jew as Model: Anti-Semitism, Aesthetics, and Epistemology in the Goncourt Brothers' *Manette Salomon*." *Modern Language Notes*, 124, no. 4 (September 2009): 825–847.

Benjamin, Walter. *Charles Baudelaire: A Lyric Poet in the Era of High Capitalism*. Translated by Harry Zohn. London: Verso, 1983.

Bernheimer, Charles. *Figures of Ill Repute: Representing Prostitution in Nineteenth-Century France*. Durham, NC: Duke University Press, 1997.

Blood, Susan. *Baudelaire and the Aesthetics of Bad Faith*. Stanford: Stanford University Press, 1997.

Brooks, Peter. *Body Work: Objects of Desire in Modern Narrative*. Cambridge, MA: Harvard University Press, 1993.

Browse, Lilian, ed. *Constantin Guys*. London: Faber & Faber/Shenval Press, 1945.

Buerger, Janet. *French Daguerreotypes*. Chicago: University of Chicago Press, 1989.

Burton, Richard. *Baudelaire in 1859: A Study in the Sources of Poetic Creativity*. Cambridge: Cambridge University Press, 1988.

Cabanès, J. L., ed. *Les Frères Goncourt: Art et écriture*. Talence: Presses universitaires de Bordeaux, 1997.

Christin, Anne-Marie. "Matière et idéal dans *Manette Salomon*." *Revue d'histoire littéraire de la France*, 80, no. 6 (November/December 1980): 921–948.

Clark, T. J. *The Painting of Modern Life: Paris in the Art of Manet and His Followers*. Princeton: Princeton University Press, 1984.

Clayson, Hollis. *Painted Love: Prostitution in French Art of the Impressionist Era*. Los Angeles: Getty Research Institute, 2003.

Cohen, Margaret, and Christopher Prendergast, eds. *Spectacles of Realism*. Minneapolis: University of Minnesota Press, 1995.

Collier, Peter, and Robert Lethbridge, eds. *Artistic Relations: Literature and the Visual Arts in Nineteenth-Century France*. New Haven: Yale University Press, 1994.

Corbin, Alain. *Les Filles de noce: Misère sexuelle et prostitution au XIXe siècle*. Paris: Flammarion, 1982.

Crary, Jonathan. *Techniques of the Observer*. Cambridge, MA: MIT Press, 1990.

Daniel, Malcom. *Edgar Degas, Photographer*. New York: Metropolitan Museum of Art/ Harry N. Abrams, 1998.

Dawkins, Heather. *The Nude in French Art and Culture, 1870–1910*. Cambridge: Cambridge University Press, 2002.

Dawson, Bruce. "Giraudoux: De Harvard au Quai d'Orsay: avril 1908–juin 1910." *Revue d'histoire littéraire de la France*, 83, nos. 5–6 (September–December 1983): 711–724.

Dean, Carolyn. *The Frail Social Body: Pornography, Homosexuality, and Other Fantasies in Interwar France*. Berkeley: University of California Press, 2000.

Dolan, Thérèse, ed. *Critical Perspectives on Manet*. London: Routledge, 2016.

———."Musée Goncourt: *Manette Salomon* and the Nude." *Nineteenth-Century French Studies*, 18, nos. 1–2 (Fall/Winter 1989–1990): 172–185.

Donovan, James. *Juries and the Transformation of Criminal Justice in France in the Nineteenth and Twentieth Centuries*. Chapel Hill: UNC Press, 2010.

Easton, Elizabeth, ed. *Snapshot: Painters and Photography, Bonnard to Vuillard*. New Haven: Yale University Press, 2011.

Edwards, Paul. "Roman 1900 et photographie: Les Éditions Nilsson/Per Lamm et Offenstadt Frères." *Romantisme*, no. 105 (1999): 135–136.

———.*Soleil noir: Photographie et littérature des origines au surréalisme*. Rennes: Presses universitaires de Rennes, 2008.

Émile-Zola, François, and Massin. *Zola: Photographer*. Trans. Liliane Tuck. New York: Seaver Books/ Henry Holt, 1988.

English, Donald E. "Anxiety and the Official Censorship of the Photographic Image, 1850–1900." *Yale French Studies*, no. 122 (2012): 104–129.

Font-Réaulx, Dominique de. *Painting and Photography, 1839–1914*. Paris: Flammarion, 2012.

Freund, Gisèle. *Photography and Society*. London: Gordon Fraser, 1980.

Frizot, Michel, ed. *A New History of Photography*. Cologne: Könemann, 1998.

Garb, Tamar. *Bodies of Modernity: Figure and Flesh in Fin-de-Siècle France*. London: Thames and Hudson, 1998.

Gay, Peter. *The Bourgeois Experience, Victoria to Freud*. 5 vols. Oxford: Oxford University Press, 1984–1991.

Goldstein, Robert Justin, Andrew M. Nedd, and Lillian Lewis Shiman, eds. *Political Censorship of the Visual Arts in Nineteenth-Century Europe: Arresting Images*. London: Palgrave Macmillan, 2015.

Goujon, Jean-Paul. *Dossier secret Pierre Louÿs-Marie de Régnier*. Paris: Christian Bourgeois, 2002.

de Grazia, Victoria, and Ellen Furlough, eds. *The Sex of Things: Gender and Consumption in Historical Perspective*. Berkeley: University of California Press, 1996.

Grivel, Charles. "Le Roman mis à nu par la photographie même." *Romantisme*, no. 105 (1999): 145–147.

Guieu, Jean-Max, and Allison Hilton, eds. *Émile Zola and the Arts*. Washington, DC: Georgetown University Press, 1988.

Haine, W. Scott. *The World of the Paris Café*. Baltimore: John Hopkins University Press, 1998.

Harsin, Jill. *Policing Prostitution in the Second Empire*. Princeton: Princeton University Press, 1985.

Hauptman, Jodi, ed. *Degas: A Strange New Beauty*. New York: Museum of Modern Art, 2016.

Hess, Thomas, and Linda Nochlin, eds. *Woman as Sex Object*. London: Allen Lane, 1973.

Hiddleston, J. A. *Baudelaire and the Art of Memory*. Oxford: Oxford University Press, 1999.

Hubert, Judd. "Symbolism, Correspondence and Memory." *Yale French Studies*, no. 9 (1952): 46–55.

Jakobson, Roman. "The Metaphoric and Metonymic Poles." In Roman Jakobson and Morris Halle, *The Fundamentals of Language*. 's-Gravenhage: Mouton, 1956, 76–82.

Kerley, Lela. *Uncovering Paris: Scandals and Nude Spectacles in the Belle Époque*. Baton Rouge: LSU Press, 2017.

Kessler, Marni. *Sheer Presence: The Veil in Manet's Paris*. Minneapolis: University of Minnesota Press, 2006.

Koetzle, Michael. *Uwe Schweid Collection—1000 Nudes: A History of Erotic Photography from 1839–1939*. Cologne: Taschen Books, 2000S.

Ladenson, Elisabeth. *Dirt for Art's Sake: Books on Trial from Madame Bovary to Lolita*. Ithaca, NY: Cornell University Press, 2007.

Lathers, Marie. *Bodies of Art: French Literary Realism and the Artist's Model*. Lincoln: University of Nebraska Press, 2001.

Leribault, Christophe. *Delacroix et la photographie*. Paris: Musée du Louvre/ Le Passage, 2008.

Linton, Anne. "Prescribed Fictions: Literary and Medical Representations of Hermaphrodism in Nineteenth-Century France." PhD diss., Yale University, 2011.

———. "Hermaphrodite Outlaws: Ambiguous Sex and the Civil Code in Nineteenth-Century France." *Representations*, 138 , no.1 (Spring 2017): 87–117.

Lloyd, Rosemary, ed. *The Cambridge Companion to Baudelaire*. Cambridge: Cambridge University Press, 2005.

———. *Baudelaire's World*. Ithaca, NY: Cornell University Press, 2002.

Matlock, Jann. *Scenes of Seduction: Prostitution, Hysteria, and Reading Difference in Nineteenth-Century France*. New York: Columbia University Press, 1994.

Mayeur, Jean Marie, ed. *Les Immortels du Sénat, 1875–1918: Les Cent seize inamovibles de la Troisième République*. Paris: Publications de la Sorbonne, 1995.

McCauley, Elizabeth. *Industrial Madness: Commercial Photography in Paris, 1848–1871*. New Haven: Yale University Press, 1994.

Plesch, Véronique, Catriona McLeod, and Jan Baetens, eds. *Efficacité/Efficacy: How to Do Things with Words and Images?* Amsterdam: Editions Rodopi, 2011.

Marder, Elissa. *Dead Time: Temporal Disorders in the Wake of Modernity (Baudelaire and Flaubert)*. Stanford: Stanford University Press, 2001.

Mesch, Rachel. *The Hysteric's Revenge: French Woman Writers at the Fin de Siècle*. Nashville: Vanderbilt University Press, 2006.

Mitterand, Henri. *Zola*. 3 vols. Paris: Fayard, 1999–2001.

Montier, Jean-Pierre, Liliane Louvel, Danièle Méaux, and Philippe Ortel, eds. *Littérature et photographie*. Rennes: Presses universitaires de Rennes, 2008.

Moses, Claire Goldberg. *French Feminism in the Nineteenth Century*. Albany: State University of New York Press, 1984.

Nazarieff, Serge. *Early Erotic Photography*. Cologne: Taschen, 2002.

———. *The Stereoscopic Nude 1850–1930*. Berlin: Taschen, 1990.

The New International Encyclopedia. Vol. 12. Frank Colby, Daniel Gilman, and Harry Peck, eds. New York: Dodd, Mead, 1906.

Offen, Karen. *Debating the Woman Question in the French Third Republic, 1870–1920.* Cambridge: Cambridge University Press, 2017.

Ogawa, David. "Arresting Nudes in Second Empire Paris." *Photography*, 31, no. 4 (2007): 330–347.

Ortel, Philippe. *La Littérature à l'ère de la photographie: Enquête sur une révolution invisible.* Nîmes: Éditions Jacqueline Chambon, 2002.

Pagès, Alain, ed. *Zola en images. Les Cahiers naturalistes*, 38, no. 66 (1992).

Pichois, Claude. *Album Baudelaire.* Paris: Gallimard, 1974.

Quignard, Marie-Françoise, and Raymond-Josué Seckel, eds. *L'Enfer de la bibliothèque: Eros au secret.* Paris: Bibliothèque nationale de France, 2007.

Raser, Timothy. *Baudelaire and Photography: Finding the Pinter of Modern Life.* Oxford: Legenda, 2015.

Rexer, Lyle. *Photography's Antiquarian Avant-Garde: The New Wave in Old Processes.* New York: Harry N. Abrams, 2002.

Rexer, Raisa. "*L'Année pornographique:* The French Press and the Invention of Pornography." *Romanic Review*, 111, no. 2 (September 2020): 260–287.

Ricatte, Robert. *La Création romanesque chez les Goncourt.* Paris: Armand Colin: 1953.

Sanyal, Debarati. *The Violence of Modernity: Baudelaire, Irony, and the Politics of Form.* Baltimore: Johns Hopkins University Press, 2006.

Schincariol, Andrea. *Le Dispositif photographique chez Maupassant, Zola et Céard*, Paris: L'Harmattan, 2014.

Schlossman, Beryl. "Baudelaire: Liberté, Libertinage and Modernity." *SubStance*, 22, no. 1 (1993): 67–80.

Schopp, Claude. *L'Origine du monde: Vie du modèle.* Paris: Phébus, 2018.

Schor, Naomi. *Reading in Detail: Aesthetics and the Feminine.* London: Methuen, 1987.

Schwartz, Vanessa. *Spectacular Realities: Early Mass Culture in Fin-de-Siècle Paris.* Berkeley: University of California Press, 1998.

Scott, Joan Wallach. *Only Paradoxes to Offer: French Feminists and the Rights of Man* Cambridge, MA: Harvard University Press, 1996.

Solomon-Godeau, Abigail. *Photography at the Dock: Essays on Photographic History, Institutions, and Practices.* Minneapolis: University of Minnesota Press, 1991.

———."The Legs of the Countess." *October*, 39 (Winter 1986): 65–108.

Starkie, Enid. *Baudelaire.* New York: New Directions, 1958.

Stephens, S. "Esquisse d'incomplétude: Baudelaire, Guys and Modern Beauty." *Neophilogus*, 89 (2005): 527–538.

Stora-Lamarre, Annie. *L'Enfer de la IIIe République: Censeurs et pornographes 1881–1914.* Paris: Éditions Imago, 1990.

Terdiman, Richard. *Present Past: Modernity and the Memory Crisis.* Ithaca, NY: Cornell University Press, 1993.

Thibaudet, Albert. "La Question *Bel-Ami.*" *Nouvelle revue française*, 230 (November 1932): 746–752.

Weinberg, Bernard. *French Realism: The Critical Reaction, 1830–1870.* London: Oxford University Press, 1937.

Wing, Nathaniel. *The Limits of Narrative: Essays on Baudelaire, Flaubert, Rimbaud and Mallarmé.* Cambridge: Cambridge University Press, 1986.

⚜ INDEX ⚜

⊴ ACKNOWLEDGMENTS ⊵

I am deeply indebted to a number of people for making this project possible. Maurice Samuels has been as exceptional a mentor as he is a scholar. I have been privileged to have the opportunity to work with him, and I could not have completed this project without his careful attention and steadfast encouragement. I have also had the great good fortune of being taught by outstanding faculty at the University of Oxford, the University of Pennsylvania, and Yale, and I have been particularly influenced by my work with Howard Stern, Howard Bloch, and Peter Brooks over my years as a student. A number of other academic mentors have also been integral to the book's development. I am grateful to Jann Matlock for both her interest in the project and her incisive reading during my revisions. And finally, Rachel Mesch has been unfaltering in her enthusiasm and overwhelmingly generous in offering feedback. She has helped me find my voice as a scholar.

My research was made possible by research funds from Vanderbilt University, by a Chateaubriand fellowship from the Consulat général de France, by a Kenneth Cornell Grant from Yale University, and by a Presidential Summer Fellowship from the University of Pennsylvania. The Getty Museum, the Société française de photographie, the Ministère de Culture de la République française (POP), the Rheinisches Bildarchiv, the Metropolitan Museum of Art, the Archives d'Éros, the Musée d'Orsay, the Archives de la Préfecture de police, and the Département des éstampes et de la photographie at the Bibliothèque nationale de France all graciously allowed me to reprint images; my particular thanks goes to Marie Robert at the Musée d'Orsay for her help with sourcing images and to Faye Richardson and Philip Nagy at the Vanderbilt Center for Visual Resources for help with scanning works in my collection. I am lucky to have Jerome Singerman as my editor at the University of Pennsylvania Press, and I thank him and the Press for stewarding the book to completion.

A vast network of friends and colleagues has also contributed to this project. Raquelle Bostow, Jonathan Cayer, Noah Chesnin, Rachel Corkle, Bettina Lerner, Mathilde Simian, and the members of the French and Francophone Studies Reading Group at Vanderbilt provided feedback on various chapters; Elizabeth Bacon Eager was of immense help in thinking through the art historical components; Octavia Bright lent her keen feminist eye to the manuscript; and Annabel Kim, Annie de Saussure, and Maya Harakawa were outstanding emergency research assistants. Daniel Dewispelare, Delphine Miroudot, and Daniel Ridge introduced me to essential materials at the outset of my research. I thank Sarah Baron and Jeremy Kahan for their friendship and generosity during the years that I have spent on this project and Andy Guthrie and Mathilde Simian for their friendship and warm hospitality during my many trips to France.

Most of all, I want to thank my family. My grandparents, Henry and Carolyn Rexer, and Lawrence and Sonia Klein, have influenced me in their wit and wisdom alike. My siblings and their partners, Jonah Rexer, Norah Rexer, Mari Vandenburgh, Azza Gadir, Josh Forman, and Dan Herstig, have been a constant source of love and support, and my father-in-law, Dan Vandenburgh, has been known to drive five hundred miles because I needed a babysitter. The inspiration for this project comes from two great writers and thinkers, my parents Rachel Klein and Lyle Rexer. My father's work as an art critic opened my eyes to new ways of looking at the world and thinking about literature; my mother's talent and dedication to her writing set the unattainable standard to which I aspire in my own work. More recently, my two sons, Leander and Lawrence, have spurred on my work as they anxiously awaited the day when my book would *finally* be finished. And last, but absolutely not least, my husband, Jonathan Vandenburgh, has been a font of love, patience, sage counsel, and, when necessary, trenchant critique. He has put up with long days and short nights, far more discussion of pornography than anyone should have to endure, and moves to France and Tennessee so that I could research and write this book. It truly would not have been possible without him.